CITY PLANNING

PERSPECTIVES IN URBAN GEOGRAPHY

VOLUME FIFTEEN

Concept's International Series in Geography

No. 1 Perspectives in Agricultural Geography (In Five Volumes) Edited by **Noor Mohammad**

No. 2 Perspectives in Geomorphology (In Four Volumes) Edited by **H. S. Sharma**

No. 3 Perspectives in Urban Geography Edited by **C.S. Yadav**

1. New Directions in Urban Geography
2. Comparative Urban Research
3. Comparative Urbanization : City Growth and Change

4.A Models in Urban Geography (Theoretical)

4.B Models in Urban Geography (Mathematical)

5. Urban Research Methods : Central Place, Hierarchical and City Size Models
6. Contemporary City Ecology
7. Slums, Urban Decline and Revitalization
8. Contemporary Urban :
9. Rural-Urban Fringe
10. Morphology of Towns
11. Cities and Housing
12. Perceptual and Cognitive Image of the City
13. Urban Economics
14. City Planning : Problems and Prospect
15. City Planning : Administration and Participation

16.A Urban Planning and Policies

16.B Urban Planning and Policies

Concept's International Series in Geography No. 3

PERSPECTIVES IN URBAN GEOGRAPHY

VOLUME FIFTEEN

City Planning

Administration and Participation

Edited by

C. S. YADAV

CONCEPT PUBLISHING COMPANY, NEW DELHI

First Published 1986

Published by

Naurang Rai
Concept Publishing Company
H-13 Bali Nagar
NEW DELHI 110015 (India)

Printed in India by

Godwall Printers
at Mohan Printing Corporation
Padam Nagar, Delhi - 110007

PREFACE

NATURE OF URBAN GEOGRAPHY

THERE are several studies on urban geography which reveal that, as a major sub-discipline, it has a long tail but a short body. However, the spectrum is so vast and broad that researchers are able to make general statements in defence of its conception, philosophy, nature and orientation. Urban geography today encompasses and interfaces with various disciplines which are interested in urban studies. As an introduction to this series, our task here is to make an attempt to briefly review the development of geographical interest in various aspects of cities.

There are several reviews of the early development of urban geography which have been dealt with by Berry and Harton (1970)[1] and Carter (1974).[2] Berry and Harton in their book, *Geographical Perspective on Urban System*, have made an attempt to introduce readers to its present-day status. They have clearly resolved that "the formative years of the social science in the late nineteenth century and early twentieth century were also the years in which urban studies first developed,"[3] thus providing the context for the geographer's emerging interest in cities. However, the emergence of urban studies dates back to the writing of Greek scholars, but as a sub-discipline, it has reached its present-day status only in the past 30 years.

In their historical perspective the works on urban geography show that the pre-20th century studies primarily concerned themselves with themes of location, size and shape of the cities. The initial findings were strongly subjective, descriptive and dependent more on observation such as the works of Hassert (1907)[4] and Blanchard (1911).[5] In the succeeding years the conceptual framework of site and situation was criticized by

Aurousseau (1924)[6] and Crowe (1938)[7], their conception being that cities were not inanimate objects in landscape, but also organic elements which involved people and their movements. The morphologist, later in 1960, truly brought the indigenous line of evolution in the sphere of urban geography and studies on the build-up fabric of cities (Conzone, 1960).[8] Smails (1955)[9] constituted the prime base of urban geography, which remained articulated without any major conceptual change till early 1960s. The studies on the morphological aspects of the urban system were influenced by external forces, consequently the methodological frameworks got impetus within the discipline. At this juncture the evolution of concepts was not based on environment but took shelter under the umbrella of economics of location, and incorporated analysis of land values and rents, and the concept of nodality and accessibility. These concepts were derived from the economic theories of Cooley (1894)[10], Weber (1899),[11] and Hurd (1903).[12]

The Chicago School of Urban Ecology hastened the evolution of urban geography. In his monumental work Park (1925)[13] developed the idea of order and analysis of towns. Further, a powerful thrust and much of the rationale was provided to the studies of urban geography by the Central Place Theory of Christallar (1933).[14]

The impact of the statistical method was powerful and it brought rapid and enormous changes in the field of urban geography. It also brought new insights into the development and application of urban geography towards increased quantification. Brian J. Berry, pioneer in the field, analysed the spatial order, size and location of towns and cities. There was widespread use innovative techniques to explore the nature of urban problems, hypotheses were tested, new theories propounded and old theories remodelled. The statistical methods were put to a variety of uses. Smith (1965)[13] evaluated the classification of settlements ; Berry and Garrison (1956)[16] examined the utility of the rank-size rule for urban populations. The models of Park and Burgess (1925),[17] Harris and Ullman (1945)[18] and Homar Hoyt (1939)[19] were tested and re-examined by various geographers.

A new impetus to urban geography came from social area

analysis which was initially propounded by Shevky and Bell (1955)[20] and later on this provided a basis for factorial ecology. The collaboration of this stream in urban geography was offered by Berry (1971),[21] Herbert (1972)[22] and Johnston (1974).[23] As a consequence of these thrusts in geography after 1960, the techniques of investigation were sharpended and this has provided the basis for a scientific explanation of cities. Attempts were made to introduce new theories and frame laws to make the explanation of events more rational and logical. Sophisticated models were propounded as urban geography entered a new era of rationalizing the subject matter of urban studies on the basis of new philosophies, new concepts, new theories, new methodologies and applications.

However, the status of contemporary urban geography has been elevated only recently by the behavioural approach. The studies of perception and cognition which have a long tradition in physiology were first introduced into the field of geography by Lynch (1960),[24] Dowson and Stea (1973)[25] Gould and White (1974).[26] At present there is a sudden spurt in the studies on the subject with a new paradigm. But the full impact of behavioural approaches upon urbon geography has yet to be realized.

The aim of this series is to seek reorientation of the discipline strengthened by new philosophies, methodologies, subject matters or application. The series has been arranged in such a way that all contemporary view points are covered comprehensively. Hopefully, this series will inspire researchers to appreciate the work already done by geographers in studying cities. Geography by nature seems to be a synthesizing field of inquiry. As such we have made an endeavour to combine some of the otherwise disparate facts garnered by other disciplines in such a manner that we can gain a better understanding of the urban system. The study of urban geography is essential if we are to analyse the human consequences of the settlements in which we live. It is useful to planners, decision makers in government and corporations and also to each one of us as citizens. Finally, it gives us a perspective on what may be happening to our cities and to the nature.

To achieve the above goal only those contributions with

originality and contrasting viewpoints were selected for inclusion in this series. In doing so the editor does not wish to compete with the journals in the field in which innovative research and methodological aspects are presented. But he does wish to convey, and convey with conviction, that significant researches are being undertaken in the different branches of urban geography and in other allied disciplines. The present series is an attempt to provide a selective reappraisal and rigorous examination of the assumptions and the urge to disseminate new knowledge created by the mutual interaction. Emphasis is also placed on the conceptualization and theorization of the subject matter so that general laws may emerge. A conscious effort has been made to organize the series in such a way that it reflects the philosophical approach parallel to that of the behavioural school. Finally, a vigorous attempt has been made to demonstrate throughout the series how geographers are basically involved in solving the urban problems.

C. S. YADAV

REFERENCES

1. Berry and Harton, *Geographic Perspectives on Urban System : With Integrated Readings*, New Jersey, Prentice Hell INC, Englewood Cliffs, 1970
2. Carter, *The Study of Urban Geography*, Edward Arnold, London. 1974.
3. Berry and Harton, 1970.
4. Hassert, K.. *Die Stadte Geographisch Betrachect*, Leipzig, 1907.
5. Blanchard, R., *Grenoble : Etude De Geographic Urbanine*, Paris, 1911.
6. Aurousseau, M., "Recent Contributions to Geography : A Review," *Geographical Review*, 1924, 14, p. 444.
7. Crowe, P.R., "On Progress in Geography," *Scottish Geographical Magazine*, 1938, 54-1-19.
8. Conzone, M.R.G., "The Plan Analysis of an English City Centre," Ink. Norkorg (Ed), *Proceedings of I.G.U. Symposium on Urban Geography*, C.W.K. Gleerup, Lund, 1962.
9. Smails, A.E., "The Urban Mes of England and Wales." *Transactions and Papers*, Institute of British Geographers 1946, 11, 85, p. 101.
10. Cooley, C.H., "The Theory of Transportation," *Publications of the American Economic Association*, 1894, 9, p. 5-7
11. Weber, A.F., *The Growth of Cities in the Nineteenth Century: A Study in Statistics*, New York, 1899,

12. Hurd, R., *Pricinples of City Land Values: New York Record and Guide*, 1903, p. 19-21.
13. Park, R.E., "Suggestions for the Investigation of Human Behaviour in an Urban Environment,,' in R.E. Park, E.W. Burgess, R.D. Mackenizie (eds), *The City*, University of Chicago Press, 1925.
14. Christallar, W., *Central Place in Southern Germany*, Gustar Fischer, Teno, 1933.
15. Smith, R.M.T., "Method and Purpose in Functional Town Classification," *Annals of the Association of American Geographers*, 1965, 55, pp. 539-548.
16. Carrison, W.L., "Applicability of Statistical Inference to Geographical Research," *Geographical Review*, 1956, 46, 427, 429.
17. Burgess, E.W., "The Growth of City," in R.E. Park, E.W. Burgess and R.D. Mackenzie (eds.), *The City*, University of Chicago Press, 1925.
18. Ullman, E.L., "The Nature of Cities," *Annals*, American Academy of Political and Social Science, 1945, 242, 7-27.
19. Hoyt, H., *The Structure and Growth of Residential Neighbourhoods in American Cities*, Washington, Federal Housing Administration, 1939.
20. Shevky, E. and Bell, W., *Social Area Analysis*, Stanford University Press, Stanford 1955.
21. Berry, B.J.L. (ed), "Comparative Factorial Ecology," *Economic Geographic* (*Supplement*), 1971,47.
22. Hrbert, D.T., *Urban Geography: A Social Perspective*, David and Charles, Newton Abbot 1972.
23. Johnston, *Urban Residential Pattern*, Bell, London, 1971.
24. Lynch, *Image of the City*, Massachusetts, Cambridge, 1960.
25. Dowson and Stea "Image and Environment," Chicago and London, 1973
26. Gould and White, R., *Mental Maps*, London, 1974.

ACKNOWLEDGEMENT

We Thank Editors Gerd-Michael Hellstern, Erithjof Spreer Hellmut Wollmann, *Heft 2*, *Vol. II* and *Vol. III*, for their permission to use material from "Applied Urban Research" Proceedings of the European Meeting on Applied Urban Research, Essen Oct. 2-4, 1981.

CONTENTS

PREFACE v

ACKNOWLEDGEMENT x

LIST OF CONTRIBUTORS xv

1. Introduction 1
—C.S. Yadav

PART ONE

CITY ADMINISTRATION AND PROVISION OF FACILITIES

2. The Politicization of American Local Executives : City Managers, Planners, and Superintendents
—Frederick M. Wirt and *Leslie J. Christovich* 31

3. Administrative Leadership in a Big City
—Harald Baldersheim 45

4. The Contribution of Evaluation to Administration
—Gerd-Michael Hellstern and *Hellmutt Wollmann* 59

5. The Reform of Metropolitan and Regional Government : A Comparative Perspective
—D.C. Rowat 91

6. Recent Trends in Planning and Management in Sweden : Some Experiences of Citizen Participation
—Ove Kalltorp 97

7. The Implications of Local Government Reorganisation : For Central-Local Relations
—Donald C. Rowat 109

8. Municipal Government as Socio-Political Entity : A Case Study
—*Arun Kumar Singh* 119

9. Financial Management of Municipal Governments : A Case Study of Five Cities of West Bengal
—*Arun Kumar Singh* 153

10. External Mandating of Local Government Service Provision : The Fiscal Consequences
—*Susan A. MacManus* 187

11. Local Implementation of External Policy : Effects of Majority and Minority Interests
—*Herman Turk* and *Lynne G. Zucker* 195

12. Integrating Manpower and Economic Development Strategies
—*Carl. E. Van Horn* and *Peter Kobrak* 211

13. Public Services in Cities and Counties
—*K. Newton* 231

14. Determinants of Urban Service Expenditures : Fire and Social Services
—*John A. Schofield* 251

PART TWO

CITIZEN PARTICIPATION

15. New Option for Participatory Democracy
—*Peter C. Dienel* 273

16. Be a Good Neighbour
—*Dan Ferrand-Bechmann* 285

17. The Historical Development and Function of Chonaikai : In a Comparative Perspective
—*Hachiro Nakamura* 293

18. New Urban Movements between Isolation and Integrations : Comparative Researches in Italy and West Germany
—Alberto Tarozzi 303

19. The Profile of Contemporary Neighborhood Movements
—Margit Mayer 311

20. Social Action Groups with Reference to Trends in the British Voluntary Sector
—Stephen Humble 325

INDEX 333

LIST OF CONTRIBUTORS

Harald Baldersheim : Institute of Public Administration and Organisation Theory, University of Bergen

Dan Ferrand-Bechmann : I.A.E.S., University of Grenoble

Leslie J. Christovich : University of Illinois

Peter C. Dienel : Research Unit on Citizen Participation and Planning Methods, University of Wuppertal, Germany

Gerd-Michael Hellstern : Center for Social Science Research, Free University, Berlin

Stephen Humble : The Volunteer Centre, England

Ove Kalltorp : The National Swedish Institute for Building Research, Swedon

Peter Kobrak : Western Michigan University

Rebort A. Levine : Editor, Sage Publications, Beverly Hills London

Susan A. MacManus : University of Houston, Houston

Margit Mayor : Amerika-Institute der Jug-Universitat, Frankfurt

Hachiro Nakamura : Institute of Social Sciences, Tsukuba University

K. Newton : Department of Political Science, University of Dundee

Donald C. Rowat : Carleton University, Ottawa, Canada

John A. Schofield : University of Victoria, Canada

Arun Kumar Singh : Human Ecologist Anthropological Survey of India, Southern Regional Office, Mysore 570 002, Karnataka

Marain A. Solomon : Editor, Sage Publication, Beverly Hills London

Alberto Tarozzi : Instituto di Sociologia Universita, Degli Studi, Bologna

Herman Turk : University of Southern California (USC)

Carl. E. Van Horn : The Eagleton Institute of Politics, Rutgers University

Frederic M. Wirt : University of Illinois

Hellmutt Wollmann : Center for Social Science Research, Free University, Berlin

Yadav, C.S. : Department of Geography, Bhagat Singh College, Delhi University, New Delhi

Lynne G. Zucker : University of California, Los Angeles (UCLA)

ONE

C.S. YADAV

INTRODUCTION

AT THE turn of the Twentieth Century, our era is labeled as the "nuclear age" ; "space age" ; "Age of materialism" ; "Age of anxiety". But it is more appropriate to call it the "age of the city" (Clinard 1970).[1] The tremendous growth of the modern urban centres has created a complex aud difficult world in terms of social relationship. Urbanism as a way of living is qualified by extensive conflicts of norms and values, by more rapid social change, by increased mobility of population, by emphasis on material goods and individualism and by a marked decline in effective communication (Anderson 1959).[2] Today, our cities are scenes of physical deterioration of housing, sanitation and health, they breed criminals, cause mental disorders, alcoholism and other forms of deviant behaviour. Nevertheless, a peculiar feature of our cities is that there has been the ever increasing institutionalization of society and individualization of man (U.N. 1959).[3] Institutionalization represents a system which provides, governmental and non-governmental services in the city. It is a system through which our cities are managed. And an inevitable result of the greater concentration of population in our cities is that the role of the government has become bigger, there are more experts to take care of various services and the active participation of individuals in the improvement of our urban affairs has diminished. As a matter of fact the lines of communication among the people, the city officials and the politicians have broken down as a result of this tendency. The individual citizen has almost ceased to feel personally involved Greer (1964).[4] Thus the institutional agencies do not have any link with those whose needs they presumably serve. In such a situation the urban dwellers are bewildered by the inpersonality of the city, the municipal government and the officials for who they work. The problems of the city are further added to them because of the urban system "cannot be perfected by clever manipulation, no matter how well trained, nor by eager philanthropists working alone and from the outside. The toughest problem is that of generating indigenous leadership and the spirit of self-help Yalvisaker).[5] Thus it is within the purview of the community development scheme that many a problem of our cities can be resolved through effective community feelings and self-help and citizen participation. Although the term "Community Development with which are associated self-help and citizen participation is quite new and usually denotes different cannotations, there is an increasing trend these days towards adoption of urban community development in different parts of the world as an approach to get rid of urban problems. Its importance can be realized from the attention paid to it by the United Nations. In 1961, the United Nations published an important document on community development in urban areas United Nations (1961).[6] Since then there has been a mounting demand for a greater degree of public participation, and planning in the 1970s faced a critical challenge in this direction. As a matter of fact, in its formative years, it covered the problems relating to cities such as urban renewal, location of various facilities and development of transport works. Nevertheless, today, it has become more widespread embracing such subjects as poverty, education and protection of the environment Derrick and Coppock (1977).[7] While this challenge is not new, it has become increasingly intense in the recent past.

Alienation towards governmental decision making

The pressure to consider citizen participation as an essential part of the planning for the solution of urban problems is rooted in its philosophical and pragmatic considerations.

According to the philosophical belief of planning, in a democratic set-up, every individual has the right to be consulted and has freedom to express his point of view on matters which are going to affect him personally. As a matter of fact in a democratic set-up, there is more reliance on the elected representative who normally bridges the gap between the governor and the governed through the ballot box, public inquiries and letters to officials or raising question in parliament and in the press. In spite of the fact that this system is effective where channels of communication are well known to the individuals involvement, in recent years there has been mounting concern that the public has developed an increasing feeling of alienation towards governmental decision making particularly concerning those issues which involve modification of environment Wengert (1971),[8] Marshall *et al*. (1972).[9]

Objectives of public participation

The ingredients of social welfare planning are the people and their problems, and the urban community development is the collective initiative of families living in the same neighbourhood and support of their efforts through services rendered to them by a higher level of government (U.N. 1961).[10] The urban community development involves democratic action, stressing citizen participation, self-help and self-determination through group action in meeting the problems created by city life Clinard (1970).[11] In this way a responsible section of the people becomes involved in responsible action directed towards solving mutual problems. Thus citizen participation in decision making is a process in which individual citizens play a direct role in the physical and social changes occurring in an urban setting.

The evaluation of success or failure in public participation depends upon the reasons for which the participation is sought. The department of environment suggests, "If the policies to be embodied in the plans are to be understood and generally accepted, and if the proposals in them are to be implemented successfully, the authorities must carry the public with them by formulating, for public discussion, the aims and objectives of the policies and then the options for realizing these aims and objectives. Giving the public the opportunity to participate in the formative stage will, when handled with skill and understanding, not only make the plan a better plan, but also do much to improve relationship between the planning authorities and the public. Thus participation is a two-way process (Great Britain, Department of Environment 1972).[12]

Thus public participation in essence helps improvement in the planning process. It is a truism that the first duty of planners is to plan, and active participation enhances this activity. As Weaver stressed, we mean by citizen participation not just a passive acceptance of what is being done, but the active utilization of local leadership and organization which can profitably assist in the community's efforts (Weaver).[13] Thus the introduction of public participation techniques into the planning process implies a movement along a continuum from representative to participatory democracy Hampton (1977).[14] Such a development may have a considerable effect on the roles which elected representatives, public servants avd citizens are expected to play. To achieve this objective, there should be much wider and more open public debate about policy issues, which may proceed to a sharing of responsibilities for decisions among a larger number of people Hampton and Pike (1974).[15]

Demand for public participation

Governments, government agencies and community development organisations all have contributed in varying degrees and in a variety of ways to the growing demand for more public participation. These responses have initiated some studies to evaluate the nature and significance of the demands and effectiveness of participation, and the passage of legislation and alteration of the administrative structure to provide some future participation. Several governmental and academic investigations relating to public participation have been undertaken to examine the question as it affects a broad range of areas of government interest (Canada, Task Force on Government Information 1969, Ministry of Housing and Local Government (1969) [16] Others are Mogulof (1970),[17] Spiegel (1968),[18] Lynch (1972),[19] Ontario Select Committee on the Ontario Municipal Board 1972,[20] Ontario Committee on

Government Productivity (1972,)[21] Poverty, Moynihan (1969).[22] Associated with these studies have been several indepth studies and experiments, aimed at assessing the effectiveness of particular avenues of participation. The movement to seek public participation in urban planning and policy making is still in its infancy in most of the countries and it is difficult to draw firm conclusions on how far it will go or what its final form will be. The specialists, who include physiologists, sociologists and geographers, have suggested an enlarged role for the public in planning and policy making. In some examples, planners, administrators and politicians have emphatically accepted greater interaction with the public particularly when it required accurate assessment of public views, obtaining additional expertise or gathering information to gain public understanding of proposed policies.

Participants

Some scholars have pointed out that greater involvement of public in decision making inevitably means that more time is taken in reaching a decision, and that the total cost of planning increases. On the other hand increased public participation will result in a reduction of power and prestige for the planner, the administrator or the politician. This notion of negative attitude has persuaded some observers to conclude that the movement towards group public participation may already be on the wane and that may soon die out (Sewell and Coppock).[23] Mazamanian and Nicnaber (1974),[24] for instance, pointed out that history is repeated with instances of enthusiasm for more direct involvement in participation, followed by distrust and even opposition. They suggest that the members of public are apathetic and unconcerned about most issues and are always satisfied whatever decisions are taken by administrators on their behalf. Now the question arises why public has taken this extreme view ? It is because when government officials are rigid and put strong resistance to change and are unwilling to alter the norms. This also has happened in communities where participants are not fully aware of their problems, either they are fully contented with the prevailing environment or they are negligent. Thus it is appropriate to decide who should participate. In prinicipal the process of decision making should take into consideration the views of all those who are legitimately concerned with the issue. Perhaps these individuals are conscious citizens or those who will receive benefits. Thus the reliance should be placed upon the interest groups whose views may be obtained through such channels as contacts with afficials, letters to newspapers or appearances at public meetings or hearings. Marshall Clinard (1970).[25] firmly believed that citizen participation is a process through which individual citizens have direct roles in the physical and social changes affecting their immediate lives. He stated that through community development action even in residents of hopless slums, latent skills can be developed to alter the environment. He pointed the following elements to achieve this goal :

1. Creation of a sense of social cohesion on a neighbourhood basis and strengthening of group interrelationship.
2. Encouragement and stimulation of self-help, through the initiative of the individuals in the community.
3. Stimulation by outside agencies when initiative for self-help is lacking.
4. Reliance upon persuasion rather than upon compulsion to produce change through the efforts of the people.
5. Identification and development of local leadership.
6. Development of civic consciousness and acceptance of civic responsibilities.
7. Use of professional and technical assistance to support the efforts of the people involved.
8. Co-ordination of city services to meet neighbourhood needs and problems.
9. Provision of training in democratic procedures that may result in decentralization of some government functions.

Thus it is clear that in order to participate in a meaningful way in decision making, the public must be well informed about the issues, problems and strategies. Equally important is the fact that continuous participation in urban planning and policy making largely depend on the fact that some useful purpose is being served. The citizens involving in planning, feel that they are participating in something that is likely to have meaningful results. As a matter of fact it is not always conducive nor possible to obtain views of every individual on every issue, however it is worthwhile to involve those individuals who are drawn from the better ranks of the better educated and those who are politically conscious. Thus the leadership and advice are often provided by those in the middle and upper classes Bell and Held (1969),[26] Babchuck and Booth (1969).[27] These interest groups are more articulate and conscious to improve the prevailing conditions in an environment. These groups help in the identification of needs, selection of priorities and carrying out of activities. Therefore to bring about change successfully, potential indigenous leadership in local areas needs to be identified and developed.

Role of government

A major problem facing the managers of public goods is the integration of public opinion into the decision making process. It has been recognized that some sort of citizen participation has always been at the level of local government, but only recently it has become a feature of Metropolitan government Wood (1977).[28] A community comprises individuals and groups. Varying in power and organization, occupying a common location, and linked by social, economic and political interactions Clark (1968).[29] In a democratic set-up individual's right to power is delegated via the elective process to politician who sets policy and makes decisions concerning social wellbeing, while a non-elected technical bureaucracy implements them through representation, jurisdiction and public participation Maars (1962).[30]

The modern metropolis is so huge and sprawling that efficient managemeut has become all but impossible as a resutl of which direct contact between the people and administrations of city services has frequently receded into the background. The very government designed to serve the people has become unwielding political units like wards are too large and the problems too complecated for one council man or alderman to handle Clinard (1970).[31]

A distinct goal of the urban community development is the effective decentralization of some governmental authority and services through neighbourhood citizen boards. As a matter of fact a well-established decentralized body in an urban setting may give better support for government and might overcome some of the apathy and hostile attitude of many urban dwellers towards government.

In a strict "top down" system of political centralism there is no chance of avoiding severe conflicts between decisions at the top and opposing individuals at the bottom. However, the political system which include local level of communities and individuals can reduce this conflict in political culture. One of the major barriers in the intercourse between administration and public is the principle of preventing public access to administration files. This fact kindles suspicions that the administration is preparing its decisions internally or in accordance with powerful private investors. Planning in alternatives seems to be reduced, decision making is a black box for the public (Klaus Turke).[32] Accordingly the principle of transparent bureaucracy might induce an atmosphere of increased trust and co-operation between administration and citizens. Turke in his analysis proclaimed that urban and regional policy and research in Federal Republic of Germany are tackling the problem of citizen participation on three different levels :

— On the neighbourhood level, citizen co-operation is a most efficient means to improve the urban environment ; rehabilitation in housing, improvement and maintenance of green and open spaces and restraint measures for inner city traffic heavily rely on a strong support by the residents. Action research and case studies can produce results transferable to other cities ;

— In citywide planning (Master Plan structure plans), citizen participation has been made obligatory during the seventies which reflect recommendations for planners,

— In infra-local planning (regional, national, sectoral) most problems of citizen participation are yet unresolved.

Finally one can-recognize that there is some symptom that time is maturing for more citizen participation.

— Stronger influence of (Administrative) courts on planning in favour of individuals and local decision making.
— More activities of citizens to express and enforce their interests.
— Growing responsiveness of planners towards citizens' wishes and fears.
— An intensive discussion on enhanced rights of individuals and interest groups.

Thus the new philosophy of a town planning propagated these days is devoted to developing the "indigenous potentials" within regions. A centrally organized distribution growth overspills out of the agglomeration areas towards peripheral regions will be replaced gradually by a bottom-up development strategy. In such a strategy, citizen participation will play an important role in creating a regional identity and checking central planning projects against needs and apprehensions within the cities,

ABOUT THIS VOLUME

The term citizen participation has come into use mainly since World War II. Earlier the poverty, hunger, disease and other problems of towns the world over were difficult to master because the social environment had not stimulated self-improvement and acceptance of technical assistance from the outside. As a result, there appear to have been an increasing disillusionment with both central and local governments. However, in recent years, there has been a wider reaction against authority in various forms. Citizens are concerned for a greater say in decisions which affect their lives and in direct action to ensure that these demands are met. As a matter of fact, whether willingly or otherwise, the need for greater involvement by those affected has been given due consideration by administrators and politicians and various mechanisms have been proposed in this front. Much of this concern has been focused on changes occurred in the built-up environment which obviously produce an effect on the quality of human life for both present and future. The theme of the present volume is thus how to manage our bewildered cities through public participation and local governmental action. In this volume those articles are included which reflect management of the cities. It also includes those articles which discuss the problems and processes of planned social change, particularly through the new approach of citizen participation. Whatever the causes, the examination of the variety of ways of securing public participation in different legal and cultural environments should be of some importance to all those who believe that planning is for the people.

The present volume is divided into two parts, (I) City Administration and Provision of Facilities, (II) Citizen Participation.

PART ONE
CITY ADMINISTRATION AND PROVISION OF FACILITIES

In modern democracies there has been increasing tension between the imperatives of popular control and the need for leadership. The popular pressure arises from a basic desire to make power responsible and responsive to citizens over whom power is exercised. Leaders, while accepting the value of this pressure, strictly confine themselves to making judgements about efficiency, utility and other criteria of public benefit for which they may lack popular support. While party system has provided channels to the pressure of popular demands, leaders of public service bureaucracies have developed a repertoire of strategies to deflect or absorb these pressures. Therefore public services traditionally have not been viewed as very open to citizen demands. A primacy of demands rather than ends and an orientation inward rather than outward produces the hallmark of modern public administration. Frederick M. Wirt and Leslie J. Christovich, in their article, "The Politicization of American Local Executives: City Managers, Planners and Superintendents", explore a major, continuing tension in modern democracies between the imperatives of popular control and the need for leadership. The central purpose of their research is to determine if recent calls for more participation in local decision making has altered the urban executives' perception of their power position in local governance in the United States. The major hypothesis is that executive perceptions of increased local demands as expressed through group activity have modified these executives' perception of their powers. The authors further hypothesize that the effect of these demands on the executives' power perceptions will vary by the context of the community and by the administrator's experience. The data for analysis consisted of a 54 per cent responses to a national mail questionnaire conducted in early 1981 from American city managers, planning directors and school superintendents. The authors raised a querry, why should the participatory thrust be evaded ? According to the authors' analysis, executives are also professionals, and by definition they receive their signals for action and their normative values about policy from professional networks as well as from politicians and citizen groups. So the strength of the executive influence lies in that acceptance of the larger norms of the professions. As a matter of fact, local power contexts strain and deflect these external signals to the executives. But, over time, the professional norms persist, while local action often does not, consequently over a period of time, the external norms become local policy. That may be why these executives can report the contradictory perceptions of greater pressure v. greater executive policy will influence an acceptance. A second reason for the dilution of the participatory thrust lies in the nature of the policy world of urban America. The authors reveal that when groups inject new ideas into the local policy system there exists extreme pluralism of political, administrative interest. So our executives can report greater group demands but they are too often unfocused, confused, contradictory and, in time, lack persistence.

If the city's problem is thought to be an environmental one, the leaders are faced with the task of renegotiating the environment. If the problem is one of organizational control, the pattern of authority may have to be revised or the distribution of loyalties redrawn. Oslo is, obviously, having problems of both environment adaptation and organizational control. H. Baldersheim, in his paper, "Administrative Leadership In a Big City", discusses three questions :

(1) How do the leaders of a big urban municipality react to the financial crisis that affects their city ?
(2) How does the structure of leadership influence the way the municipality handles the crisis ?
(3) How is the role of the administrative leader in particular affected by growing financial problems ? What are the manager's strategies in handling the problems ? To what extent is he able to maintain organizational control, and what sort of external networks does he try to establish in order to renegotiate the municipality's environment ?

Baldersheim's paper is a report from a study of the role of city managers in a big city, Oslo. The study forms part of a larger project on leaders and leadership in Norwegian cities. The process described in this paper seems to demonstrate that the influence the city managers can hope to have in the organization to a large extent depends upon the interest and the energy his officers invest in a project. The author arrives at a conclusion that being relatively few in number, the city manager's officers cannot influence all issues they deal with equally. The key to managerial control seems to lie in the choices his officers make when they decide whether or not to take extra interest in a particular issue. One way for the city managers to control the organization is by influencing these choices. At the managerial level, the chief mechanisms for achieving such influence is probably through recruitment policies, motivation and socialization.

Several years ago, only a few people were willing to consider evaluation research in the Federal Republic as a legitimate enterprise. But there has been a spectacular rise in the past few years in the number of evaluation researches. Evaluations were called a "political planning tool" in the late sixties. As part of a feedback process to increase purposeful co-ordinated government action, they gained importance as a tool to increase efficiency in a time of recession in the mid seventies, when decisions had to be made about the allocation of scarce governmental resources. Finally, evaluation demand has recently increased due to the need in accountability and responsiveness, as a counter-balance for the destabilized power system undermined by growing citizen action and changing political party structure. Gerd-Michael Hellstern and Hellmuttwoll Mann, in their article, "The contribution of Evaluation to Administration", reveal that evaluation is intended for use and the demand for evaluation has come mainly from administration. The authors think that having a strong administrative tradition Germany as a rapidly "developing country" in evaluation research is an inteıesting case study, illustrating the interrelationships among the administrative machinery, the political process and evaluation research and offering some informed guesses about the perspectives and utilization of evaluation in such a setting. In describing the connection between administrative needs and responding evaluation tools and strategies the authors concentrate on the necessity of evaluation to address the special problems created by the administrative process. The authors also make an attempt to analyse the different models and instruments which developed in West Germany in response to the various needs of the policy arena and administrative and political environments.

In this respect four broad questions illustrate the current state of evaluation to administration in this respect :

(1) What was the impetus shaping the evolution of evaluation ?
(2) What links will increase administrative and political use of evaluation ?
(3) What forms of evaluation have emerged for new assessment tools taking into account the German political and administrative system ?

(4) How does the German experience compare with the American one and what modifications are required ?

D.C. Rowat, in his brief paper, "The Reform of Metropolitan and Regional Government : A Compaiative Analysis", discusses general trends and metropolitan and regional reform. The comments made by the author are derived from the International handbook on the reorganization of local governments, edited by the author himself. In the present paper the material is present in two parts : structural reform and its implications for control—local autonomy.

The effects of the citizen partcipation experiments in planning and management are somewhat contradictory as far as increased public control is concerned. It is highly questionable if these measures have resulted in any real control by citizens. But no doubt the municipal planning procedures have become more open to the public than previously. More information about plans is distributed through the mass media, exhibitions, pamphlets, etc. And citizen groups have been invited to information meetings, study groups, etc. Ove Kalltorp, in his article, "Recent Trends in Planning and Management in Sweden—Some Experiences of Citizen Participation", analyses some experiences of and tendencies in the recent citizen participation experiment in Sweden. The author has encompassed three different but related fields : Municipal planning, housing management and community work. Kalltorp evaluates from several case studies the effects of citizen participation in terms of increased influence on planning procedures and results. The social background of institutional participation experiments is discussed briefly, as well as their positive functions for the municipal and housing authorities. The author arrives at a conclusion that participation exercises have had only marginal effects on planning, housing management and community work. A major reason why participatory experiments have been executed is that politicians, planners and managers have found it necessary to respond to citizen demands for direct influence in order not to lose public confidence in the democratic character of planning and management procedures. Another reason is that the need to gain control of the rising level of political conflicts. The grounds for citizen demands are found in the structural reorganisation that has occurred during the 1950s and 1960s and the social problems that followed. Now citizen participation in planning and management seems to decrease in number and scope, but at the same time new forums of institutionalization of citizen demands and protest appear. A new development was made possible by the recent law in decentralized local government. Instead of spending money on community work projects, the municipal authorities and housing companies are now supporting the established voluntary associations.

In recent years local government has been reorganized in a remarkable number of countries. This development has been worldwide, including both developed and developing countries and countries with wide variety of types of political regimes. Donald C. Rowat, in his article, "The Implications of Local Government Reorganization for Central-Local Relations", tries to seek answers to the following questions : What are the causes and consequences of structural reorganization ? Are the causes common to all countries or are they different (for different) types of countries ? What are the implications or consequences of this reorganization ? The author clearly evaluates that the general impact of the recent reorganization of local government has been to promote centralization through their stress on the objective of technical efficiency at the expense of citizen access and participation. There have been many nationwide consolidations of local government at the lowest level, thus creating larger units of local government that are more distant from the citizens. The growth of cities has created more populous units of local government that are also more distant from the citizens. The author reveals, though there has been a new movement to create or strengthen regional governments, they are still not autonomous enough, and tend to be controlled by the central government. The cumulative effect of these developments has been to increase the degree of central control, to reduce the autonomy of local government, and to make government more remote from the citizens. The author therefore believes that there is need for the invention and adoption of new devices for citizen access and participation and for decision making at the local level. He proposes that there is need of a new kind of decentralization, a decentralization not only of structures but also of decision making. Real decentralization and the local autonomy cannot be achieved unless important decisions are made at the local level.

All organizations require care for maintaining continuity of usefulness. The cities for their effective running also require management services. Normally these management services are organized and maintained through an institution of city government. In India the city governments are commonly described by the term municipal government which is a specific instance of institutional intervention in the freedom of choice of the resident population. This can also be seen as the logical necessity arising from the incapacity of individual citizens to regulate the affairs of a very large community. For these reasons, municipal governments are required to be created and to be emplaced within the commitment of the citizen to sustain them. Arun Kumar Singh, in his article, "Municipal Government as Socio-Political Entity : A Case Study", makes an attempt to analyse five selected urban centres with various types of character and way of development : Burdwan, Hoogly-Chinsura, Howrah, Chandernagar and Durgapur. The author analyses the status and performance of these municipal governments. He concludes that functional integration between factors of the urban growth, public consciousness, statutory devolution of powers of government or management of the civil infrastructure has not taken place.

Arun Kumar Singh, in his second article, "Financial Management of Municipal Government : A Case Study of Five Cities of West Bengal", argues that a better appreciation of the problem of financial management could be obtained through an inquiry into the sources of municipal governments and then matched by an inquiry in the utilization of the resources through expenditure. The author, of course, takes up the inquiry in the income of municipalities. It would be sufficient to mention that by reversing the order of inquiry in the manner the author has proposed will permit us to ascertain the way the needs of the municipality emerged in their observed preference between diverse items of expenditure undertaken by the five municipal governments under inquiry. This provides a better appreciation of the municipal governments about their attitude to improve their resource status. The organization of the study undertaken in this article is simple enough to follow. This has been arranged not only to examine the attitudes of the individual municipality regarding the relative importance of different service sectors but also to appreciate the differences of such attitudes between the five municipal governments.

A state mandate is a responsibility, procedure, or activity that is imposed by the state government on its local governments by constitutional, legislative or judicial action. Susan A. MacManus, in his article, "External Mandating of Local Government Service Provision : The fiscal consequences", examines (1) The relationship between 20 state spillovers or services, mandates and municipal fiscal condition and (2) the combined effect of service and fiscal constraint mandates on municipal fiscal condition. The units of analysis are the central cities of all U.S. Standard Metropolitan Statistical Areas existing at the time of the 1970 census. The study finds that not all types of service mandates are associated with municipal fiscal decline (only transportation, leisure and recreation and education mandates). It also shows that not all fiscal constraint mandates advance the worsening of municipal fiscal condition (only non-property tax fiscal constraints). Finally the study demonstrates that where both service and non-property tax constraints are imposed, the likelyhood of municipal fiscal declines increases.

Applied urban research has, in a large measure, concerned itself either with identifying problems and evaluating corrective policies or with describing the distribution and activation of citizen interests. Herman Turk and Lynne G. Zucker, in their article, "Local Implementation of External Policy : Effects of Majority and Minority Interests", reflect this emphasis. The autors clearly evaluate that California's proposition 13, whose overwhelming passage nearly halved local revenues from property taxes, has provided a quasi-experiment in mandated state-wide fiscal change. Though the sweeping "experimental treatment" was constant, wide variability occurred in its local implementation. The authors indicate that their emphasis is not upon taxation, which varies from one nation to the next, but rather upon the neglected areas of local government's implementation of external policy and upon its responsiveness to citizen interests, with which all nations are concerned. The authors have been able to compare the immediate effects of local preferences—here choices by rote—on the budgets of 43 California counties. Affording a possible resolution to the issue of the previously prevalent mass models versus the newer, organizational models of social movements and counter-movements are finding what support the following :

1. Where local decision is subject to external mandate, it is effected more by an organized minority's accord with that mandate than it is by the unorganized majority.
2. But where local decision is not subject to external mandate, it is effected more by the unorganized majority than by an organized minority. The authors conclude that the results present a paradox : political influence in geographically organized—even in systems that do not depend on the immediate expression of citizen preferences—wards, districts, cities, counties and regions. But political interests are not always geographically organized, depending as they do on occupation, ethnicity, gender, age, party membership, etc. Still the analysis of the data suggests that the degree to which interests are met—especially those of the minority—depends upon their concentration within political jurisdictions. The paradox is this : as long as geography defines concentrations of political influence, segregation, not integration, is a main device that assures representation of minority interests in the local decision process. Should melting pot planning be re-examined ?

During the late sixties and seventies, a series of Federal initiatives evolved in the U.S.A. relating to manpower and economic and community development. Unfortunately, however, these efforts remained uncoordinated and lacking in sufficient resources individually to achieve a significant impact on the employment and other economic needs of disadvantaged individuals residing in aging central cities and rural poverty areas. Carl E. Van Horn and Peter Kobrak, in their article, "Integrating Manpower and Economic Development Strategies", try to demonstrate that the Targeted Jobs Demonstration Programme addresses an important set of policy issues about the mix of public and private sector strategies to foster urban revitalization. At the heart of this policy question is the search for the appropriate mix of concessions and incentives to private firms, on the one hand, and requirements and sanctions placed on them, on the other. Specifically, TJDP and similar policies raise the question : What can/should the government demand from private firms in return for public assistance for urban economic development ? To what extend should policy makers emphasize efficiency concerns over equity concerns in fashioning urban revitalization policies ?

Traditionally, U.S. government policy makers have segmented programmes aimed at stimulating private sector investments in urban areas from programmes aimed at directly fostering the employment of low income people. Consequently, the typical urban economic development programme doesn't demand equity benefits from the private firm. Within the past few years a growing number of federal, state, and local policy makers have begun to challenge the traditional isolation of equity and efficiency concerns in urban economic development. The willingness to place demands on the private sector in return for public assistance has increased, but it is still not widespread. What has brought about this movement and change ?

There is a growing dissatisfaction or unease among longtime supporters of urban economic development programmes that they don't produce many jobs in relation to the investment. Federal, state, and local elected officials have been asking some tough questions about economic development projects, such as whether economic development assistance is a windfall or a necessary incentive. Moreover, various studies have demonstrated that the job generating outcomes of economic development assistance are much lower than claimed by the applicants for aid. One way to demonstrate that economic development aid is worthwhile is to tie it with other public purposes, such as hiring unemployed city residents.

Local officials are also becoming more sophisticated, or perhaps more cynical about the economic development process. They are beginning to question the assumption that a modest provision of tax incentives and low-cost money will alter the behaviour of private firms. Business location and expansion decisions are very complex and governmental inducements may be marginally important. Much more salient are such factors as the availability of suitable labour and access to markets to which the firm can sell their product or service. Government decision makers are gaining more knowledge about how to intervene in the economic development process and what they can reasonably expect from business in return for public support.

A set of policy initiatives have also contributed to changing attitudes and practices regarding urban economic development assistance. During the Carter Administration, Federal officials initiated several programme demonstrations and promulgated policy statements supporting the concept of obtaining jobs for the structurally unemployed from economic development aid. The only one of these initiatives to reach maturity was the Targeted Jobs Demonstration Programme, but the widespread discussion and promotion of job targeting has influenced the thinking of policy makers at state and local levels. According to one recent study of 25 cities, 18 cities targeted their economic development projects to either a specific resident population subgroup such as minorities, women, or youth or to the structurally unemployed.

Finally, the impact of scarce Federal resources has helped renew emphasis on enter-agency co-ordination and programme consolidation. Federal, state and local officials are looking at the range of programmes in their jurisdictions and trying to devise ways to achieve public benefits with less money.. As resources shrink, strategies that might guarantee higher returns on investments become more attractive. A programme that ties job benefits to economic development assistance thus becomes more appealing to hard pressed administrators and elected officials.

Given the increasing interest in job targeting policies and practice, the Targeted Jobs Demonstration Programme bears careful examination. The task of targeting jobs from economic development projects for low-income and long-term unemployed residents is very difficult. Local officials must support jobs and business targeting. Two and probably more agencies must cooperate with each other by sharing information and resources in a timely manner. Procedures for tracking economic development projects must be established and implemented. The local economy must remain vital enough to sustain the private firms who obtain public assistance. Despite the obstacles to effective job targeting an increasing number of local officials are finding it an attractive strategy for gaining direct public benefits from economic development programmes.

Conventional attempts to explain the variations in public expenditure on the pait of local authorities in the Western world have not proved particularly successful. K. Newton, in his article, "Public Services in Cities and Countries", attempts to explain the spending of state and local governments in West Europe and in North America but these have not been particularly successful, in that they lack theoretical coherence and have generally produced unsatisfactory results. The work reported here deals with the top tier of the local government system of England and Wales, 1960-1973. The study tries to fill some gaps in the literature by showing that among the main determinants of local spending patterns of any given authority are : its position in the national or regional system of cities, its location with respect to other urban areas, its regional location and historical factors such as war-time bombing damage.

Investigation of the determinants of expenditure on local public services has enjoyed an active tradition. The thrust of research has frequently been directed to the question of whether scale effects exist in the provision of municipal services and to the related question of optimum city size from the point of view of efficiency in service provision. Despite its relevance for purposes of planning public service developments very little work along these lines has been undertaken. John A. Schofield, in his article, "Determinants of Urban Service Expenditures—Fire and Social Services", explores the separate influence of selected socio-economic, geographic and political factors on the supply of and demand for municipal fire and social services. The analysis is applied to what were non-London boroughs of England and Wales in 1971-72. While the data are thus some few years old they are the most recent available so far as required census is concerned. And while local government reorganization has occurred in the meantime, lessons can be provided for current practice. In the second section of the paper, the estimating model is developed. In the third section results are presented and in the fourth section conclusions drawn. Details of definitions and sources of variables are given in Appendix I.

PART TWO
CITIZEN PARTICIPATION

The discussion on the necessity of enlarged citizen participation has more or less reached a point on general consensus. Controversial, however, is the question of how to introduce the necessary participation into the different processes of dicision making. The classic instruments of parliamentary democracy as well as the commonly used techniques of citizen participation are of limited capacity. They cannot be enlarged without negative side effects for the situation involved and for society as a whole. We are therefore forced to look for new ways if we want to increase opportunities for participation. Peter C. Dienel, in his article, "New Options for Participatory Democracy", clearly evaluates that in addition to the existing channels of political participation, social research needs to outline new supplementary instruments of participatory democracy. One way to achieve this goal is to break down issues of public interest into workable parts so that they can be handled by people at random : the so-called "Planning Cell" and the "Citizens" Report are instruments of this kind. This paper presents these new participatory techniques, their intentions and results. The question concerning the status quo and the substance of what is termed "society" in other words concerning the forms of collectivity which are still present today in cities and urban districts beyond bureaucratically and commercially mediated relationship was posed unequivocably by Ms. Ferrand Bechmann in her paper, "Be a Good Neighbour". In her contribution she reported on the analysis of neighbourhood relationship in a French urban district. The background to this inquiry was provided by previous research projects in which investigation had been made into the counter-productive effect of professional "social work". Counter-productive in the sense that this sort of social work does not succeed in filling the vacuum resulting from the destruction of informal social relationships of mutual help which is a consequence of a relationalization of daily life and an individualization of the people involved. Inquiries were made into the types of informal solidarity with respect to housing problems, financial help, emotional relationship, advice information, and help with the shopping, etc.

Hachiro Nakamura (Japan), in his article, "The Historical Development and Functions of Chonaikai—In a comparative perspective", reported, after Reffield-Wirth, the urban study has turned its attention to a number of other topics, say, community power, urban social networks, quality of life, Marxian challenge to existing theories. In dealing with cities in developing countries, the private city, the culture of poverty, core peripheral and dependent theories and so on have been appealing to the research interest of today. Whichever of them may be in vogue currently, the institutionalized neighbourhood organization called Chonaikai has constantly been the object of study among urban sociologists of Japan, though the above topics and approaches are also pursued by them. H. Nakamura reported in his contribution on the traditional form of popular and social self-organization in Japan, the "Chonaikai". The requisition and integration of this system as a sort of internal arrangement during the period of Japanese Totalitarianism in the 1940s had rendered a study of its significance impossible. However, in the context of communal politics incorporating elements of participation and collectivity, the study of the "Chonaikai" and its long history has gained a new relevance.

Questions were posed, although not answered, concerning the extent to which new forms of community development can be biased on this sort of tradition.

A. Tarozzi's article, "New Urban Movements between Isolation and Integration", seemed to be particularly interesting because he provides the clearest historical perspective to the question of mediation possibilities, form of co-existence, corporations and cooperation between new social movements and government policy. The forms of participation chosen today by initiatives and new movements are just as provisional as the movements themselves. Tarozzi prefers to view these movements as a embryonic pre-forms of something which could, in the context of an identity crisis of the traditional large social movements, develop into a single new social movement. From this perspective the question of participation can be reformulated. In his paper Tarozzi assumes that what the new movements have in common is a new concept of living which affected the spheres of working and living and their traditional structure and interrelationship. A comparison of the developmental history of Italian and German movements from both sectors (young unemployed people and workers in Italy and the environmentalist movement in West Germany) should at the same time demonstrate when the most important obstacles to such a process are to be found. The question remains to what extent a positive form of negotiation with the established political and administrative bodies can be achieved—beyond the extremes of total rejection and ghettoization and of integration of new sectoral demands (e.g. self-help as self-administration of the poor). According to Tarozzi's argument this at the same time is the contemporary formulation of the problematic nature of the participation and conceptualization in which the traditional machanism of exclusion and subordinate integration should not be repeated.

The underlying concepts in Ms. M. Mayer's paper, "The Profile of Contemporary Neighbourhood Movements" (FRG/USA) were those of autonomy and "disintegration" of such new forms of social association, concepts which were not themselves explained. Every form of "bargaining" with the current political parties, organizational and administrative bodies appears in this context as a perspective which, although perhaps unavoidable, is a primary danger to "autonomy". She reported in her contribution on one aspect of comparative research into the role of new social movements and the forms of their self-organization and mediation with the political system. On the basis of a typology of urban-based grassroots political activity, which has emerged around localized problems or issues generated by structural changes in economic, social and spatial relations, the concern of Ms. Mayer is to identify and compare the changing modes and consequences of the states' response over time to this grassroots mobilization in the United States, and in Germany. In this sense Mayer sees this type of corporate participatory institutionalization of social and cultural initiatives as a process-maintaining alternative to the more exclusive and repressive form of dealing with social and cultural initiatives which can be observed today.

In British urban studies, it has been customary to deal with the organizational and structural problems of central and local governments since these are the major providers of public welfare. With the current reduction in public expenditure has come a new debate about the limits of the welfare state and an emphasis upon the contribution that the voluntary sector and social action groups can make. S. Humble, in his article, "Social Action Groups With Reference to Travels in the British Voluntary Sector", examines that debate and points out some pitfalls in the recommendations for a new pluralistic system of voluntary statutory provision.

The contribution of S. Humble offers a different formulation of the problem of "participation and social movements" to that of Dienel, but forms a similar perspective.

FOOTNOTES

1. Clinard, M.B. 1970., *Slums and Community Development*, Collier-Macmillan Canada Ltd., Toronto.
2. Anderson, Mels., *The Urban Community : A World Perspective*, New York, Holt, Rienhart and Winston, Inc.
3. United Nations, 1959, "European Seminar on Community Development and Social Welfare in Urban Areas", Bristol, England.

4. Greer, Scott, 1964, *The Emerging City : Myth and Reality*, New York, The Free Press.
5. Yalvisakar, P.N., *Community Action : A Response to Some Unfinished Business*, New York, the Ford Foundation, n.d., p. 4.
6. United Nations, 1961, Secretary-general of the United Nations, "Community Development in Urban Areas"-
7. Derrick Sewell, W.R.D. ; Coppock, J.T., 1977, "A Perspective on Public Participation in Planning", in *Public Participation in Planning*, John Willy and Sons Ltd.
8. Wengert, M., 1971c, "Where Can We Go With Public Participation in the Planning Process", the paper presented at a sympsoium on Social and Economic Aspects of Water Development, Cornell University.
9. Marshall, Dale Rogers et al. (1972), *Minority Perspective*, Baltimore, Johns Hopkins Press.
10. United Nations, Secretory-General, "Community Development in Urban areas". p. 1.
11. Clinard, 1970, op. cit.
12. Great Britain, Department of Environment, 1972, Circular 52/72, London : HMSO.
13. Weaver, From an Address to the 50th Anniversary Meeting of the Family Service Association of America, New York City.
14. Hampton, W., 1977, "Research into Public Participation in Structure Planning", in Sewell, W.R.D. and Coppock, J.T., *Public Participaiton in Planning*
15. Hampton, W. and Pike, P., 'The Open Council and Public Participation : The Liechhardt Experience", *Policy and Politics*, Sept., 1974, Vol. 3, No. 1.
16. Canada, Task Force on Government Information 1969, *To Know and Be Known*, Ottawa, Owen's Printer, 2 Vols.
17. Mogulof, M.B., 1970, Citizen Participation :A Review and Commentary of Federal Policies and Practices, The Urban Institute, Washington D.C.
18. Spiegal, Hans B.C., (ed.), 1968, *Citizen Participation and Urban Development* , Washington D.C., Center for Community Affairs, NIL Institute for Behavioral Science, National Education Association, 2 vols.
19. Lynch, Thomas D. (ed.), "Symposium on Neighbourhoods and Citizen Involvement," *Public Administration Review*, May-June.
20. Ontario Select Committee on the Ontario Municipal Board, 1972, *Final Report*, Toronto.
21. Ontario Committee on Government Productivity, 1972 *Citizen Involvement*, Toronto, Queen's Printer.
22. Moynihan, Daniel P., 1969, Miximu n Feasible Misunderstanding : Community Action in the War on Poverty, New Yonk, The Free Press.

23. Sewell and Coppock, op. cit., p. 6.
24. Mazamanian, Danniel A. and Nicnabar Jeane, 1974, 'Citizen Participation in Agency Decision Making : Can it Survive ?", paper presented at a meeting of the Public Choice Society, Newhaven, Conn., March 21-23.
25. Clinard, op. cit., p. 126.
26. Bell, Daniel and Virginia Held, 1969, "The Community Revolution", The Public Interest, Summer, 142-177.
27. Babchuck, N. and A Booth, 1969, "Voluntary Association Membership : A Longitudinal Analysis", *American Sociological Review*, 34 (1), 31-45.
28. Wood Colin, J.B., 1977 ''The Use of Threat in Community Decision Making : The Gold Stream Case, Victoria B.C.", in Swell and Coppock (eds.), *Public Participation in Planning*, John Willey and Sons Ltd.
29. Clark, T., 1968, (ed.), Community Structure and Decision Making : Comparative Analysis, San Francisco, Chandler.
30. Maars, A. *et al.*, 1962, *Design of Water Resources Systems*, Cambridge, Mars, Harvard University Press.
31. Clinard, Marshall, op. cit., p. 333.
32. Klaus Turke, "Federal Research Institute for Regional Geography and Regional Planning" in Heft, Vol. II.

PART ONE

CITY ADMINISTRATION AND PROVISION OF FACILITIES

TWO

FREDERICK M. WIRT
LESLIE J. CHRISTOVICH

THE POLITICIZATION OF AMERICAN LOCAL EXECUTIVES
City Managers, Planners and Superintendents

PARTICIPATION AND BUREAUCRACY IN DEMOCRACY

The administrative stance

THIS paper explores a major, continuing tension in modern democracies between the imperatives of popular control and the need for leadership. The popular pressure arises from a basic desire to make power responsible and responsive to citizens over whom power is exercised. Leaders, while acknowledging the value of this pressure, find independence from it is desirable in making judgements about efficiency, utility, and other criteria of public benefit for which they may lack popular support. Efforts to mediate this tension in the past have fallen largely to the informal governance provided by party life in the United States. While party life has opened channels to the pressure of popular demands, leaders of public service bureaucracies have developed a reportoire of strategies to deflect or absorb these pressures. Hence, public services traditionally have not been viewed as very open to citizen demands. A primacy of means rather than ends and an orientation inward rather than outward produce the hallmark of modern public administration—lack of responsiveness and responsibility to public pressures. This syndrome is termed here the *Administrative Stance*.

Paper presented at the "European Meeting on Applied Urban Research", Essen, Oct, 2-4, 1981.

The participatory thrust

But there have also been recurrent calls for more controls on such bureaucracies to meet democratic requirements of responsiveness and responsibility. One of these calls has been a challenge of the autonomy granted by society to trained specialists whose services are deemed of vital importance. This is the "revolt of the client" or the challenge to professionalism (Wirt 1981). The call has regularly featured the need for more popular participation in decision making.

Sometimes the participation urged is direct, e.g., referenda, citizen advisory councils. But there is also an indirect form of citizen participation to control leadership, but much harder to capture empirically than those above. Formulated as "the law of anticipated reaction" by Carl Freidrich or "the zone of tolerance" (McGivney and Moynihan 1972) in administrative theory, the concept assumes that leaders are conscious of and respond to implied popular limits on their actions. It is more often been analyzed in the links between citizens and elected leaders, and hence has formed part of the pluralist concept of democracy (Dahl 1961).

Such participation constitutes a potential challenge to the Administrative Stance and its autonomy in decision making. However, these participatory modes share with electoral modes a characteristic citizen inattention and inactivity, a dominant feature of American politics and policy making. Yet their potential can become a reality. When activated, such control constitutes what we term here the *Participatory Thrust*.

Where stands this tension between the Participatory Thrust and the Administrative Stance at the urban level, after 15 years of new programmatic responses to group pressure in the United States ? Specifically, what have been the consequences of this Participatory Thrust for these urban leaders ? It is such major questions that that research was directed in the project here reported. The particular question addressed in this paper tests the proposition that *perceived increased local public demands—expressed through group action—have modified these local executives' powers, as mediated by the context of the community they serve and by their experience*.

RESEARCH DESIGN AND METHODOLOGY

Our primary framework of analysis is that of field theory. That is, the immediate field in which one interacts produces a mental map of actors, events, and behavioral norms. This understanding has featured political analysis since at least Plato's cave analogy. The concept places a cognitive screen between the stimuli of reality and the consequent behavior, a screen mediating between a confusing set of reality signals and purposive action. One cognition relevant to this is the executive's perception of the presence of political actors within one's decisional field, and their relationship to others' and one's political self. Our hypotheses will explore linkages among these others and the self within the local political world.

The testing of the central research question rests on the assumption, well validated in urban politics, that increasing the bases of political demands increases the potential for political conflict, and further, that role behaviors differ under conflictual vs. consensual conditions (Minar 1966 ; Boyd 1976 ; Catanese 1978 : Chap. 5 ; Rabinovitz 1969). Consequently, the guiding hypotheses to be tested in this first report of our research are as follows :

> *Hypothesis*$_1$: Perceived executive influence will not increase, and greater group demands will not be perceived, in larger cities or in different locales (city, suburban nonmetropolitan).
>
> *Hypothesis*$_2$: Urban executives' perceptions of group demands will not be affected by the salience of certain groups to their positions and by some groups' newness to local policy making, holding experience constant.
>
> *Hypothesis*$_3$: Urban executives' perceptions of group demands will not be affected by their experience, holding city size constant.
>
> *Hypothesis*$_4$: Executive influence with policy makers and citizens will not be conditioned by the degree of group demands, holding city size and experience constant.

The data for analysis consist of responses to a mail questionnaire conducted in early 1981 among American school superintendents, city managers and planning directors. All large and middle sized cities, plus a sample of small towns, were used. Thus 750 names were selected, one third to each executive type. There were 406 returns, or 54 per cent, distributed almost equally among superintendents, managers, and planners (33, 32, and 36 per cent respectively).

DISTRIBUTION OF GROUP TURBULENCE

Group Turbulence is central to this analysis, referring to an executive's perception of the current volume of demands compared to "earlier in this job". Executives were asked to rate eight local and state groups along a range of this demand volume over time. The number of the eight groups marked as making More or Much More demands for each executive constituted that person's score on a Group Pressure Index (GPI), ranging from 0-8. The hypothesis underlying the GPI is that communities should be quite different for those executives who reported no or little change rather than much change. Table 2.1 displays the distribution of the perception of their demand contexts by executive types on the GPI.

A little more than half (54 per cent) of the respondents perceived that four or more of the groups had increased their demands. Superintendents perceived the most increased demands (62 per cent vs. 54 and 46 per cent for managers and planners). Overall, Table 2.1 indicates that all three executive types perceived increased group demands, for only 4.6 per cent reported no increase.

There was no expectation that each subset of executives would view each group in the same way. After all, the three do not overlap in function and only rarely in authority. Rather, our expectation was that executives would report a segmented policy politics, with each executive type reporting a different perception of its demand world. Table 2.2 enables us to test this empirical assumption, indicating that there are indeed differing perceptions of demand worlds. While there are some similarities among executives (e.g., Business groups), each type generally perceives a different cluster of groups to be salient. For example, 62 per cent of the superintendents

TABLE 2.1 : Percentage distribution of Group pressure index by executive type

Executives	*Number of Groups Perceived as Increasing Demands*									
	8	*7*	*6*	*5*	*4*	*3*	*2*	*1*	*0*	N
Superintendents	5.8	3.3	20.8	12.5	20.0	15.8	11.7	7.5	2.5	131
Manager	2.7	3.5	3.5	19.5	24.8	16.8	15.9	7.1	6.2	127
Planner	1.5	1.5	4.5	19.4	19.4	26.1	14.9	6.7	6.0	*144*
All Executives	3.3	2.7	9.6	17.2	21.3	19.9	14.2	7.1	4.6	402

perceive that Labor has increased demands, but only 14 per cent of the planners do so, and city managers fall in between. Conversely, the fewest superintendents identify Elected Local Officials as making increased demands, but the other two types are much more than this set. Overall, superintendents appear to be experiencing the most in increased demands (Wirt 1976.)

TABLE 2.2 : **Frequency distribution of "More" and "Much More" demands by executive and Group types**

Demand Group	*Supt.*	*Manager*	*Planner*
Business	48% (62)*	45% (55)	52% (73)
Labor	62% (81)	46% (57)	14% (20)
Clientele	52% (66)	39% (46)	39% (54)
Minorities	50% (63)	35% (41)	35% (49)
Elected Local Officials	34% (44)	60% (73)	66% (94)
State Officials	50% (65)	42% (51)	34% (48)
Federal Offiicials	54% (70)	46% (56)	40% (56)
Lay Opinion	61% (77)	46% (56)	60% (84)

* The first figure indicates the per cent of respondents perceiving that the group had increased its demands. The second figure indicates the N of each executive type ; multiple choices of groups means that the Ns add up to more than 100 per cent.

DISTRIBUTION OF PERCEIVED POLICY INVOLVEMENT

A second perception sought was the degree of movement away from policy neutrality toward policy involvement. A special scale tested the respondent's sense of the changing nature of the profession as experienced throughout his or her career. The results were remarkably uniform, for there was no significant diffierence among the three executives in reporting their heavily increased involvement. Of the three executives, 68-77 per cent registered some degree of increased policy involvement, and only about 5 per cent reported any decrease (the remainder marked no change). This self-reporting confirms what scholars have long contended, that there is no line between policy making and administration, and that administrators increasingly define their work as influencing the policy they are thereafter to administer.

DISTRIBUTION OF EXECUTIVE INFLUENCE

Involvement is not the same as influence, however. So the executives were asked to use a special scale to judge the degree of acceptance of their professional judgments, by 1) their superordinate, authoritative agency (board, council, commission) and also 2) citizens in the community. In both authorities and citizens, there was no significant difference. Most of these executives reported *increases* in acceptance of their judgments by their authorities (50-57 per cent) and by citizens (55-62 per cent). Few reported decreasing acceptance (7.5 vs. 3.0 per cent respectively). Too, a strong minority reported no change in political and citizen acceptance, about 40 per cent for both. A self-inflating factor could operate here, of course, as professionals like to think their advice is acted upon. However, another factor may work against this inflation, namely, these professionals' reticence to report publicly their real influence with law authorities. The inference is clear that growing group demands has not deferred these executives from advancing their own judgments and gaining acceptance from the sources that count in democratic politics.

We see in these descriptive findings a picture of local executives as "politicians". That is, they negotiate among conflicting group demands in order to secure adoption of their own policy preferences, as different professions increasingly report (Cuban 1976 ; Catanese 1978 ; Catanese and Farme 1978). Their reported greater involvement and success, no matter how inflated, point to their greater policy participation and so a greater chance for executive influence, well beyond their professions' norm of policy neutrality.

COMMUNITY CONTEXT AND DERCEIVED PEMANDS

Description is not the same as explanation, of course, so we move to the central hypotheses about variations in these executives' perceptions.

First, is the amount of perceived group demands a function of different qualities of cities, such as size and socio-economic status of citizens ? Factor analysis scores of these qualities in the responding executives' cities were regressed against an interval measure of such group turbulence (how many of the groups in Table 2.2 were reported to bring heavily increased demands). The size of population, often thought to be a surrogate for the intensity of urban politics, was measured in several ways.

The result were uniform and clear, namely, no matter the type of executive, these community characteristics did little to predict the respondents' scores on the GPI. The R^2s for the equations of the superintendents, managers and planners were .13, .04 and .11 respectively ; none was significant at the .05 level. Population alone was also a poor predictor ; the R^2s were abysmal ranging from .01 to .07.

The null hypothesis is clearly accepted. That is, the degree of perceived turbulence, for all executive types is not at all related to the size of jurisdiction,[1] reformism, citizen status, suburbanism, and region. The results suggest, rather, that group turbulence may be so pervasive on the urban scene that it is a systemic factor.

GROUP SALIENCE AND PROFESSIONAL TENURE

Second, is it the case that these perceptions of group turbulence are not differentiated by the group's salience to a profession, regardless of executive experience ? That is, another potential explanation of perceptions may be one's length of experience in office. That is, the more one has been in the office, the more one should be aware that the volume of demands is greater now than in earlier periods of time. But there emerged little significant difference in mean group turbulence scores, by executive type, except among the least and most experienced planners (significance=.003). The direction of the means is as the hypothesis suggests, i.e., more executives perceived more demands with more experience, but little of it is significant.

Another measure was devised to test the volume of group demands and its relationship to tenure. For each demand group perceived, we looked for differences in the mean amount of demands made between each experience category, by executive type. However, difference of means tests revealed no significant differences. When even those with short experience report increased demands, then turbulence must be pervasive throughout urban political systems, regardless of community type.

THE URBAN CONTEXT AND PERCEPTION OF TURBULENCE

Third, is it the case that executives' perceptions of group turbulence are not a function of their urban context, as influenced by length of their experience ? We have noted in treating Hypothesis$_1$ the lack of a linkage between group turbulence and both community context and professional experience. What is the relative influence of these two upon perceived turbulence ? The theoretical assumptions undergirding such tests are straightforward. The greater variety of urban context may well generate more perceived turbulence regardless of city size, the more one perceives increased turbulence ; too, newer executives may lack a grasp of earlier, less turbulent urban politics.

A simple test was to regress context and experience against the measure of group demand volume. Neither predicted the degree of perceived group turbulence ; the R^2s ranged only from .01 to .13. Again, the results suggest a systemic demand pattern in urban policy making, regardless of the type of executive, of community or of experience.

GROUP TURBULENCE AND EXECUTIVE INFLUENCE

Finally, is it the case that group turbulence does not affect executive influence, regardless of other factors like community context and experience ? There was much evidence reported from the three respondents that what we have termed Participatory Thrust has definitely been perceived on the increase. Could we determine whether increases in group turbulence depressed executive influence upon their elected boards or upon citizens, as democratic theory calls for ?

To measure executive influence, we subtracted what *had been* one's influence with what it now *was*. As the original influence scale ran from 0-9, a revised scale covered -9 to $+9$.

One receiving a +9 on this revision had seen one's influence originally at 0 but now at 9 ; a −9 score started at +9 but now is at 0. The resulting 19-interval scale became our dependent variable, with two versions of changed influence —one each for political officials and citizens. Against these two measures were regressed our measures of the volume of group demands, community context and experience.

If, as some argue, administrators resist group pressures, then there should be no relationship in these regressions ; more group turbulence would not be associated with executive influence. However, if as others argue, the Participatory Thrust can overcome such resistance because of its power or legitimacy, then the associations should be negative ; reports of more turbulence would be associated with less executive influence. As shown in Table 2.3, the dependent variables were the executives' reports of acceptance by their political authorities and citizens of their ideas since entering their current position. The independent variables were community context, experience, and the volume of group demands.

In the resulting 12 regressions, there was no evidence that the volume of group demands related to either kind of acceptance. No relationship was found for *managers* or *planners* in their reports of citizen or political authorities' acceptance. For *superintendents*, only one of the four equations revealed a possible linkage (R^2=.24), but even here the volume of group demands was not significant (.073). Nor was the size factor significant ; rather, experience, reformed government, and suburbanism are the elements that relate the two. That is, superintendents who report greater acceptance of their views by political authorities are more likely to be less experienced and to work in a nonpartisan, suburban environment. This finding points again to the special policy world of this particular executive.

Let us not lose sight of the major thrust of the concluding analysis set out in Table 2.3. It suggests strongly that executives, while perceiving more group demands, do not find this Participatory Thrust inhibiting the authorities. In short, we see throughout this paper evidence of the strength of the Administrative Stance concept. Executives see more turbulence, but it doesnt's interfere with their influence in policy making. Indeed, they report very strongly that their policy influence has grown over time.

TABLE 2.3 : **Regression of size, group demand volume and experience on political and citizen acceptance of executives**

Dependent Variable	*Superintendents*	*Managers*	*Planners*
Political Acceptance[1]			
R^2	.05	.14	.01
significance	.137	.001	.741
Citizen Acceptance[1]			
R^2	.03	.09	.01
significance	.389	.013	.705
Political Acceptance[2]			
R^2	.24	.07	.02
significance	.025	.771	.978
Citizen Acceptance[2]			
R^2	.15	.06	.04
significance	.225	.820	.892

1. Experience, volume of group demands, and jurisdiction population regressed against acceptance of executives policy recommendations.
2. Experience, volume of group demands, and community context (city size, race, reform government, region, suburban type) regressed against acceptance of executives' policy recommendations.

INTERPRETATION

Why should the Participatory Thrust be evaded ? The literature suggests several reasons. First, executives are also professionals, and by definition (Wirt 1981) they receive their signals for action and their normative values about policy from professional networks, as well as from politicians and citizen groups. So, the strength of executive influence lies in that acceptance of the larger, norms of the profession. Of course, local power contexts strain and deflect these external signals to the executive. But over time, the professional norms persist, while local action often does not. And so over time, the external norm becomes local policy. That may be why these executives can report the contradictory perceptions of greater pressure vs. greater executive policy influence and acceptance.

A second reason for the dilution of the Participatory Thrust lies is in the nature of the policy worlds of urban America. The muffling of group turbulence reported here arises in part from the segmented nature of the urban political system, which produces what Yates (1976) has termed "street-fighting pluralism." That is, when groups inject new ideas into the local policy system, they face.

> . . . a political and administrative system that is fragmented to the point of chaos. Further, there is no coherent administrative order to implement and control new policies. What exists instead is an extreme pluralism of political, administrative, and community interests . . . and in this context, the likely fate of the new policy initiative is that it will be ripped apart in the street fight between political interests (Yates 1976 : p. 149).

So our executives can report greater group demands, but they are too often unfocused, confused, contradictory, and, in time, lack persistence. In the want the professional local executive has the resources that count—maze wisdom, persistence, group cohorts, etc.

Future analysis of these data will explore other consequences of the executive's role-taking and career development. But there, as in this paper, we face a local figure who is part of a natural network of resources and a local subculture of administration that makes him or her truly a political actor.

FOOTNOTE

1. No difference was found using this total measure and a five-category range ; the latter. however. is inappropriate for regression analysis. An alternative measure of size was the rough but familiar distinctions among central city, suburban and non-metropolitan areas. However, it produced no strong relationship with the GPI ; again this categorization is inappropriate for a regression analysis.

REFERENCES

Boyd, William L.. Community Status and Conflict in Suburban School Politics. Beverly Hills. CA. ; Sage, 1976.

Catanese, Anthony J., *Planners and Local Politics : Impossible Dreams.* Beverly Hills, CA. : Sage, 1978.

Catanese, Anthony J. and W. Paul Farme (eds.), *Personality, Politics, and Planning : How City Managers Work.* Beverly Hills, CA. : Sage, 1978.

Cuban, Larry, *Urban School Chiefs under Fire.* Chicago : University of Chicago Press, 1976.

Dehli Robert, *Who Governs ? New Haven,* Conn. : Yale University Press, McGivney, Joseph and William Moynihan, "School and Community". *Teachers College Record* 74 : 317-56, 1972.

Minar, David W., "The Community Basis of Conflict in School System Politics." *American Sociological Review* 31 : 822-34, 1966.

Rabinovitz, Francine F. *City Politics and Planning.* New York : Atherton, 1969.

Wirt, Frederick M., "Political Turbulence and Administrative Authority in the Schools." In Louis H. Masotti and Robert L. Lineberry (eds.), *The New Urban Politics.* Cambridge, Mass. : Ballinger, 1976.

Yates, Douglas, "Service Delivery and the Urban Political Order". In Willis A. Hawley and David Rodgers (eds.), *Improving Urban Management.* Beverly Hills, CA. : Sage, 1976.

[illegible]

[illegible] Personnel [illegible]

[illegible] of [illegible]

[illegible]

[illegible]

[illegible] Orientations [illegible] In [illegible]

THREE

HARALD BALDERSHEIM

ADMINISTRATIVE LEADERSHIP IN A BIG CITY

INTRODUCTION

This paper is a first report from a study of the role of city manager in a big city—Oslo. The study forms a part of a larger project on leaders and leadership in Norwegian cities.

Oslo's leadership structucture evolved as a response to a continuous expansion of local services. It was probably well suited to such a situation, in which the main political and administrative problem was that of effective implementation. When the period of expansion was over around 1976, and stagnation became the order of the day, the leadership structure emerged as a source of growing organisational friction.

From one point of view, a financial crisis is an environmental problem for the city, i.e. the emergence of an environment which denies the city the resourses it needs or is used to have for its services. From another point of view the crisis can be regarded as one of organisational control, i.e. an inability to control, the processes of spending and consumption in the organisation, for example the inability to reduce spending in the light of reduced resources.

If the city's problem is thought to be an environmental one, the leaders are faced with the task of *renegotiating* the environment (Thompson 1967 ; Mintzberg 1979). If the problem is one of organisational control, the pattern of *authority* may have to be revised or the distribution of loyalities redrawn (Mayer 1979). Oslo is, obviously, having problems of environmental adaptation

Paper presented at the "European Meeting on Applied Urban Research," Essen, Oct. 2-4, 1981.

—the input of resources from the environment is diminishing while substitutes have not yet been found—and also problems of organisational control—since spending has continued to grow. The problems that confront the urban leaders are illustrated below.

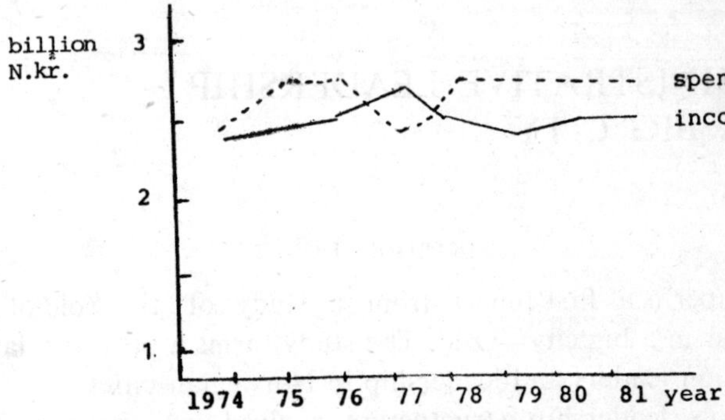

Fig. 3.1 : *Olso's net income and spending 1974-81, fixed Prices* (*1974*)
Source : Oslo Kummnee : Dokument nr. 3 Oslo bykasses pudsjett, 1981, p. 23.

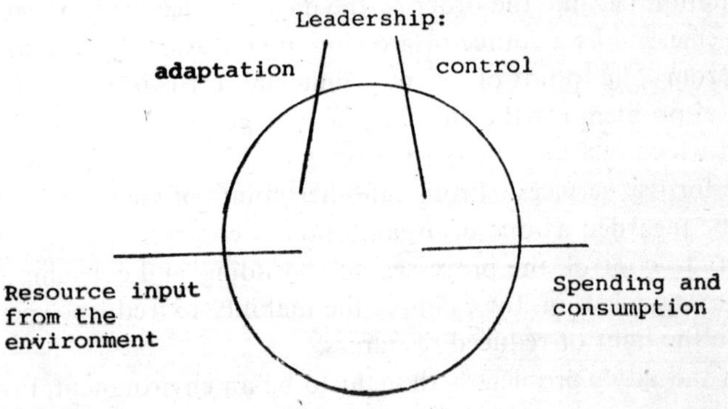

Fig. 3.2

The figure describes three processes :

1. Resources coming from the environment, (2) spending on and consumption of services, and (3) leadership, which is concerned with a) adapting to and negotiating with the en vironment, and with b) acquiring control over the organisation's spending.

Which strategy of leadership is emphasised when a mismatch between resources and spendsng occurs : taking financial imputs as given and increasing organisational control, or taking spending as given and searching for new sources of finances ? And what are the preconditions for succeeding with either strategy ? And how is city manager involved in either strategy ?

Leadership as organisational control

If organisational control is thought to be insufficient, why can't the leaders simply tighten it up and thereby bring the spending units to heel ? The answer to that lies in the ambiguous nature of authority found in most local government systems. Claims to organisational control, i.e. authority, are based on three different sources of legitimacy : electoral success, professional expertise, and hierarchical position. Local government systems vary as to how much weight they attach to elected personnel, professionals, and managers/hierarchical positions when it comes to allocating control over spending, but the three groups will nearly always be present in local government. In practical reforms the question is : how much control should by exerted by the elected representatives, how much by the technostructure, and how much by the managers ? At what stage of the process should the various groups participate, what should their contribution be, and how much weight should be attached to their respective contributions ? From the point of view of empirical research the interesting question is : what sort of consequences flow from the various ways of dividing work between the leaders ?

Ambiguity of authority is inherent in local government because of the leadership structure. The ambi uity is probably reinforced by size and complexity, which are characteristics of local government in cities. In an organisation where authority is highly ambiguous, processes of control will be *competitive* : control is expected to depend less on formal authority and more on the ability of groups and individuals to monopolise "pockets of uncertainty" (Crozier 1961). That means that the city manager's agenda will be filled with issues, the manager's authority over which is unclear or contested. The influence he is able to exert will depend very much on his ability to assert his office and his functions vis-a-vis other groups of leaders. Under such circumstances influence goes to those who are able to take an initiative and to hang on to it, i.e. to those with the time, energy, and analytical capability to think up new issues, problems, or solutions, and with the ability to put those on the agenda of other groups in the organisation (Cohen and March 1974 ; March and Olsen 1976).

Leadership as environmental impact

Like any other organisation local government depends on a favourable environment for its operations.

The transactional structnre of the voter/representative relationship is well covered ground in political theory and empirical research. The client/bureaucrat relationship is not so extensively treated, but it is not unmapped ground either. In contrast, the urban manager and his environmental relations is a dark continent. What is his contribution to a negotiated environment for the municipality ? Whom does he see ? What are the network to which he has access, and with what results ?

An organisation's participation in inter-organisational networks is a mark of dependence on external resources. The Hage/Aiken hypothesis offers both a model of inter-organisational dynamics and also an explanation of why local authorities, devoted to upholding organisational autonomy, become involved in external networks in the first place. They hold that dependence on external resources arise out of internal complexity and an accompanying propensity to innovate (Aiken and Hage 1968). Urbanisation is associated with organisational size, complexity and professionalisation of the local government machinery. Therefore, one would expect big, urban authorities to depend on a more far-flung and complex network than smaller, or less urbanised authorities. Furthermorc, the leaders of big-city authorities are probably involved in larger external networks than leaders of smaller authorites.

Consequently, by examining the city manager's network we should be able to map those parts of the environment on which the manager depends for the performance of his duties.

But we expect, once more, that the environmental impact of the manager depends on the time, energy, and analytical effort that go into the contacts with the environment. Since "networking" on behalf of a large organisation hardly is a one-man job, he will have to draw upon the resources of the organisation. This again means that he needs organisational control to make an impact on the environment. The greater his organisational control, the greater are his chances of influencing the environment. And, as a corollary, his chances are bounded by the competitive nature of organisational control in local government.

In this paper, only one of these aspects of the leadership processes will be examined : What problems or organisational control arise for the city manager as a result of the way authority is divided between elected representatives, the technostructure, and the city manager ?

The division of authority in Oslo

A Norwegian *city manager* is appointed by the local council, but the office is generally regarded as belonging to the administrative sphere of local government. The incumbent is expected to be above party politics, although some managers have held political office before their appointment.

The chief duties of the city manager are budgeting, accounting, planning, and financial forecasting. He is also policy adviser to the council, the council's executive board, and the financial committee. The Local Government Act stipulates that all action proposals that are to appear on the agenda of the council and the executive board must be routed through the city manager, if the proposals entail significant financial consequences for the authority. Since most proposals do entail such consequences, the manager is formally in a good position to make his views known to the political bodies. He is also in a position to give an unbiased view irrespective of the party colour of the political majority, since the authority cannot fire him without approval from the central government.

Expenditure proposals originate for the greater part in the technostructure, which nominally is subordinate to the city manager. His coordination of the technostructure is mainly, but not exclusively, of a financial nature. However, the city manager's influence over the leaders of the technostructure is limited. The manager has to submit the proposals from the technostructure to political bodies for consideration. He does not have the power to refuse to pass on a proposal with which he disagrees, although he will make sure the politicians are informed of his views.

The city manager's position represents an institutionalisation of financial rationality in the decision-making processes of the local authority. That means it is his duty to ensure that a *balanced* draft budget is presented to the political decision-makers, that the authority's cash flow is not endangered, and that borrowing is kept within reasonable limits.

The leadership of the *technostructure* is divided among seven branch directors along functional lines (transport, health, social services, etc.). Each director is head of a bundle of more or less related service departments. It is a peculiarity of traditional urban administration in Norway that the directors are granted access to the political bodies on an equal footing with the nominal head of administration, the city manager.

The directors not only submit proposals to the standing committees in their fields and to the board and the council, but they also have the right to meet and to speak in these bodies, including the financial committee.

Problems of organisational control

All organisations which practice specialisation of work have to divide up authority among the members. Organisational control is no problem when the division of authority is accepted and understood by all members of the organisation under all circumstances. The larger the number of issues, the authority over which is contested or ambiguous, the more unpredictable organisational control will be, and the more difficult it will be for the top management to retain leadership.

The city manager and the branch directors : who controls the purse ?

As mentioned, the branch directors have direct access to the political bodies of Oslo. Their access to the standing committees in their respective fields is of particular importance as regards organisational control. Through the close contacts which develop over time between the directors and the politicians on the committees, opportunities arise for short-cutting the City Manager's control over pl anning, budgeting and spending.

For a number of reasons service departments often have to ask for extra resources in addition the resources allocated through the normal budgetary process which takes place once a year. However, departments are encouraged to husband with their resources so that extraordinary allocations are avoided.

What are the City Manager's chance of success in the political bodies if he disagrees with one of the directors over requests of this nature ? Table 3.1 gives the figures for the number of requests for extra money which appeared on the agenda of the executive board, and where the City Manager *dissented* from the requests from the branch director. A total of 65 requests with a dissent were registered for 1978 and 1979 combined. The executive board decided *against* the City Manager's recommendation in 85 pct. of the cases, and, in other words, in favour of the directors. The City Manager has only a 15 pct. chance of persuading the executive board if he disagrees with a director over the allocation of extra resources. If his disagreement is with the Cultural Director, he only has a 5 pct. chance of succeeding. He has, in other words, a minimal degree of control over one of his core functions, financial management. As pointed out above, to understand how this lack of control arises, one has to bear in mind the organisation of the decisional process at the preparatory committee stage.

The material has been rearranged for the purpose of this paper. An example of influence wielded :

The transport plan and the motorway project

There seems to be no clear-cut relationship between the number and types of issues which appear on the City Manager's agenda, and his formal authority. Still, there are, of course, numerous instances of influence being exerted by the City Manager. What are the circumstances which favour managerial control in an organisation like the city of Oslo ?

TABLE 3.1 : **No. of requests for extra resources, with the City Manager dissenting, by branch—1978 and 1979 combined**

Branch	*Requests with dissents, no.*	*Requests granted by the Executive Board, — of column 1*
Culture	21	96
Social services	19	79
Housing	11	72
Health	9	89
Engineering works	3	100
Personnel	1	0
Transport	1	109
Sum	65	85

Source : Ida Borressen : Finansradmannens innflytelse i tilleggsbevilgningssaker. En undersokelse av tilleggsbevilgninger gitt Oslo kommune i 1978 og 1979, Institutt for statsvitenskap, Universitetet i Oslo, 1980.

Under conditions of ambiguous authority organisational control is expected to be heavily dependent upon the time and analytical capability available to the actors. More idiosyncratic factors will also play a part, such as an actor's interest in a project, or the enthusiasm he brings into an aspect of his job. The story of the transport plan and the motorway project illustrates this point.

In 1979 and early 1980, a new policy plan for Oslo was being prepared for the period 1980-90. The work was coordinated by the Policy Planning Unit. Transport was one of the subjects covered by the plan. A project group was set up to make the transport plan. The group included members from the Transport Director (traffic and urban development) and the Director for Engineering (highways).

The group discussed three alternatives for the transport plan : alternative A, which was status quo with regard to the use of private cars in the central parts of Oslo, in consequence, several large highways would have to be built ; in alternative B the emphasis was on the improvement of public transport combined with moderate restrictions on cars ; alternative C gave the highest priority to projects improving traffic safety for pedestrians and cyclists ; the improvement of public transport was also included whereas heavy restrictions on cars in the central parts of Oslo were recommended ; consequently, a low priority was given to the construction of highways. The group concluded its work by recommending the adoption of alternative C for the policy plan.

However, alternative C was highly controversial among the branch directors, among the employees in the City manager's office, at the political level, and among the public.

Not even the Transport Project Group were unanimous in its views. The members from the Highway Office left the group when work was at an advanced stage in protest at the way highways were being treated.

In the technostructure opinions were mostly in favour of adopting alternative A (October 1979) :

Director of Engineering	Alt. A
Highway Officer	,, A
Harbours Director	,, A
Traffic Officer	,, A
Director of Transport	,, B
Officer for Urban Development	,, B
Officer for Subway Projects	" B

The Transport Committee recommended alternative C (with a 4-3 majority), while the Highway commitee favoured alternative B. The parties in favour of C were Labour, the Liberals, and the Left Socialist Party. The Conservatives were for B. The alternative most wanted by the majority of the technostructure, A, had no support at the political level.

Independent of the policy plan and the Transport Project Group plans for a large motorway project through the centre of Oslo (grunnlinja) were being finalised. The project had been under way since the 1960's, and by late 1979 it had progressed to the stage where contractors had been hired. The bulldozers were literally pitched to start, just waiting for the go-ahead sign.

In November/December 1979 the necessary documents for the executive board's go-ahead signal were being prepared in the City Manager's office. At the same time, the City Manager and his Policy Planning Unit were making up their minds to accept the Transport Project Group's recommended alternative, the pedestrians- and cyclist-alternative (C). Then in January 1980, an officer in the Budget Unit, newly arrived there and temporarily brought into the Policy Planning Unit to work on the transport plan, wrote a memorandum arguing that building the central motorway was incompatible with adopting alternative C for the policy plan. Even though the preparation of the documents concerning the motorway was assigned to another officer, being responsible for the transport plan, he felt it his duty to point out the interconnection between the two projects, he said.

The motorway would take so much money for so long, he argued, that the resources needed for the traffic safety and public transport projects might not be available till after 1990. And if Oslo's resource base continued to shrink at the present rate, it would be particularly hard to find the necessary money. This was an unacceptable consequence in view of 1) the draft policy plan's emphasis on redistribution in favour of the underprivileged, and 2) the choice of alternative C for the transport plan.

The head of policy planning and also the City Manager accepted this line of reasoning. The City Manager went on to recommend that the executive board should suspend work on the motorway till the council had the opportunity to discuss the whole transport plan. Then the council would be able to review the motorway project in the wider context of the policy plan.

The City Manager's rccommendation on the motorway project was on the agenda of the executive board on the 11th of February 1980, but a decision was postponed. In the financial committee the majority rejected the City Manager's recommendation, however, some days later. The issue came on the board's agenda again on the 15th of February, and once more a decision was postponed. Then on the 5th of March the board voted to reject the Manager's advice with a 11-9 majority.

But a week later the council decided to discontinue work on the motorway till after the debate on the policy plan in August. The vote was 43-42 in favour of the City manager's proposal.

After the debate and the votings it was still uncertain what the majority of councillors would prefer with regard to alternative for the transport plan and the motorway project. One argument had been used against alternative C from the very beginning : Oslo would stand to "loose" substantial sums of money from the central government if highway construction was stopped. This argument came from the Highway Officer, among others. Most of the highway projects discussed in Oslo were national highways. 82% of the costs of national highways is shouldered by the central government. If Oslo, for example, decided to reject a national highway project costing 100 mill. kr., it would save an outlay of 18 mill. but would "loose" a highway worth 100 mill. kr.

Countering this sort of argument was thought to be important for the fate of the plan in the approaching August debate. The force of the argument could be reduced if it could be demonstrated that the central government was willing to contemplate a transfer of national resources earmarked for highways in Oslo to other projects in the transport sector, such as public transport, which was a wholly local responsibility. During the Spring of 1980 the planners had received signals indicating that the central government might indeed be willing to discuss such transfers of resources. But it was also clear that transfers would not be discussed unless it was satisfactorily documented that it would be in the national interest to do so.

What would be regarded as "satisfactory documentation" did not become clear until early June, after a meeting with the Minister for Transport (of the Labour Party government). Since the local debate was to be held in August, time was running short, the more so because the peak of the holiday season was approaching.

A project group to provide the necessary documentation was set up. The officer who had started the ball rolling with the memorandum on the central motorway was appointed the

City Manager's deputy for coordinating the group. The group included 10 members from the Department for Urban Development, another coordinator from the Transport Director's office, and an observer from the Highway Officer, who remained rather passive. A firm of consultants was used for special analyses.

The group commenced work around the middle of June, and a copy of its report was sent to the Ministry on the 1st of August, eleven days before the Minister was due to visit Oslo to be briefed on Oslo's problems in the transport sector. The effort was the more impressive since several of the members of the group had to take their summer holiday in this period. The report ran to 230 pages, not counting a separate summary of 30 pages. In 9 chapters most aspects of Oslo's transport system were covered.

The forces behind this effort was no doubt the City Manager's deputy in the group. He sacrificed most of his own holiday to participate in all phases of the project. His work included producing some of the analyses, editing the report, rewriting chapters, proof-reading the report, and supervising the printing.

The City Manager's proposal for a policy plan was debated on the 28th and 29th of August. The project group's report was submitted as an integral part of the policy plan. A majority of Labour, Left Socialists, Liberals, and the Christian People's Party emerged as the majority, choosing alternative C 2 for the transport plan. This alternative presupposed the transfer of national highway resources for use on local public transport projects. The central motorway ended up being supported by the Conservatives only.

The process described here seems to demonstrate that the influence the City Manager can hope to have in the organisation, to a large extent depends upon the interest and the energy his officers invest in a project. Being relatively few in numbers, the City Manager's officers cannot influence all issues they deal with equally much. The key to managerial control seems to lie in the choices his officers make when they decide whether or not to take an *extra* interest in a particular issue. One way for the City Manager to control the organisation is by influencing these choices. At the managerial level, the chief mechanisms for achieving such influence is probably through recruitment policies, motivation, and socialisation (Laegreid and Olsen 1978). One would expect other mechanisms like detailed supervision or review to have little chance of succeeding, given the type of work management at this level requires (Mintzberg 1973), and given the sheer number of issues the City Manager has to deal with.

REFERENCES

M. Aiken and J. Hage, Organisational Interdependence and Inte-organizational Structure, *Am. Soc. Rev.*, 33, 1968.

M.D. Cohen and J.G. March, *Leadership and Ambiguity*, N.Y., 1964.

M. Crozier, *The Bureaucratic Phenomenon*, Chicago, 1964.

P. Laegreid and J.P. Olsen *Byrakrati og beslutninger*, Bergen, 1978.

J.G. March and J.P. Olsen, *Ambiguity and Choice in Organizations*, Bergen, 1976.

M.W. Meyer, *Change in Public Bureaucracy*, London 1973.

H. Mintvberg, *The Nature of Managerial Work*, N.Y., 1973.

H. Mintvberg, *The Structuring of Organizations*, Englewood Cliffs, 1979.

J.D. Thompson, *Organisations in Action*, McGraw-Hill, 1967.

FOUR

GERD-MICHAEL HELLSTERN AND
HELLMUTT WOLLMANN

THE CONTRIBUTION OF EVALUATION TO ADMINISTRATION

EVALUATION, is intended for use, and the demand for evaluation has come mainly from administration. Having a strong administrative tradition, Germany as a rapidly "developing country" in evaluation research is an interesting case study, illustrating the interrelationships among the administrative machinery, the political process, and evaluation research and offering some informed guesses about the perspectives and the utilization of evaluation in such a setting. In describing the connection between administrative needs and responding evaluation tools and strategies, we shall concentrate on the necessity of evaluation to address the special problems created by the administrative process. We shall also analyze the different models and instruments which developed in Germany in response to the various needs of the policy arena and administrative and political environments.

Four questions illustrate the current statc of evaluation to administration in this respect :

1. What was the impetus shaping the evolution of evaluation ?
2. What links will increase administrative and political use of evaluation ?
3. What forms of evaluation have emerged for new assessment tools taking into account the German political and administrative system ?

4. How does the German experience compare with the American one, and what modifications are required ?

THE GROWTH OF EVALUATION IN GERMANY

Several years ago, only a few people were willing to consider evaluation research in the Federal Republic as a legitimate enterprise. The spectacular rise in the last few years in the number of evaluation research endeavors was evident from a computer search, with the help of the Informationszentrum Sozialwissenschaft in Bonn. Of approximately 30,000 social science research projects in Germany during the last six years, around 1,600 may be considered evaluations. The proportion, as well as the absolute number, of these research projects has been growing steadily to nearly 15 to 20 per cent of all research projects in the social science field, quadrupling from 1971 to 1977.

There is a considerable time lag between the American explosion of evaluation research into a major business field and the German evolution of evaluation as a social science research field. Nevertheless, the comparative analysis of the growth and evolution of evaluation in his country helps to clarify the underlying interests in evaluation research and to explain the commn reason for such a development. The different uses, forms, and types of evaluation research in Germany may increase the creative use and the development of alternative evaluation research tools. The most astonishing feature of the evolution of evaluation in Germany, next to its growth, is its metamorphosis during the last few years. Evaluation research activities were shaped by different forces stemming from changing administrative and political needs. In response, it had different goals and models. For analytic purposes, three purposes for evaluation may be distinguished :

(1) evaluation as a *rationalization tool* in times of political planning euphoria ;
(2) evaluation as an *effectiveness tool* in times of financial difficulty ; and

(3) evaluation as an *accountability tool* in a time of need for responsive and well-legitimated government action.

Evaluations were called upon as a "political planning tool" in the late sixties. As a part of a feedback process to increase purposeful coordinated government action, it gained importance as a tool to increase efficiency in a time of recession in the mid-seventies when decisions had to be made about the allocation of scarce governmental resources. Finally, evaluation demand has recently increased due to the need in accountability and responsiveness, as a counterbalance for the destabilized power system, undermined by growing citizen actions and changing political party structure.

Creating demand

German evaluation research had its beginnings in the reform movement of the late nineteenth century.[2] However, its evolution as a major activity in government and administration may be limited to the last ten years. In the aftermath of the reform movement during the late sixties and early seventies, German evaluation research blossomed. The economic recession in the mid-sixties marked the initiation of great concern and interest in planned governmental intervention (Mayntz and Scharpf 1975 ; Johnson 1972 ; Ashford et al. 1975). This was ushered in by the "Great Coalition" in 1966, which took the first steps to translate rhetoric into action programs. The introduction of regular state intervention activities had its official foundation in the amendments to the "Basic Law" (the West German constitution) in 1969, in which relatively new tasks for governmental intervention were formally outlined. This intervention was intended primarily to stabilize the economy by extending the range of governmental activities. The main elements are as follows :

—the need for intervention as a federal task was formally recognized :

—new intergovernmental relationships among federal, state, and local governments ("cooperative federalism") were established to regulate and channel this new flow of intervention activties ; and

—new rules for financial cooperation aimed at a coordinated economic policy were established to streamline action throughout the different federal levels in the complex and fragmented decision-making structure, characteristic of West German administration.

The policy areas covered by these constitutional revisions were different from those addressed by the American "War on Poverty". Governmental activities were more concerned with promoting infrastructural change than with legislating institutional change or changing social conditions. The areas covered concentrated on policy with a great need for capital investment. According to the amended Article 91a, 91b, and 104a of the Basic Law, spending activities (Reissert 1978 ; Spahn 1978) were in the fields of

—regional economic policy,
—agricultural reform and coastline protection,
—university development and education,
—urban transportation,
—urban development and renewal, and
—hospital building and reforms.

By introducing the new programs, the bureaucratic behavior which traditionally followed "conditional rules" changed to more goal-oriented functional and "programmatic behavior", which emphasized purposeful administrative action and decision-making. At the same time, those changes increased a process of political and administrative centralization, the amount of legislation delivered, led to increased regulation in many policy fields, and increased the size of governmental control.[8]

Effective demand for evaluation arose for very practical reasons. Stressing the experimental and preliminary character of new programs helped the administration and the majority party to secure the acceptance of innovative changes. Insecurity resulting from the newness of the programs created a demand for ongoing evaluation to optimize the program structure and avoid possible unforeseeable side effects. By requiring an evaluation, Parliament relieved the administration from the burden of proving success of a program in advance. Local reaction to educational reform and urban renewal programs called attention to the lack of information on impact and the proper implementation of the programs. Parallel with the increase of centralization, threats of the state and local levels to systematically displace the foregoing federal goals increased. Evaluations should improve program implementation by providing information on its achievements. The reports of newly installed commissions aiming at rationalization and reform and the evidence of the evaluation research results which were implemented stimulated a new wave of understanding regarding the difficulty in achieving the ambitious domestic reform programs through extensive regulations, the necessary extension for local (or situational) flexibility, and the need for new management and analytical tools.

Evaluation was becoming an important tool in four respects :

—External impact evaluation increased to provide information on the execution of programs in a politically fragmented, multilevel structure.

—Requirements for internal administrative evaluation increased to keep a check on goal-oriented programmatic behavior of the different agencies.

—Assessment of the effects of programs on th victims of change, such as through displacement in the Urban Renewal Program, was increasingly recognized as a necessity.

—As constitutional problems increased, the need for control mechanisms for Parliament to oversee administrative and executive agencies increased.

POLICY ANALYSIS CREEPING INTO ADMINISTRATION

The climate for social science analysis likewise changed. Evaluations, in the heyday of reform between 1969 and 1973, were expected to provide more rational decision-making and streamlining of the administrative and constitutional basis of government and to make "politcial planning" and "reform" feasible. Social science analysis was called upon to help in meeting ambitious aims of the reformers in three ways:

—as an instrument to change the administrative structure of government,
—as a means to regulate constitutional problems and conflicts arising out of the new power distributions, and
—as a "feeler" for social problems and actions needed.

The work of four commissions may best highlight those problems.

Changing administrative structure

The need for change in the institutional and administrative machinery was formally recognized by the establishment of two commissions or task forces. The major purpose of the executive Task Force on Governmental and Administrative Reform (Projektgruppe Regierungs-und Verwaltungsreform) in 1969 was to streamline and rationalize governmental actions, add an analytic capability, and develop coordinating mechanisms and feedback devices to improve the effectiveness of governmental programs.[4] Despite some minor successes, the departmental powers proved too strong to allow for a coordinated overall policy. When the task force was resolved in 1975 only a task sheet remained from the envisioned comprehensive planning system to desrcibe current programs and actions to the different ministries. In 1971, following the establishment of the task force, a parliamentary commission for the reform of the civil service (Dienstrechtsreformkommission) was set up to suggest changes in the bureaucratic personal structure to allow for a more adequate "task-oriented" personal structure, which was hoped would facilitate the implementation of reform programs. Despite a long report in 1973, the translation of the commission's recommendations into effective reform is still not visible. What has remained is the intrusion of "evaluation ideas" into different departments and great concern on the part of the Civil Service Academy for a goal- and result-oriented management system (Verwaltung und Fortbildung, 2, 1979).

Solving emerging constitutional problems
The new activities and domestic reform programs affected not only the operation of the internal administration but, more visibly, the balance of power in the federal system. In 1971 an "Enquete Commission" for the reform of the Constitution was established. The commission was expected to find new ways to balance the system, to increase parliamentary control, and to find modalities to improve the relationships between the federation (Bund) and the states (Lander). It was hoped that the commission would succeed in institutionalizing some kind of parliamentary control or supervisory procedures of government activities and would be able to find a new balance for the working relation of the federal system between the states and the federation. The promise of the interim report which emphasized different forms of evaluation procedures or regulations to strengthen the supervisory function of Parliament was not met in the final report, which avoided the issue of planning control and evaluation. Despite widespread disappointment, Parliament succeeded in defending its own interests by taking advantage of established traditional tools. Reporting requirements and termination clauses for new programs proved more successful than the plea for institutionalized evaluation procedures. In addition, political changes at the state level brought the political centralization to a sudden halt ; the states in control for the implementation of the reform measures were gaining in political weight due to the changing favor of the voters at the state level. The Bundesrat and the Ministerkonferenz of the state governors proved to be the counterweight to any central domestic reform, which often lacked clear goals and rules for implementation.

Responding to social needs
A broad mandate to survey the need for change and to set goals for change was received by the "Commission for Social Change" in 1973. In a mammoth approach the commission surveyed the field of social changes and necessary governmental changes with the help of more than 150 (published) reports. The commission recommended changes in nearly all fields, from

ex ante evaluation problems in the field of technology assessment to ex post evaluations of governmental programs. But the breadth of their approach and the altered political and social climate by the time the report was delivered in 1975 largely undermined the immediate utilization of the report's recommendations. Their demand for better technolgy assessment and environmental impact assessment systems, for program monitoring and continuous evaluation procedures, remained unfulfilled.

The second face of evaluation

"After the reform" in the mid-seventies, the press to establish a rational decision-making base came to a sudden halt, the restrictions on positive planning tightened, and the limits for governmental actions became clearer (Hanf and Scharpf 1978). The focus of action changed from the executive federal level to the local and state levels. Some of these new directions came from a recognition of the difficulty of planned change in the federal system with varying political forces, from the unanticipated consequences of the measures taken, and from the growing unwillingness to accept further change. The restrictions on the available funds, which drastically limited the range of possible reforms, came from the sudden realization of the limitations on resources, the population decline, and the beginning of the energy shortage, The impetus for evaluation changed from the planning units to the financial budgetary offices to the comptroller general, the BRH (*Bundesrechnungshof*). The best indication of the changing mood was the recognition of the administrative order coming out of the §7 Budget Law (BHO, Bundeshaushaltsordnung of the new Budget Law in 1973), which provided the first legal basis for ex post evaluation. A major concern for the financial consequences of reform programs developed, especially at the local level. Self-evaluation as a tool for setting priorities with regard to various local tasks and for streamlining the task program (by introduction of "task critique"—*Aufgabenkritik*) became popular in larger local government departments (Banner 1979). The treasurer became involved in the evaluation of programs to coordinate investment programs.

The rise of responsive management

The new concept of increased financial responsibility and local autonomy merged with a renewed interest in administrative accountability for public accountability. The growing demand for increased institutions is manifested in the growing unwillingness to accept governmental decisions ; for example, in the field of environmental policies and transportation. The attempts of political planning and domestic reform became the subjects of attack under the slogan "debureaucratization and private sector control" of governmental activities ; attempts were made to deregulate activities and to speed up the decision-making processes. The new mood is reflected in the appointment of "debureaucratization" committees since 1977 at the federal level and in many states which intend to decrease federal paperwork and to increase administrative flexibility and responsiveness to citizens.

In this process, parliament gained new muscles ; politicians became increasingly aware of their unused power potential and insisted on reports about the effects and outcome of certain policies and decisions. The willingness to accept administrative actions and reports without questioning diminished. The awareness of the small increments for political change possible given an energy shortage and population decline increased. The political split between the states and the federal level gained in importance. Administration became less concerned with monitoring subordinates ; career-oriented administrators became more interested in their own managerial evaluation and became increasingly interested in proving their responsiveness to citizen's needs. As a result of these diverse trends, evaluation needs emerged which responded to the new power distribution. Evaluation became less an administrative tool to regulate subordinates and increasingly recognized as an instrument in the policy-shaping process. Evaluations became more political, and their use as a strategic weapon increased. The growing interest in interactive process-oriented management tools reflects this new administrative mood. The attempt to add subjective indicators to the "objective" measurement of impact is part of this trend.

The emergence of social science

In order to understand the current boom in evaluation activities, analyses cannot be confined to the field of politics and administration. One has to take into account the dynamic change which has occurred over the years in the social science as well. The explosion in the social sciences during the last ten years may be measured by the number of new departments and faculties created, the number of faculty members added, and the mushrooming number of students. It has brought changes in the professional perspectives of the younger social scientists, who no longer can find their fields in the realm of education, no longer can reside in an ivory tower, and are increasingly forced to work in institutions and organizations outside the universities. They not only enter the administration as a task force for change (like the Task Force for Government and Administrative Reform), but increasingly take up regular posts in the administration, thus providing a necessary link between the social science research and administrative perspectives. With their entrance into the federal, state, and local government levels they change the framework and background of their agency, often raising the standard of work delivery, increasing the planning and organizational capacity, and providing the kind of receptivity which is needed to use the social science information (Mayntz 1977).

With the recognition of the need for change and reform, new institutions were founded to engage in applied research (such as The Center for Science in Berlin, the Deutsches Institut fur Urbanistik, a national urban institute). Existing governmental research institutions were enlarged (like the National Health Institute) ; even the states founded their own government research institutions (iike the Institute for State Planning and Urban Research in Dortmund). New independent research enterprises sprang up, and universities started to build their own applied research centers. The traditional focus of applied research previously limited to the field of economics changed to reduce the interest in macroeconomic studies. There is now greater concern with the outcome of governmental actions than with tabulating governmental output. Increased demand for an understanding of the administrative process, of the link between intention and outcome, has emerged. This change of focus is reflected not only in the creation of new institutions for the study of public administration in Speyer, Konstanz, Bielefeld, and Berlin, but much more in the new perspective of public administration. The change has been from a legal perspective to one increasingly grounded in the social sciences.

For evaluation, the picture which emerges shows signs of great diversity. The current change is accompanied by a greater concern with program management, organizational development, and procedural change. The new interest in public realities is leading more and more evaluators to question some of their social scientific criteria, with questions of relevance replacing criteria of generalizability. Attempts have been made to combine traditional approaches to an understanding of the sciences with the methodological tools of behavioral sciences. The changing role of social science has led to the fear of increased exploitation of the social sciences—the use or misuse of social science by directing and designing the fields of research. This has led to an intense and critical discussion on the future directions of the social sciences in our society. It may also equally be seen as a new potential for increasing the relevance and influence of the social sciences and evaluation research.[5]

DEVELOPING BASES IN ADMINISTRATION

The overview of the driving forces in the growth of demands for evaluation in Germany illustrates some of its diversity (which partly accounts for its potentials) and its dependence on the administrative and political interests of administrators and policy makers. As in other countries, evaluation in Germany depends on liaisons with the political and administrative process. As a result, evaluation should be organized along traditional channels of information and administrative work production. Government reporting and record-keeping are traditional devices for information processing, cornerstones for evaluation research. The further development of a government reporting (political accounting) system may still prove a strong basis for ensuring evaluation an instant link to parliament. New dimensions for administrative evaluation and monitoring may be opened by the introduction of the computers, which offers new possibilities for joint record-9eeping and informations system.

Transmitting evaluation into the political process

The number of official governmental reports which find their way back to Parliament has increased steadily over the last ten years. Whereas the frequency of reporting nowadays is decreasing, the number of required reports is still increasing. These now total around 100, half of which must be delivered at regular intervals. The reports themselves vary greatly in content and are often of limited value as an evaluation instrument, since the information given in the report is, by and large, determined by the agency being evaluated or checked.

Several types of reports may be distinguished, such as comprehensive report from fields of actions (such as "Planning Reports"), programs or issue-specific reports (for example, "Reports on Housing Problems"), and reports required regularly by law and specific ad hoc reports. These last are increasingly becoming a parliamentary tool to force administrative action. In general, the trend is to move first from analytical to programmatic reports and from there to more evaluative reports. This is best illustrated by the reports in the fields of regional policy, social policy and agriculture (Federal Ministry of Regional Planning, 1977). Most of them appeared for the first time in the mid-sixties as programmatic report, whereas today they contain some measures of goal-achievement and output production.

Reports alone cannot substitute for more intense evaluation research, nor can they serve as a parliamentary control instrument. However, they can provide an evaluation stimulus, ensure continuing interest in evaluating the policy field, or transmit evaluation research results to a larger public and parliament to keep interest alive in some policy areas. Their constant pressure for evaluation and coordination in the process of report preparation should not be underestimated.

From administrative control to a computerized accounting system

Whereas report requirements are often the outside stimulus for evaluation, the collection of administrative data is often the precondition for a successful evaluation. The use of administrative data generated by the processes of application, internal reporting, and spending is very often hampered by the insufficient procedures of recording the data. Only in a few cases have administrative data been systematically used for monitoring purposes. However, with the increasing computerization of administration, the potential use of administrative records and data will become easier, increasing the possibilities for evaluative purposes. Three different appoaches may be currently distinguished :

—the building of systematic observation systems from different data sets ;

—the use of the financial acounting system to provide information on the flow of resources ; and

—the use of particular program statistics to develop a program-related data bank.

"Observation systems" are often part of the federal and state statistical service. These systems contain a set of structural data mostly as background information. They measure, for example, the quality of life (provision of services, financial health) in different communities. These data banks, which are developed mostly outside the regular administrative system, provide only limited information on the administrative achievement in certain programs. Their aim is to provide background information on the state of a region or city, drawing their data from the official statistics. Examples are the observation system of the Bundesforschungsanstalt fur Raumforschung und Landeskunde (BflR), the "structural data sheets" of some state statistical agencies, or the indicator system of the Ministry for Labour and Social Affairs. More important for evaluators are attempts to provide some baseline information on governmental spending and to build up program or project statistics.

These uses of data banks, however, bring out a major limitation. Both in the states and in such federal agencies as the Department for Economic Cooperation and the Department of Transportation, the uses of data for evaluative purposes so far have been limited by the political sensitivity of the process monitoring its implementation. The system, well known for its high sophistication, includes evaluated observable effects of the highways as data and as part of the decision making and priority-setting process. But the experience so far also shows how difficult it is to separate such information from various political interests. The past history of the data bank's usage shows how sensitive such a statistical data bank is to political distortion and outside pressures.

Although the agencies recognize the need for a more computerized information system and a more sophisticated evaluation system to maintain monitoring functions, the manpower and the knowledge required to use those computerized recording systems is lacking in many offices and agencies responsible for the programs. Computerized information systems are mainly regarded as increasing the complexity of the information without providing an adequate reduction mechanism or flexible handling of individual cases. For officials, who are empirically knowledgeable but untrained in statistics, computerized project statistics are both too complex and too unsophisticated to serve as a tool for information. Most experienced administrators therefore tend to supplement computerized "early warning systems" or complicated reporting systems by informal controls. They base evaluation activities on the informal mechanism of regular site visits, ratings and judgments by the operating unit, or problem-oriented evaluations by external evaluators for more rigid reviews. Through the use of flexible interrogative technique a better check can be made on possible distortions, and political and administrative constraints can be better taken into account. Political turmoil and clashes can often be better dealt with by early individual consideration of the individual situation than by relying on the formalized, politically inflexible accounting system. In order to improve evaluation systems, one has to find the right balance between the improvement of the recording base and the use of informal scanning and information procedures.

THE DIFFERENTIAL USE OF EVALUATION IN THE FEDERAL GOVERNMENT

Evaluation research handbooks often give the impression that evaluation is the last stage in the planning-reform cycle : from analysis, planning, programming, implementation, to evaluation. This picture needs correction, because of numerous overlapping and simultaneous actions. In this process, evaluation is a focus which has its source in very different administrative and political activities, such as bookkeeping, accounting, and financial assessment, and which is brought in at very different stages of such planning-evaluation cycles. A large number of heterogeneous approaches stemming from those activities, shaped by different policy arenas and research traditions, have fostered a multiplicity of evaluation approaches at the federal level. For example, the heterogeneity and multiplicity of evaluation approaches may demonstrate the need for adapting evaluation research to the particular needs of the surrounding administrative and political environment. Five different approaches have merged which demonstrate the various uses of evaluation in the federal government :

1. The most ambitious model of evaluation practice tries to link evaluation to a *comprehensive program-building* process with clear goals and operational objectives. This attempt is best illustrated by the Department of Agriculture.
2. Less ambitious but still noteworthy is the case of the Department of Economic Cooperation. Here an *institutionalized evaluation office* is responsible for continuous routine and ad hoc evaluation.
3. Limited in their approach, but easier to institutionalize, are program evaluations which use program related *monitoring systems* to help shape program decisions. The Regional Economic Policy serves as an example of such a program.

4. There are numerous *model projects* accompanied by evaluation research mainly to demonstrate the usefulness of the model. The connection of those projects to administration is weaker and the use of evaluation results more uncertain. This approach has often been taken in the field of education and social policy.
5. The use of *experimental programs* to introduce change is increasing. This approach is mostly limited to fields in which a highly technical problem is involved ; for example, telecommunication or transportation. Often administrative and political decisions have already been shaped, and the experimental program is designed only to demonstrate the usefulness of such programs or provide information for program adaptation and implementation.

Evaluation as program development

A comprehensive planning program-evaluation system has long been the aim of many administrative reformers. During the heyday of programmatic policy reform in government, the planning staff in the Federal Chancellor's Office tried to develop and implement the first stages of an integrated planning system. According to the federal-level plan, all departments were to be included in a regular feedback system channeled by a "task-data-sheet" (*Aufgabenblatt*). Despite all initial efforts, the separate departmental administrative interests proved far too strong to allow for streamlined planning and evaluation activities under the auspices of the chancellor. The current practice of the Chancellor's Office is therefore to select only single interdepartmental problem areas for evaluation (Steinhausen 1979).

The development of an integrated planning and evaluation system seems to have been achieved inside one department, rather than among a group of departments. After many attempts, the Task Force for Governmental and Administrative Reform (Projektgruppe Regierungs-und Verwaltungsreform) finally succeeded in enlisting the cooperation of one "pilot department"—namely, the Department of Agriculture and Forestry (Bieler 1979).

Case illustration—rationalization with no imp act

The Department of Agriculture and Forestry had lost many of its former departmental tasks to the EEC. Public criticism was growing when, in 1973, it decided to introduce a new program structure which would integrate task structure and finance programming. A special evaluation unit was set up to be responsible for conducting evaluation studies and cost-benefit analysis.

In each program section, an authorized planning representative who is at the same time a member of a cross-sectional "planning-group" is responsible for planning programming and evaluation tasks in each program section. Programs and projects for evaluation are selected yearly in a brainstorming session by the planning group or suggested by the various program section. The evaluations are mostly carried out by outside evaluators ; one of the main tasks of the evaluation unit is to stimulate discussion and cooperation between the programe section and the evaluators. Despite its rational outlook, the system often has difficulty dealing with the political pressures arising in different programs and the need to respond to the complicated decision-making process created by the EEC in the field of agriculture. The transfer and utilization of the evaluation research results therefore still create a bottleneck. Increasing publication is one of the strategies to improve the diffusion and utilization of evaluation research results, however, despitel the rational approach to synthesize programmatic, organizational, and evaluation structure, the impact in the politica arena has yet to be felt.

Establishing governmental evaluation units

Evaluation activities may be found in all government departments, even at the local level. Very often they are connected with the planning or policy units. At the local level, evaluation-related activities are often carried out by the budget office of sectional agencies (such as in the welfare office). Sectorial evaluations usually prove to be more successful in the acceptance of their findings and the implementation of their evaluation results than their cross-sectional counterparts. Despite many attempts, real evidence of an institutionalization of evaluation rarely can be found. Only a few agencies and cities have their own evaluation office ; the earliest and most often cited example of this at the federal level is the inspection (or evaluation) unit of the Department for Economic Cooperation.

Case illustration—outside stimulus, inside restrictions
Since the UNESCO Conference on the Effectiveness of Social and Technical Assistance to Underdeveloped Countries in 1954, discussion in the Department for Economic Cooperation (BMZ) has never ceased on how to best evaluate its own program. As a consequence of the UN proclamation of the first Development Decade, the department issued a policy paper in which constant evaluation of its policies was suggested as part of its program. In 1970 an evaluation unit was created which still exists ; it forms no part of the administrative hierarchy and reports directly to the concerned program unit and program managers. For purposes of evaluation, projects are chosen partly according to systematic (serial) procedures that cover most of the projects at least once during their respective periods of existence, and projects are selected partly on an ad hoc basis according to special problems brought to light from the regional offices or indicated by the department's "early warning system". This system, called projects statistic, forms a data bank containing, by and large, information on the financial flow and the progress of project activities. The evaluation procedures used by the BMZ largely stem from the World Bank discussion on project appraisal ; evaluation is carried out by staff members assisted by some suborganization of the Ministry (the Gesellschaft fur Technische Zusammenarbeit, the Organization for Technical Cooperation, GTZ, is particularly important in this regard) and selected experts from outside.

The evaluation is conceived as a "goal-analytical process" which centers around four criteria :

—effectiveness,
—efficiency,
—significance, and
—transferability.

Despite the rather elaborate evaluation system, many of the evaluations are either economic or descriptive. The quality of the evaluations varies, and their validity is often questionable.

The fact that the results of some of the program evaluations have been used as political weapons by the opposition has only served to aggravate an already difficult situation for the special evaluation unit in the department. Willingness to cooperate among the regional and program agencies still remains rather weak ; the fear of negative sanctions and repercussions is hard to overcome. However, willingness to cooperate has begun to increase since strict confidentiality for the results of the research was promised and finally achieved to some extent.

The difficulty of including political criteria in the evaluation and of taking into account the dynamic political process in some underdeveloped countries often makes it necessary to alter set goals and objectives, making clear evaluation more difficult. Increased feedback and discussion have helped to increase acceptance of the evaluations. Organized feedback procedures and frequent participation of the program managers are now essential features of the system.

Monitoring

When comprehensive evaluations are not possible, the institutionalization of program-related evaluations is still a possibility. Attempts to continuously monitor programs are increasing. The best examples can be found at the local level, where data are readily available (for example, for the measurement of environmental quality). Data systems for efficient monitoring at the federal level are harder to develop. After the failure of the Central Planning Agency of the Chancellor's Office to establish a regularly updated (Reform) project data bank, some departments developed their own data banks and indicator systems (such as the Department of Labor and the Department of Transportation). A good example of the attempts to introduce some kind of systematic monitoring and evaluation can be found in the field of regional economic policy (Kohn 1979).

Case illustration—monitoring : stalemate

Regional economic policy is a shared task of the federal government and the states, introduced by Article 104 of the Basic Law in 1969. It aims to secure the same standard of living throughout West Germany and to counter-balance the adverse effects of structural changes. To aid those areas, whose economic potential has lagged considerably behind the federal average, and to mobilize unutilized or insufficiently utilized production factors by stimulating job creation of safeguarding jobs, some 700 million DM a year are spent as investment aids to private enterprises and for infrastructure and industrial sites. In a four-year plan, which is updated annually, progress and planning decisions are reported. To guide the decision-making and to regulate competition between the states, a monitoring system was developed which sought to measure the needs and potential of each region in the Federal Republic. A common indicator was constructed which included measurements of infrastructure, unemployment, and income. All regions falling below a certain level were to be included. The success in reaching a final agreement on the indicator construction created mixed feelings. Critics pointed to the crucial questions of the validity of the indicator regarding to the possibilities of statistical distortion. Using job creation as a tool for measuring success, numerous studies have shown the limits of these current measures. Changes in the indicators may not reflect program-induced change but result of other ongoing processes. Long-term effects may be missed or overrated by the current system, which also may not be able to provide information on the action necessary to guide structural change. Information on side or adverse effects of the program is lacking. The indicator seemed to have been created to fit crucial political needs, with the size and borders of a region largely determining the results of the measurement process. Political bargaining determined the final decision. Monitoring succeeds only so far as consensus can be achieved on the selection of the right indicators. As a consequence, one may state that political decisions cannot be avoided by referring to a (mechanical) technical tool, as has been attempted so far.

The use of models

Evaluation has become a major enterprise in the Federal Republic, not only in the field of social policy, but also in education. In both fields, the federal government is limited in its action by the Basic Law. To bring about innovations in these fields, it has often financed model programs to demonstrate the usefulness of some alternative approaches to social and educational problems. A joint federal-state educational commission (*Bund-Lander-Kommission fur Bildungsplanung und Forschungsforderung*) decides on most of the model-research program for educational purposes. As a new variation, they now attempt to build up model regions to integrate and combine different models and the so far often isolated and noncomparable projects.

Similar demonstration programs are conducted in the social fields (for example, for pregnancy consultation). Evaluation has played an important part in demonstrating the effectiveness of these programs. For example, at the preschool and primary school levels the federal government spent some 64 million DM in 1978 ; but the largest and most discussed issue is the introduction of "experimental comprehensive schools". Some 125 million DM have been spent by the Bildungskommission for these projects.

Case illusartion—action as evaluation

The Federal Republic tended to produce only a small percentage of students with university educations as compared with other western countries in the sixties. The *Bildungsrevolution* (educational revolution) brought about a major departure from the human-oriented ("*geisteswissens-chaftlichen*") approach to a more empirically oriented approach in education. The Max-Planck Institute (founded in 1963) was one of the forerunners of this development. Preliminary steps for educational reform were taken in the late sixties. In the early seventies most reforms were concerned with implementing new educational systems, as in the preschool curricula programs and the comprehensive school models. Most of the accompanying research projects used a practice oriented approach, stressing development and substituting action for evaluation.

The evaluation of the German Youth Institute (Deutsches Jugendinstitut) may serve as a characteristic example of such an approach. Most of their efforts went into curricular development evaluation. Rigid evaluation designs were disregarded, since (1) the priorities differed in the different states (the states are responsible for cultural and educational affairs), (2) the program implementation procedures and regulations differed between the states, and (3) the differences in the population of the model schools impeded the implementation of simple experimental design rules.

For their "practice-oriented" approaches they stressed the use of soft designs, using group discussion, expert interviews and parental involvement, communications and organizational development as their main tools. The immediate success of a curriculum took priority over "scientific rigor". Tests were not regarded as suitable instruments for comparison. Instead, research concentrated on judgmental data-rating schemes, group discussions, and the like. The stress on qualitative approaches to evaluation, the need for success and the uncoordinated and unconnected evaluation attempts diminished the transfer value of the institute's evaluations. As in other model projects, the model character and the evaluation activity had to serve to conceal the introduction of new programs and to help to make the program "a success". The available evaluation tools in most cases were too rigid to allow for the hidden political aims of the evaluations. More qualitative approaches maintaining the scientific standards of qualitative research procedures are needed fit this task.

Experimental programs : limited to technical issues ?

Experimental programs are found mostly in the field of technical experimentation ; for example, the introduction of cable TV, new traffic schemes, or noise reduction programs. Some published examples are the "highway speed reduction" experiment and the experiments preceding the introduction of a "phone tact" system (limiting local phone calls in time). One nontechnical experiment with far-reaching implications has been developed in the process of legal reform (Geck, 1977).

Case Illustration—Limits to Reforms as Experiments

For a long time, legal education in the Federal Republic followed a two stage pattern. The first stage of university training was followed by a practically oriented traineeship. Reform came under discussion in the late sixties and early seventies, accompanied by much resistance in the profession. In order to make reform possible, a federal statute—§5 Richtergesetz (Law for the Judges)—for the first time authorized the states to combine university studies and practical training (one-stage education). Eight universities introduced new experimental programs which were carefully observed by the alerted profession. A steering group was established to evaluate the results of the experiment. A combination of factors made it difficult to set up any kind of reliable evaluation procedures : the attacks by more traditionally oriented faculties, and the sudden student explosion combined with the resulting financial squeeze of the reform models. Most of the research time had to be spent in fighting for the new concept, developing curricula, securing financing, and defending the new program to allow them to work, thus also preventing any kind of systematic evaluation. With termination of the experiment imminent, the different political interest groups still do not agree on what the purpose of the evaluation should be. Should the traditional training system be compared with the new reform models ? Or should the reform models be conceived as a form of planned variation ? Finally, what should the goals be on the basis of which one could evaluate the models ? And how can one terminate the different models, for each shows differing qualities which make it difficult to select the most advantageous ? With termination set for 1981, the confusion is still increasing, and political decisions seem to replace scientific experimental evaluations.

THE NEED FOR DEVELOPMENT

No longer is social science found exclusively in universities and limited to teaching and (basic "pure") research. Growing numbers of social scientists are being placed in governmental programs. This change will influence both the program pers-

DIRECTIONS FOR EVALUATION RESEARCH IN GERMANY

Despite all improvements, different forms and usages of evaluation will develop. They all substitute for the political process, but they will increasingly help to shape policies, to improve the management of programs, and to increase the understanding of the consequences and impacts of policies.

If one tries to formulate some "informed guesses" based on our theory of evaluation research as to the future development and perspectives of evaluation research, the need and demand for (outside) evaluation research on the part of politicians and administrators will continue to increase. There are distinct differences between the American and the German political and administrative systems.

1. As compared with the American federal system with its maze of governmental unit, intergovernmental relations, and dependencies, the West German federal system appears almost "orderly". Governmental units on all levels are less numerous and heterogeneous—for example, the number of local governments was cut from 24,000 to about 8,000 during the communal territorial reform in the sixties and seventies. Their intergovernmental relations are more clearly prescribed as constitutionally fixed systems of matching-grants funding in specific policy areas. Both factors make the implementation process and the outcome patterns more easily foreseeable and calculable in Germany than in the United States and make the need for policy information through outside research less pressing.
2. While the American administrative system tends to run "experimental" programs through "new" organizations, German administrative tradition and culture tend to implement new policies through established public units and procedures, thus also increasing the possibility of foreseeing the process and its outcome to some extent.
3. Administrative recording and statistical systems in the

of social science methods. Reflective methodological mix of different methodological tools is seldom limitations, and administrative and political factors are not taken into account in most research. Only approaches which take into account the administrative and political action (maneuver) room which are able to integrate the organizational environment of a program, will improve the value of the evaluations conducted. Approaches like evaluability assessment may help in this process.

The inadequate use of theories. Closely related to the inadequate methods is the inadequate use of social theories in evaluation research. If used, they are discipline-oriented or based on a theory-testing model that is inadequate for social action. Well-founded theories and the development of alternative theories are only now evolving ; the formation of a theory is only slowly being recognized as part of the evaluation process. There is a need for "basic applied social research" which takes into account the *Handlusspielraum*" of the administrative and political system relating basic theory to the action potential.

The lack of administrative receptivity to using social science information. Administration is still largely dominated by legal or technical professionals. Understanding and use of the social sciences are largely confined to statistical reasoning and discussion ; the interpretation and translation of social science research into the administrative and political process fails. Evalution is of use only in a very strict intrumental sense, as justification for their action. The connection between program managers and the departmental research unit is often weak ; to strengthen it, more target oriented research should be conducted. Strategies for incorporating evaluation research into the political and administrative processes must be found.

The lack of trained evaluators. Most evaluators have never worked in administration. They often receive only theoretical or empirical training. Their interest in evaluation differs and often hinders effective evaluation. Career patterns in political and research are different. The potential for an interchange between both systems should be improved.

pectives as well as the relation of administration to evaluation research. Concurrently, administration is changing. It is more receptive now to social science knowledge. More social science information is required to respond to the needs of politics. At the same time, evaluation research must be tailored to the administrative process. New methods have to be developed which are able to respond to the varying political and administrative requirements. So far, social socientists are still used at best for their intelligence, as social bookkeepers of the bureaucracies. They generate information on impacts and process, compile facts, and serve in a monitoring and data-gathering capacity, but they usually fail to play a major role in contributing to the shaping of policies. Political decisions are made elsewhere. Evaluation research has largely failed to have a major impact on governmental or departmental policies and programs. Its use has been limited to soft-issues—education, social policy, economic aid, and manpower policy ; even in these areas it has never succeeded in integrating its findings into the political administrative machinery. Some may regard this as a failure, others may regard it as a necessary condition in a democratic society, where research usage should be part of and not dominating the political process. But even then some restrictions have so far limited the wider use of evaluation research.

The lack of adequate methodology. The methodological developments are still borrowed from the (pure) science model. Methodological tools and policy-oriented criteria for policy analysis are slowly responding to the needs of program action and management. The problem of integrating criteria of relevance with the requirements of social science has not yet been solved. Pure scientific methods, still dominate evaluation research. Most quantitative or qualitative evaluation research designs are not able to accommodate the administrative and political "*Handlungs*" structure. Far more expectations of administrators and policy makers are oriented to the use of scientific models, numbers, and figures, even then when only of limited value. Action research models are rarely found. When used, they were often a substitute for nonreflexive usage

United States appear to be in better shape than in Germany, thus allowing at least embryonic forms of internal book keping and program and project statistics. Together with the increasing computerization of administrative data storage, it seems likely that this field will constitute a growing domain of administrative "in-house" evaluation.

4. German parliamentary evaluations are largely underdeveloped. Given the administrative outlook and orientation of the West German political system and the lack of the resources of the GAO, parliamentary evaluation will never acquire the same importance as in the U.S. context. To improve these evaluations, the influence of the highly complex system of committees, party fractions, and congressional research service has to be recognized, as well es their different interests in evaluation as part of their power play. Evaluation research in this context will always take a rather informal and piecemeal approach ; comprehensive evaluation systems are not to be expected.
5. A driving force may develop from the interests of the independent Rechnungshof, the Comptroller General's Office, but its research will be limited to in-stall evaluation. By evaluating departmental policies, it will increase the willingness of others to introduce their own departmental evaluation system to be betteı prepared for the BRH evaluation.

Further growth of the publicly funded "research money market" can be foreseen, especially if one takes into account the growing interest in evaluations at the state and local levels.

The response on the part of evaluation researchers may be differentiated as to government-related research institutions, private (commercially run) research firms, and university research institutes. As far as government-related research institutions are concerned, it is safe to forecast further expansion. A case in point for this kind of government-related (albeit independent) research is the Science Center Berlin—Wissenschaftszentrum Berlin—funded by federal and Berlin money. This organization responds to the information needs of politics ; for instance, by regrouping a major research unit to do large-scale research on labour market policies. A second example is the German Institute for Urban Studies (Deutsches Institut fur Urbanistik, Berlin, funded by major German cities). These two research organizations probably constitute the closest German analogy to the Brookings Institution or the Urban Institute in the United States. Yet, a structural impediment to gaining a comparable visibility and impact vis-a-vis policy makers and administrators may be seen in the fact that, in contrast to the United States, where constant circulation takes place among government, research, and university personnel (Brookings being a conspicuous example), there is hardly any circulation of that sort on the German scene, due to the fact that the German civil service system makes such an exchange difficult, if not impossible.

Regarding private (commercially run) research institutions, a further expansion of research capacities and a sharpening of competition in the "bidding market" of evaluation research can be foreseen. In the past few years, some of these private research organizations have specialized in specific policies and corresponding public bureaucracies, building clientele relations which may structure the research market to some degree. Due to an interest in reaching some "economies of scale" in terms of computerized data collection and data handling, they may tend to push for further research based on indicators, survey data, and quantitative research designs.

As to the development of evaluation research in university settings, a set of contrasting factors have to be considered. On the one hand, the expansion of research manpower (at least potentially also available for evaluation research) has been dramatic in the course of the university reform and expansion during the sixties and seventies. We illustrate this point with a story : While the entire university community of sociologists could have gathered in a major lecture hall in the late fifties, it took the newly inaugurated, monumental International Congress Center in Berlin to embrace the number and also the self-esteem of this years's meeting of the professional association of sociolcgists. German social science is more firmly rooted in the tradition of *Verstehen*—sociology (with its implications in terms of research design and techniques, such as historical case studies, the reconstruction of processes on the basis of the actors' perception and interpretations, and also in terms of its openness to interactive research methods such as action research) than its American counterpart. Imbued as it is with a spirit of theoretically derived and supported "societal criticism" (such as the "Critical Theory" of the Frankfurt School), it could be a sort of natural candidate for engaging in a direction of evaluation research which might meet both the administration's need for detailed, process outcome-oriented research, backed by intensive empirical fieldwork, and at the same time social science's standards of critically detached, theoretically supported analyses. On the other hand, university social science research has undoubtedly had difficulties in claiming and holding its ground in the field of evaluation research due to habitual organizational features of the academic trade which will be hard to change : organizational ineptitude in handling a large-scale research, individualistic reputation and production patterns, and the inability to produce readable and transferable research prose and to deliver it in time. Yet, as noted above, there are indications that policy research at the universities is better suited to cope with the challenges and possibilities (or potential) of evaluation research.

FOOTNOTES

The following notes and references are limited to books published in English. Only documents are cited.

1. To stress this point (which has been explored in another paper), the growing receptipn of Habermas' writings in the United States seems to be reliable indicator for the growing interest in the European tradition of social science research methods. The number of new books on qualitative research approaches, the foundation of a special sociological journal with an applied section on qualitative sociological methods ("Qualitative Sociology") may be an additional illustration of those developments.

2. Early predecessors to the current evaluation research activities may be found in the social reform movements of the late nineteenth century. The "Verein fur Sozialpolitik".

3. This discussion has been frequently repeated. Attempts have been undertaken to privatize public sector activities in many fields to speed up administrative procedures and at the moment growing call from the local level is the quest for more global granting ("Pauschalistering") replacing the conditional grants (a discussion comparable to the American Block Grant Discussion). For a comprehensive survey of the German subvention practices and problems see Juttemeier and Lammers (1970). A result of discussion may be the appointment of the Transfer Commission to analyze the Social Security System at the Chancellor's Office.

4. A short treatment is included in Mayntz and Scharpf (1975). The main results have been published in three volumes. *Projektgruppe fur Regierungs and Verwaltungs, reform beim Bundesministerium des Innern* (1969-1972).

5. The discussion of "what steers the search for truth", "is modern science largely functionalized ?" has been stirred up by Bohme et al. at the Max-Planck-Institut zur Erforschung der Lebensbedingungen der wissenschaftlich-technischen Welt in Stranberg (1976 : 306-336) ; Bohme (1977 : 319-358, and Pfetsch, forthcoming).

REFERENCES

Ashord, D. et al. 1975, Biblography of Comparative Public Policy in Britain, West Germany, Japan and France. STCA Occasional Papers, Harward.

——(ed.) (forthcoming) Financing Urban Government in the Welfare State, London : Croom Helm.

Bieler, U. (1979), "How we have tried to get along with institutionalization of evaluation. Presented at the American-German evaluation research workshop, Berlin.

Bohhme G. (1979), Models for the developments of science in Spiegel, Rosing, D. Solla (Ed.), Science, Technology and Society. Beverly Hills, Calif., Sage.

Bohhme, G. ; W. Daele, and 'W. Krohn (1976), "Finalization : science." Social Science Information 15 : 306-330.

Bundesministerium des Innern (1969-1972), Reports I-II, Projektgruppe der Regier ungs-und Verwaltungsreform, Bonn.

Dorn, H. (1979), 'The control of success by the Federal Auditors' Court (BRH)". Presented at the American-German evaluation research workshop, Berlin.

Enqaete Kommission (1976), Final report. BT Drs. 7 5924 of 12 9 76.

Enquaete Kommission (1972), Interim report BT Drs VI. 3829 of 9 1272.

Federal Ministry of Regional Planning, Building and Urban Development (1975a), The 1975 Urban Development Report, Bonn.

——(1975b), Federal Regional Planning Program Publiketten Series, Regional Planning, Bonn.

——(1974), Regional Planning and Development. Overview of the Federal Regional Planning Program, the 1974 Regional Planning Report.

Geck, W.K. (1977), "The reform of legal education in the Federal Republic of Germany." *American Journal of Comparative Laws 25* : 86-119.

Hanf, K. (1973), Administrative developments in West and East Germany. Political Studies 1 : 35.

Hanf, K. and F.W. Scharpf (eds.) (1978), Inter-organizational Policy Making Limits to Coordination and Central Control, Beverly Hills, CA : Sage.

Johnson, N. (1972), Government in the Federal Republic of Germany: The Executive at Work, Oxford, Pergamon.

Jottemeier, K.H. and K. Lammers (1979), Subventionen in der Bundesrepublik Deutschland, Kiel : Kieler Diskussionsbeitrage.

Kohn, H. (1979), "Efficiency analysis in the Federal Ministry for Economic Affairs." Presented at the American-German evaluation research workshop. Berlin.

Landesregierung Baden-Wurttemberg (1979), Burgernahe in der Verwaltung Stuttgart.

Lotz, R.E. (1979), "The institutionalization of evaluation research---experience from government". Presented at the American-German evaluation research workshop. Berlin.

Mayntz, R. (1977), "Sociology, value freedom, and the problems of political counseling." in C.H. Weiss (ed) Using Social Research in Public Policy Making. Lexington. MA. D.C. Heath.

Mayntz, R. and F.W. Scharph (1975), Policy Making in the German Federal Bureaucracy, New York.

Hetsch, E. (forthcoming), "The finalists debate". Social Studies of Science.

Reissert, B. (1978), "Responsibility sharing and joint tasks in West German federalism," in P.B. Spahn (ed.) Principle of Federal Policy Coordination in the Federal Republic of Germany. Basic Issues and Annotated Legislation. Canberra : National University Press.

Spahn, P.B. (1978), Principle of Federal Policy Coordination in the Federal Republic of Germany Basic Issues and Annotated Legislation. Canberra : National University Press.

Steinhausen, J. (1979), "Statement to : How we have tried to get along with the introduction of evaluation." Presented at the American-German evaluation research workshop, Berlin.

Studienkommission fur die Reform des Offentlichen Dienstrechts (1973), Bericht der Kommission, Vol. 1 ff.

FIVE

D.C. Rowat

THE REFORM OF METROPOLITAN AND REGIONAL GOVERNMENT

A Comparative Perspective

In accordance with the objectives of this international meeting, I will discuss general trends and problems of metropolitan and regional reform. My comments will be based mainly on the international handbook that I edited on the reorganization of local government around the World. My presentation will be in two parts : structural reform, and its implications for central-local relations and local autonomy.

I. The Structural Reform of Local Government

Much structural reform has been at the level of metropolitan areas and regions below the level of the state in federations. Why has there been so much structural reform of local government in recent years? The answer may be summed up as due to the growing industrialism and urbanism throughout the world since World War II. By 1970 one-quarter of the world's population lived in urban centres with a population of over 100,000. In developing countries the extent of urbanization since the war has been astounding. Both industrialism and urbanism are centralizing forces, leading to :

1. greater control by central governments, and
2. larger units of local government, in order to provide the services required of modern government on an efficient basis.

Paper presented at the "European Meeting on Applied Urban Research". Essen, Oct. 2-4, 1981.

Larger units give greater economies of scale and wider tax base, as well as other advantages. A result of geater central control is a weakening of local government, while a result of larger units is their remoteness from the citizens, making public participation more difficult. It seems almost a contradiction in terms to call a city government for over one millions persons "local". One of the provinces in Canada has a population smaller than several of Canada's cities. Yet, these cities have one city government. How can they any longer be called local ?

One of the central problems of local government in the modern world is how to meet two pressing, yet contrary, needs : the need for larger units for greater efficiency, and the need to keep local government close to the people for easy access and participation. The case studies in my book on reorganization show that many recent reorganizations have been guided by the need for centralization and efficiency rather than for participation. For instance, L.J. Sharpe has complained in a recent article (1981) that the structural reorganization in Britain was aimed almost exclusively at the objective of greater efficiency, to the neglect of the criteria of citizen access, participation and local democracy. And his study of the financial crisis of local government in Western Europe (1980) shows that inflation has favoured centralization, for it has increased the revenues of central governments at the expense of local governments.

With this as a background, let us now analyze the kinds of metropolitan and regional reorganization that have been tried in recent times.

Metropolitan reorganization

The traditional types of metropolitan reorganization have been :

- annexation or consolidation of the suburbs with the central city, and
- cooperation of the municipalities in a metropolitan area.

The difficulty with the first solution is that it enlarges the unit too much and creates greater remoteness, and usually comes too late in the sense that new suburbs soon spring up beyond the new boundaries. Cooperation may be criticized as both too late and too little. Because the cooperative agreements are voluntary, usually because of disagreement they do not go far enough. Since the metropolitan area is in many ways a single social and economic unit, it needs a single government over the whole area for many purposes.

What I call the two-tier solution to the problem of structure is newer, though there are some well-known older examples, such as the Greater London Metropolitan Authority. It involves creating a government for the whole metropolitan area but leaving the existing units of local government with substantial powers and autonomy. It is a kind of local government federation. An outstanding example is the government for metropolitan Toronto, which is often referred to as a metropolitan federation. Most other large metropolitan areas in Canada now have such a two-tier system of local government. This type of government for metropolitan areas has the great advantage that it is a middle ground between the conflicting objectives of efficiency and closeness to the citizens. The upper tier of government is responsible for those services that must be provided on an area-wide basis for reasons of efficiency. While the local units remain to help meet the objectives of access, participation and local democracy. It is mainly for this reason that I (and the authors of the overview essay on metropolitan government in my book, Victor Jones and Patrick O' Donnell) favor the two-tier or federal form of metropolitan government.

Regional reorganization

Regional government, like the metropolitan federation, is also a two-tier solution, but it means creating a whole new level of government between the local governments and the central government (or the state government in federations). The Canadian province of British Columbia is an example of a province or state that has created such a level of regional government. It may be looked at as a way of fighting greater centralization and control by the higher level (or levels) of government, because services and controls can be decentralized to the regional level. At the same time, it is a compromise between the objectives of efficiency and participation, because the local units need not be consolidated, and may be left mainly as they were before, to meet the objectives of closeness and local democracy. However, to ensure that regional governments are not mere agents of the central government, or lean too heavily toward the objective of efficiency, it is crucial that they be elected bodies and have a high degree of autonomy.

THE IMPACT OF REFORM ON CENTRAL-LOCAL RELATIONS

The implications of reform for local autonomy and participation have often been neglected, and yet are of key importance. Often so-called reform has been hidden centralization, especially in developing countries, but even in developed countries the weight may be too much on the objective of efficiency. Yet, in many countries local governments are so small that there is a real need for the centralization of certain services to at least the regional level for the sake of efficiency. In his overview essay on regional government in my book, Fred Bruhns argues that the needs for centralization and decentralization vary from one country to another. In some countries, regional government is needed because government is too centralized, while in others it is needed because government is too decentralized, that is, local government is too fragmented and autonomous. As examples he places Belgium, France and Italy in the first category and Australia and Canada in the second. In general, regional government is desirable because of the tremendous pressure toward centralization in the modern world. It is a way of ensuring that too many services of government are not provided or controlled by the central government. But, for this to be true, it is absolutely essential that the regional government be elected and be granted a high degree of autonomy, and also that the local governments be left with as much power and autonomy as possible.

REFERENCES

Rowat, D.C. (ed.) : International Handbook on Local Government Reorganization : Contemporary Developments. Aldwych and Greenwood Presses, London and Westport, Conn., 1980.

Sharpe, L.J. : "Is there a fiscal crisis in Western European local government ?", *International Political Science Review*, Vol. 2, No. 2 (1980), 203-226.

Sharpe, L.J.: "The failure of local government moderniza.ion in Britain : a critique of functionalism", *Canadian Public Administration* 24, 1 (Spring 1981).

SIX

Ove Kalltorp

RECENT TRENDS IN PLANNING AND MANAGEMENT IN SWEDEN

Some Experiences of Citizen Participation

At the end of the 1960's and the beginning of the 1970's a wave of public opinion with strong demands for participant democracy aroused in Sweden. This was a new feature in the political life of this country. Sweden has a highly organized democracy with various levels of representational bodies within political parties, municipal councils, labour unions and other civic organizations. But now many people called for more direct participation and influence on politics, work conditions, education and civic life. This phenomenon was not unique for Sweden, of course, but was common to many other countries in Europe and America.

The social and political causes of the rising democratic demands in Sweden can be traced back to the rapid structural transformation of the whole society during the 1950's and 1960's. Some of the most important traits with direct significance for planning and housing management should be mentioned here. The capitalist economy was still expanding and concentrating to a few urban areas in central and southern Sweden. This led to a great migration wave to these areas. Many new housing areas were built. Some of them were much criticized because they were said to bring about isolation, anonymity and passivity. Whether true or not this type of criticism implied that public planning and housing management was challenged. Sometimes the criticism was also widened to apply to the whole political and administrative structure of Sweden, as a result of influence from radical political movements and events in other countries and also facilitated by a rising educational standard.

The structural transformation was also connected to rising demands for national and local state interventions to handle the big planning tasks as well as the social problems that accompanied expansion and ongoing urbanization. The municipalities had become too small to finance and manage the expanding public planning and management bureaucracies. Therefore a municipal reform was carried out in the beginning of the 1970's, reducing the number of municipalities by one tenth. Quite naturally this meant that politicians and officials lost contact with the citizens. And many citizens found it very difficult to get their views through to those who decided on their behalf. This development helped to strengthen the criticism against those in power. Another reason why public planning and administration became a main target for protests and criticism was that living conditions was becoming increasingly dependent on measures taken by the national government or municipal bureaucracies.

The rising demands for participation and influence from the citizens could not be totally rejected without a loss of political confidence. And there were also many politicians and officials within the public bureaucracies who considered the demands justified. Some of them were probably also aware of the favourable consequences of institutionalizing the increasing citizen activity. Organized participation could possibly aclm down conflicts that might otherwise grow out of control. Public confidence in the democratic character of the political system could be strengthened too. And some planners and officials saw the demands as a potential support for their own position when competing for resources within the bureaucracies. For these different reasons several national and local authorities responded to the demands in the 1970's by permitting some insight, organized participation and, sometimes limited influence on planning and management procedures. By organizing limited experiments the authorities tried to handle the contradictions and antagonisms that social development and state intervention in social life had brought about. Some managers within public housing companies also hoped that the readiness to pay the rising rents would increase with the help of various participatory practices.

In the following section an attempt is made to give a preliminary answer to the question whether the public participation experiments in fact have had any apparent effect in terms of citizen influence and whether they have strengthened the democratic character of municipal planning or the housing management or community work projects. The probable future development of authorized participation activities is shortly discussed, too. It should be pointed out that the experiments are not evaluated in terms of goals that are formulated by the initiators. These goals have been of various kinds, such as : to inform the citizens ; to listen to their demands ; to activate those concerned etc. Nor is any attempt made to be complete by considering all the different goals that various participant categories have had. Instead it is here assumed, that the most important motive for citizens, or tenants, or users, to participate in planning and management is that they might influence the outcome of these processes.

Some effects of participatory experiments

The effects of the citizen participation experiments in planning and management are somewhat contradictory as far as increased public control is concerned. It is highly questionable if these measures have resulted in any real control by the citizens. But no doubt the municipal planning procedures have become more open to the public than previously. More information about plans is distributed through the massmedia, exhibitions, pamphlets etc. And citizen groups have been invited to information meetings, study groups etc.

In the case of community work the projects have seldom had any obvious effects on planning or management. Many people have been involved in various activities and many independent action groups and ad hoc organizations have started with the aim of influencing the authorities. But these groups have been successful on minor issues only. And the results very often have been short-lived.

Considering the tenant participation experiments several concrete but small effects have been achieved. The tenants have gotten greater insight and also some influence on management through new channels of information and decision-making between the tenants and the housing companies. But while information could be obtained on most matters the right to decide has been restricted to the day-to-day management jobs within a limited housing area : repairs, cleaning up, social activities among neighbours etc., all within a budget decided upon by the management. Yet it is likely that the fact that tenants now are organizing themselves around minor issues may to some extent improve the bargaining position of tenants as a collectivity on the local level. On more central levels the tenant associations are well established and they have considerable power in negotiations with the housing companies' association.

The number of participants in the different experiments vary. In some cases several hundred people have discussed municipal plans or more detailed plans for specific housing areas, but very seldom has the fraction of citizens participating in such authorized activities exceeded a few per cent of the concerned population. In community work projects for housing areas it has been possible to reach a majority of the inhabitants in various activities, but for a period of a year or more there are normally only a few persons who are constantly active. The same kind of experience pertains to the experiments with tenant participation. Those active are seldom or never socially representative of the inhabitants of the municipality or the neighbourhood. Participation in planning shows the most biased selection in this respect. In most cases the middle aged men with good social position come to meetings, join the citizen planning groups etc. In the community work projects and in the tenant participation experiments other social strata participate to a greater extent. There, the percentage of active women is also larger. This quite naturally follows from the simple fact that the action areas for community work and local tenant organizations are the main social arenas for many women.

The number of participants has been much larger in some cases when independent action groups have campaigned against planning proposals or concrete measures such as demolition of housing areas, construction of motor-ways etc. This kind of intervention in the urban environment has often aroused thousands of protesters and has also led to cooperation between several locally based ad hoc-groups.

The participation experiments in public planning and management have pointed out several political problems concerning how citizen participation should be organized, in what institutional forms and by whom. There is no political agreement concerning direct versus indirect representation, the role of the political parties etc. The demands on increased participation in planning and management as well as the various campaigns and experiments have in most cases aimed at mobilizing people and demands. This mobilization points to failings in the existing representative democracy. It has often been argued that formal democracy to a growing extent takes on the character of a rigid bureaucracy with centralized decision-making, and deficient contacts between citizens, politicians and officials. This promotes specialist rule and leads to great difficulties to get an overview of the political and administrative process. Therefore the participation experiments have had the positive function of alleviating some imperfections of the political and administrative system by improving its ability to give and take information, thereby also enhancing the sensitivity of politicians and officials to local demands and wishes.

One consequence of this is however that the role of the established political parties as well as the position of the big organizations has been altered. Part of the political demand articulation process has bypassed them and has instead been channeled through new groups and movements and in campaigns initiated by officials, not political representatives. In the planning participation experiments, for example, officials in the municipal administration very often have played an important role by initiating the experiments, choosing participants, prepairing informational or educational material and by organizing the whole process. Thus the established political parties and big organizations have had good reason to consider some of these experiments as a threat to their own position and in some cases they have reacted accordingly. A common feature of these reactions is the aim of tying the independent participants to the established political and administrative structure. The recent neighbourhood government reform described below may possibly be seen as the final stage in a process of institutionalization of the citizen protests and participation campaigns from the 60's and 70's.

It has been argued above that the participation experiments have had their foremost function in facilitating the flow of information while the effects in terms of concrete influence on important matters have been minor. There are several basic characteristics on the experiments, which contribute to explain this. Participants in authorized campaigns oblige themselves to follow the rules laid down by the authorities. They are bound to wait for initiatives taken by politicians or officials and if nothing happens the participants can do very little about it except to withdraw and thereby lose their credibility in the eyes of the authorities. Their only hope then is that the authority may also lose its credibility by not responding to citizen demands. Another basic reason why the concrete effects have been very small—at least in the planning experiments—is that the scope of municipal decision-making is quite limited. The municipalities are forced to follow government regulations, and they are very often constrained by contracts with private firms or by harsh economic realities. At present munipalities are very reluctant to accept anything that might raise the costs of management. Yet another reason—which of course is strengthened by the economic crisis—is that limited experiments bring to the fore competition about resources between different localities, social strata and administrative sectors. A participation campaign directed towards a specific housing area or local district with possible favourable effects in terms of allocated resources may be seen as an unfair privilege in the eyes of neighbouring areas. Housing areas are very often differentiated with respect to social class and social antagonisms may also be aroused.

In the community work projects the question of influence must be stated somewhat differently. This is because those experiments have aimed at mobilization of citizens in various social activities with no clear view of what kind of results should follow. Instead the ideology has been that the goal of the activities should be stated by the participants themselves. Partly for this reason no formal channels have been provided for communicating issues to housing companies or municipal councils. As a consequence these authorities have not felt any obligation to respond to citizen demands on concrete measures. And therefore the opportunities to exert influence have been very small.

In the tenant participation experiments, on the other hand, influence on management decisions has been an important goal and the scope of participation in decision-making was agreed on early in the process. But the right to decide has been bought to the price of very strict delimitation of the relevant issues. Instead the question of mobilization and articulation of interests has not been regulated at all but has been handed over to the tenants and their associations. It should also be added that the scope of tenant participation in housing management is, like planning perticipation, very circumscribed.

It should be noted, however, that action groups have sometimes been successful in pressing for their claims without having any formal position, or channels to the authorities. These cases are, however, not characterized by a high degree of conflicts. There have also been at least some decision alternatives left and those who have pressed on have been well-informed and have had the means to win acceptance for their demands. Most often such action groups have been established independently of the kind of participation experiments discussed here. In fact autonomous action groups and authorized participation campaigns seem to be contradictory. When the former type of activity develops, the authorities most often seem to take shelter behind the normal bureaucratic procedures while on other occasions, when no opinions have yet been formed, they sometimes try to anticipate independent action by initiating a participation campaign.

From the citizen's point of view there are obvious risks associated with authorized participation. Politicians and officials have the ability to decide the issues and the forms of activities and thereby disarming the citizen claims. Experiences from community work projects do however indicate that this does not always occur. On the contrary some of those experiments have triggered underlying conflicts between groups of tenants and housing companies or municipal authorities. This has led to that they now less often initiate community work projects and, when they do, the procedures are more strictly regulated.

SOME CURRENT TENDENCIES IN CITIZEN PARTICIPATION EXPERIMENTS

Is the wave of citizen participation experiments during the 1970's only the result of a temporary mobilization of citizen demands and activity which will be followed by a return to the established indirect forms of government and management ? Or are those experiments only the first stage of a process of integration where participatory practices will become routine in most political and administrative processes ?

As far as tenant participation experiments are concerned they seem to have had instrumental as well as symbolic functions for the housing companies. Besides the necessity of legitimizing their management procedures, these companies are also in need of means to decrease the costs of management in the face of the rapidly increasing building and maintenance expenditures. By delegating some part of the management to the tenants themselves the rent increases might be reduced to some extent. But will this result in any real influence for the tenants ? Judging from the experiments, very far-reaching administrative changes must be made within the housing companies in order to guarantee tenant influence. Visible results are required to stimulate the tenants to take part in management work. During recent years several agreements on the forms and scope of tenant participation have been entered between tenant organizations and housing companies. These agreements seem to show that the contradiction between management requirements and tenant demands is now being regulated in a way that was established by industrial companies and trade unions in the early 1970's : an order of conflict regulation in the Swedish labour market that has been formulated as a law.

Very few community work projects are now underway or being started. The economic recession plays an important role here. The municipal authorities choose to cut temporary activities which are not part of the normal administrative procedures. The fact that some community work projects have caused bureaucratic trouble and political embarrassment probably increases the inclination of the authorities to stop this kind of activity. Instead there is now a tendency to allocate the decreasing resources to existing voluntary associations which try to uphold various social activities in the housing districts. But are there reasons to believe that all community work projects will disappear? Probably not. The same type of social problems that motivated the initiation of such projects ten years ago still exist in many areas. The problems may become even worse as a result of increasing unemployment and government cutbacks of economic support to tenants and housing companies. If this happens political demands on the social authorities for preventive measures will grow.

What are, finally, the prospects for future participation experiments in municipal planning? The main positive functions for the authorities seem to have been that they smoothed over conflicts and that they legitimized the planning procedures. But these functions have lost some significance during recent years. Firstly the planned large-scale building activity has decreased since the middle of the 1970's. Secondly the authorities have acquired more experience in handling the existing conflicts within existing institutions. But most important of all is that unwillingness to respond to demands and protests can be very well legitimized by reference to the economic recession. This very likely has a restraining effect on the part of citizen demands.

But other tendencies in recent years may increase the need for participatory planning precedures. The current trend towards urban renewal will mean that large groups of inhabitants will be more directly affected by various interventions in their immediate surroundings. Experiences of renewal projects in Sweden have so far shown that those who live in or adjacent to renovation blocks can very easily be mobilized and that strong protests often arise. If planning proposals in the future are concerned with such areas, politicians and planners will have reasons to initiate a direct participation by the people in the neighbourhood.

Recent experiences also indicate that an influence pse-requisite is decentralization and local coordination of the municipal administration. This has great significance in planning for renewal of existing urban areas. It is probably more effective for citizen groups to influence the political process where the principles of various planning decisions are developed than to protest against specific plans at a late stage in that process. From this perspective the introduction of comprehensive neighbourhood government may be a way for local opinions to influence planning decisions with relevance for the immediate neighbourhood. A national law now permits municipalities to establish neighbourhood councils on a trial basis and several experiments are in progress. There is now a political cleavage as to whether the neighbourhood councils should be locally elected or appointed by the municipal council. Social democrats most often favour the latter procedure for the reason that the political representation should be uniform in the whole municipality. Liberal and conservative politicians more often favour strictly local elections, sometimes saying that this would lead to more true democracy. Behind the rhetoric there may be more strategic motives. The social democrats have their own decentralized political party structure in many municipalities while other parties very often have none. Directly elected neighbourhood councils may alter this difference in political organization. The neighbourhood councils which have been established up to now have no real planning capacity but have acted as enforcers of decisions taken more centrally. If the authorities want people to become involved in local planning issues, it is probably of great importance to give the neighbourhood councils an independent responsibility within certain limits. Only then one can expect that people will consider it meaningful to participate.

At last it must be reminded, that neighbourhood councils alone cannot guarantee the democratic character of the planning and management procedures. At best they can promote more effective channels for communicating demands and arguments. There is still the risk that the new channels will be used primarily by people who are well-educated and have good social positions or are already involved in the decision process. Other ways to stimulate the participation of broader categories are therefore still needed.

REFERENCES

Ahlgren, B. and Miller, T. (1975) Conflict and Participation in a Renewal Process in Stockholm : Birka, in Appleyard, D. ed, (1979) *The Conservation of European Cities*. MIT Press, Cambridge, Mass.

Almqvist, A. et al. (1980) *Medborgarinflytande i bostadsomradesplane—ring—Rissne i Sundbyberg* (Citizen participation in the planning of a housing district). Meddelande M 80 : 10, Statens institut for byggnadsforskning, Gavle.

Anton, T. (1974) The Pursuit of Efficiency. Values and Structure in the Changing Politics of Swedish Municipalities, in Clark, T. ed, *Comparative community politics.* Sage John Wiley and Sons, New York, N.Y.

Anton, T. (1980) *Administered politics. Elite political culture in Sweden.* Martinus Nijhoff Publishing, Boston, Mass.

Boaden, N. et al. (1979) Public participation in planning within a representative democracy, in *Policy and Politics*, Vol. 7.

Boaden, N. et al. (1980) Planning and Participation in Practice : A Study of Public Participation in Structure Planning. *Progress in Planning*, Vol. 13 Part 1/2, Pergamon Press, Oxford.

Breitbart, M. and Kasperson, R. (1974) *Participation, Decentralization and Advocacy Planning.* Association of American Geographers. Washington, D.C.

Butcher, H. et al. (1980) *Community groups in action : case studies and analysis.* Routledge and Kegan Paul, London.

Cockburn, C. (1977) *The Local State. Management of Cities and People.* Pluto Press, London.

Coser, L. (1956) *The Functions of Social Conflict.* Free Press, New York, N.Y.

Hjarne, L. et al. (1979) *Hyresgastinflytande—pa vems villkor ? Utvardering av ett forsok med hyresgastinflytande i bostadsforvaltningen* (Tenant influence—on what terms ? Evaluation of a tenant participation experiment). Byggforskningsradet. R 115 : 1979, Stockholm.

Hjarne, L. et al. (1981) *Kvartersrad pa bostadsforetagets villkor* (Tenant councils on the terms of the housing company). Byggforskningsradet, T 26 : 1981, Stockholm.

International Union of Local Authorities (IULA) (1971) *Participation, Studies in Comparative Local Government*, Vol. 5 No 2.

Kaase, M. and Marsh, A. (1979) "Political Action. A Theoretical Perspective", in Barnes, S and Kaase, M. et al. *Political Action,*

Mass Participation in Five Western Democracies. Sage, Beverly Hills.

Miller T. (1980) *Medborgardeltagande. Politiskt inflytande eller . . .?* (Citizen participation. Political power or ... ?). Byggforskningsradet, T 4 : 1980, Stockholm.

Miller, T. and Osterberg, R. (1977) *Medborgarinflytande i kommunal planering. Forsok till utvardering av trafiksamradet i Stockholm 1973:74* (Citizen participation in municipal planning. Evaluation of traffic planning in Stockholm 1973-74). Byggforskningsradet, R 30 : 1977, Stockholm.

Miller, T. and Burell, U. (1978) *Kunskap och inflytande. Utvardering av planeringssamrad i Hedemora 1975-77* (Knowledge and influence. Evaluation of municipal planning in Hedemora 1975-77). Byggforskningsradet, R 82 : 1978, Stockholm.

Offe, C. (1972) *Strukturprobleme des kapitalistischen Staates*. Suhrkamp, Frankfurt am Main.

Olsson, S. (1979) *Fororten, grannskapsarbete och forandringsmojligheter* (The suburb, community work and prospects of change). Delegationen for social forskning, Rapport 1979 : 1.

Saunders, P. (1979) *Urban Politics. A Sociological Interpretation*, Penguin Books, Harmodsworth.

Thornley, A. (1977) Theoretical Perspectives on Planning Participation, *Progress in Planning*, Vol. 7, Part 1, Pergamon Press.

The Europe Council (1979) *Information and Communication about Local Affairs*, No 17 in Study Series on Local and Regional Authorities in Europe, Strasbourg.

SEVEN

DONALD C. ROWAT

THE IMPLICATIONS OF LOCAL GOVERNMENT REORGANIZATION

For Central-Local Relations

IN RECENT years local government has been reorganized in a remarkable number of countries. This development has been world-wide, including both developed and developing countries and countries with a wide variety of types of political regimes. It immediately raises some interesting questions : what are the causes and consequences of this structural reorganization ? Are the causes common to all countries or are they different types of country, such as developed and developing : What are the implications or consequences of this reorganization ? If the causes are the same, will the consequences be the same ?

These questions are difficult to answer because of the lack of an adequate methodology for the comparative study of local government. Comparative cross-national studies of any kind are difficult to do. For local government they are particularly difficult because of the larger numbers and different types of units involved, and because local government cannot be divorced from the political system of which it is a part.

As a result, the comparative studies of local government that have been done so far cannot be of much help in answering our questions. Very few of these studies have been genuinely comparative. They may be classified into three types. The first is the case-study type. It is a study of local government in two or more countries or of a single feature or structural aspect of local government in two or more countries. This type of study proceeds country by country and provides no real comparison. The second type of study has a problem focus. It takes a particular problem related to local governments, such as urbanization, and discusses how each country deals with that problem, but does not deal specifically with local government as such.[1] The third is what might be called the compendious type of study. It takes one feature of local government such as structure or finance and investigates this feature in many countries, again on a country-by-country basis. An outstanding example of this type of study is the volume by Humes and Martin, *The Structure of Local Government : A Comparative Survey of Eighty-one Countries.*[2] The difficulty with all of these types of study is that they consider local government in isolation and do not look at it as part of the total political system of a country .

Despite these difficulties, one must try to understand the common causes of trends and problems in different countries, and if one takes a common phenomenon, such as the reorganization of local government, it may be possible to reach some general conclusion about causes and consequences. This was my objective in editing my recent volume on the reorganization of local government around the world. It belongs to the compendious type of study because it is a collection of forty-eight essays by different authors, mainly on particular countries. However, an attempt was made to arrive at comparative insights by having some of the authors write comparative essays on several related countries in a region, and by including a number of comparative essays at the end. These provide an overview of reorganization separately for developed and developing countries, and for metropolitan areas and regional or country government. My final essay seeks to identify common causes, problems, and consequences of local government reorganization. This brief paper, then, will attempt to sum up some of the general conclusions about the reorganizatiom of local government that are revealed by our compendious study in its five concluding essays, with emphasis on the implications of reorganization for central-local relations and on the nature and implications of metropolitan and regional reorganization.

Causes of reorganization

Our comprehensive survey reveals that two basic causes of local reorganization everywhere in the world are the growth of urbanism and industrialism. Since the Second World War these trends have affected both developed and developing countries at an accelerating pace. The result has been to crowd more and more people into urban centres, and to turn a larger and larger proportion of the working population into earners of wages or salaries.

By 1980 more than one quarter of the world's population lived in urban centres with a population of over 100,000. In developing countries the extent of urbanization since the war has been astounding. The rapidly rising urban population has had serious results for local government. One of the most far-reaching results has been to increase remarkably the average population of urban municipalities and, by the same token, the distance between the citizen and his local government. Since many cities now have a population well over a million, it seems a contradiction in terms to call the government of such cities "local". For instance, Canada's two largest cities now have populations larger than some of its provinces, yet these cities have a single government. How can it any longer be considered local ? Another consequence of urbanization has been the development of huge metropolitan areas. In most cases local government is fragmented within them and there is no overall unit of metropolitan government. Thus, one of the central problems of local government in the modern world is how to meet two pressing, yet contrary, needs : the need for larger units for greater efficiency, and the need to keep local government closer to people for essay access and participation.

The rise of industrialism is closely connected with the growth of cities. It results in a growing integration of a nation's economy and in problems that must be dealt with on a nation-wide rather than local basis. Personal and regional differentials in wealth increase and, for the sake of equity, this wealth must be taxed and redistributed by the central government. Because of the insecurity of employment for wages, there arises a need to provide social and other services at an acceptable minimum standard across a nation. And because of economies of scale, these services can be provided more cheaply and efficiently by larger units of government. Also, rapid industrial development requires central direction and control. In other words, there is a general trend toward centralized government in order to promote uniformity, equity, efficiency, and industrial development. In many countries it has become painfully evident that units of local government created for an agricultural economy are too small and financially weak to provide at an acceptable level the great variety of local services that the public demands in the modern industrial state.

Thus, both urbanism and industrialism are centralizing forces, leading to larger units of local government, more control by the central government, and more centrally administered services, in order to provide the many services required from modern government on a more efficient basis. Larger units and centrally provided services give greater economies of scale and a wider tax base, as well as other advantages. However, larger units are more remote from the citizens, making public participation more difficult, while more central control and services weaken local government and all of the democratic values that it serves.

As Professor Subramaniam's overview essay on developing countries shows, a serious problem for many of these countries is the impact of striving for national integration and economic development on the strength of local government. The need for national integration does not admit much decentralization of power to local government, while economic planning and development require strong direction from the central government in the formulation and implementation of national plans.

Implications for central-local relations

All of the authors of the concluding essays in our volume have stressed that the impact of reorganization on central-local relations is of key importance. It raises the question : will the reorganization centralize or decentralize the national political system ? One should therefore ask : what are the real objectives of the reorganization ? Are they designed to promote democratic values—to increase the autonomy of local governments, local decision-making, the participation of the citizens in government, and the easiness of their access to government ?

Or is the chief objective to gain greater efficiency in the provision of services, or to promote national integration or the development of the economy? Our study of recent reorganizations reveals that in most of the research studies preparatory to reorganization and in most of the reorganizations themselves the main objectives have been the latter rather than the former, with serious implications for central-local relations : political systems are becoming more centralized at the expense of the above-mentioned democratic values. Similarly, L.J. Sharpe has complained in a recent article that the recent structural reorganization in Britain aimed almost exclusively at the objective of greater efficiency, to the neglect of the criteria of citizen access and participation.[3] And his study of the financial crisis of local government in Western Europe shows that inflation has favoured centralization, for it has increased the revenues of central governments at the expense of local governments.[4]

Metropolitan reorganization

Since much of the world's population now live in metropolitan areas, let us turn to the nature and implications of recent reorganizations of local government in metropolitan areas. To solve the problem of the urban population spilling over the boundaries of large cities, the traditional types of metropolitan reorganization have been :

1. Annexation or consolidation of the suburbs with the central city ;
2. Cooperation of the local governments in a metropolitan area ;
3. The consolidation of all local units into a single government for the area.

The difficulty with the first solution is that it enlarges the unit too much and creates greater remoteness, and usually comes too late in the sense that new suburbs soon spring up beyond the new boundaries. Cooperation may be criticized as both too late and too little. Because the cooperative arrangements are voluntary, they emerge very slowly and rarely go far enough. Since the metropolitan area is in many ways a single social and economic unit, it needs a single government over the whole area for many purposes. However, the third type—the creation of a single government for the whole area —overstresses the value of efficiency and creates a government that is too remote from the citizens. One way of trying to meet this problem is to divide the metropolitan area into numerous districts that have elected consultative or advisory councils. An experiment such as this was tried recently in the Winnipeg metropolitan area, when the previous two-tier system of metropolian government was replaced by a system popularly called "Unicity". But it was not particularly successful because the local councils had no real decision-making powers.

The deficiencies of the traditional types of reorganization have led to the growing popularity in recent years of a fourth type : the creation of a second level of government for the whole metropolitan area, but leaving the existing units of local government in their place with substantial powers and autonomy for local purposes. It is a kind of local-government federation, with the upper tier forming the central government of the federation and with a division of powers between the two tiers. Outstanding examples of this kind of local government are the greater London metropolitan authority and the government of metropolitan Toronto. The Toronto system, which was created in 1953, provided an example or prototype for other large metropolitan areas in Canada, and by now most of them have a two-tier system of metropolitan government.[5] The Toronto system has also been widely discussed in the United States, but so far not many American metropolitan areas have adopted a version of it.

This type of government for metropolitan areas has the great advantage that it is a middle ground between the conflicting objectives of efficiency and of closeness to the citizens. The upper tier of government is responsible for those services that must be provided on an area-wide basis for reasons of efficiency, while the local units remain to help meet the objectives access, participation and local democracy. It is mainly because of this advantage that I and the authors of the overview essay on metropolitan areas, Victor Jones and Patrick "O" 'Donnell, favour the two-tier or federal system of metropolitan government.[6] However, a serious problem faced by most existing examples of this system is that the central city of the metropolitan area has usually retained its local government in substantially its previous form. This means that it serves much too large a population to meet the objectives of local decision-making, participation and easy access. A solution would be to break up the central city into several districts with their own self-governing councils so that the local units within the metropolitan area would all have relatively small populations.

Regional reorganization

Regional government, like a metropolitan federation, is also a two-tier form, but it means creating a whole new level between the central and local governments, or between the state and local governments in federations. The Canadian province of British Columbia is an example of a province or state that now has such a level of regional government. It may be looked at as a way of fighting greater centralization and control by the central government, because services and controls can be decentralized to the regional level. It is a compromise between the objectives of efficiency and participation, because the local units need not be consolidated, and may be left mainly as they were before, to meet the objectives of closeness and local democracy.[7] However, to ensure that regional governments are not mere agents of the central government, or lean too heavily toward the objective of efficiency, it is crucial that they be elected bodies and have a high degree of independence from the central government. Many recent reorganizations of county or regional government have been more concerned with efficiency than autonomy, and have therefore led to greater centralization. However, in Sweden there has been considerable concern for regional autonomy, and in France it has been one of the central objectives of the new movement toward decentralization.

CONCLUSIONS

The general impact of the recent reorganizations of local government has been to promote centralization through their stress on the objective of technical efficiency at the expense of citizen access and participation. There have been many nationwide consolidations of local government at the lowest level, thus creating larger units of local government that are more distant from the citizens. The growth of cities has created more populous units of local government that are also more distant from the citizens. Though there has been a new movement to create or strengthen regional governments, they are still not autonomous enough, and tend to be controlled by the central government.

The cumulative effect of these developments has been to increase the degree of central control, to reduce the autonomy of local government, and to make government more remote from the citizens. There is therefore a need for the invention and adoption of new devices for citizen access and participation and for decision-making at the local level. What we need is a new kind of decentralization, a decentralization not only of structures, but also of decision-making. Real decentralization and greater local autonomy cannot be achieved unless important decisions are made at the local level. Often so-called reform has been hidden centralization, especially in developing countries, but even in the developed countries the weight has been too much on the objective of efficiency at the expense of participation.

In the long run this will weaken a country's democratic foundations and lead to the strengthening of a centralized bureaucracy that is remote from the people. Those planning the reorganization of local government would therefore be well advised to look at the implications of any proposed reorganization in terms of the centralization or decentralization of the whole political system in a country. The value of efficiency must not be pursued to the exclusion of the values of democracy.

FOOTNOTES

1. A good example is A.H. Walsh, *The Urban Challenge to Government* (New York : Praeger, 1969). It is based on separate case studies of thirteen urban areas. Attention is focused on urban problems and the governmental machinery for dealing with them, regardless of whether it is designated as local government.

2. The Hague : International Union of Local Authorities, 1969.
3. "The Failure of Local Government Modernization in Britain : A Critique of Functionalism," *Canadian Public Administration* 24, 1 (Spring 1981).
4. "Is There a Fiscal Crisis in Western European Local Government ?" *International Political Science Review* 2, 2 (1980), 203-226.
5. The Toronto and other Canadian metropolitan governments are described briefly in my *Your Local Government* (Toronto : Macmillan, 2nd ed. 1975), 20-21.
6. The advantages of the two-tier system are more fully explored in my *The Canadian Municipal System* (Toronto : McClelland and Stewart, 1969), 72-80.
7. The advantages of a regional level of government are discussed in *The Canadian Municipal System*, 139-146.

EIGHT

ARUN KUMAR SINGH

MUNICIPAL GOVERNMENT AS SOCIO-POLITICAL ENTITY
A Case Study

INTRODUCTION

ALL organisations require care for maintaining continuity of usefulness. The cities also require management services. Normally these management services are organised and maintained through an institution of city government. In India the city governments are commonly described by the term Municipal Government. The municipal governments can be seen as specific instances of institutional intervention upon the freedom of choice of the resident population. This can also be seen as logical necessities arising from the incapacity of individual citizen to regulate the affairs of the very large community. For these reasons municipal governments are required to be created and to be emplaced within the commitment of the citizen to sustain there. Therefore these are symbols of collective will. We propose to examine this reality in the present exercise. For this purpose we have selected five urban centres (Fig. No. 1) with various types of character and way of development. Burdwan being the oldest nucleus of this region has developed mainly as an administrative headquarters right from the time of Burdwan Raj, and a service centre for its vast fertile and developed agricultural region. Hooghly-Chinsura, a class I town (1971 census) in the Calcutta conurbation, a district headquarter of Hooghly District and divisional headquarter of Burdwan Division has developed as river port, trading centre and also the first European settlement in the Ganga plain after the down fall of 'Sapthgram' the famous port of medieval India for ocean going ships on the same of Hooghly. Hooghly-Chinsura served as a main commercial centre for the European traders till the development of Calcutta. Chandranagar developed as a headquarter of the French till 1947, it was a place of political rivalry between the French and the English. Howrah developed as a trading centre, than industry, railway terminus and presently a growing centre for the engineering industries in the Calcutta Metropolitan Development Authority area with the second largest population after Calcutta. Durgapur developed after 1955 as an industrial complex with a modern plan for its various functions such as residential, commercial etc.

Hierarchic placement of the municipal governments

In India the principal functions of the municipal government consist of construction and maintenance of roads, their cleansing , watering and lighting, abatement of public nuisances, regulation of dangerous and offensive trades, granting of trade licenses, water-supply, drainage, maintenance of hospitals and dispensaries, conducting vaccination, construction of and maintenance of public markets, slaughter houses, and sanitary conveniences, arboriculture, education (specially primary) etc. These functions are regulated by an elective body of commissioners or councillors. These are also assigned exactly defined revenue sources. According to Article 12 of the Constitution, the state of India, 'includes the Government and Parliament of India and Legislature of each states and all the local or other authorities within the territory of India or under the control of the Government of India'. India has thus a three level system of government i.e., the Union, the States/ Union Territories and the Local Government. The government at these levels are constituted on the basis of three fundamental democratic characteristics : popular authorities, assigned revenue resources and thirdly specified spheres of responsibility.

The Constitution prescribes the legislative, administrative and financial powers of the Union and the State only. It does not specify anything so far as local government is concerned. In other words, the municipal governments of India do not draw their powers from the constitution directly. The Municipal government as one of the many other forms of local government, is just one of the sixty-six subjects assigned exclusively to the States. The State governments have the authority to design and also to grant powers to the Municipal Governments. It is also noteworthy that while organisation of village panchayats is one of the directive principles of the State Policy fundamental in the governance of the country, urban local government does not find a place there.[1] This means that the collective will of the people behind the municipal governments encompass a much larger body-polity than the citizens of any individual city.

Types of city governments

The Municipal Institutions have evolved over past one century and their form have largely been determined by the extent of control exercised by the State administration and its functionaries. Since independence, this concept has undergone some changes and Municipal authorities are now working in keeping with the views of the local needs and importance of the local area. There are at present five types of urban government in West Bengal.[2]

(a) Municipal Corporations
(b) Municipalities
(c) Notified Area Authority
(d) Town Area Committees and
(e) Contonment Boards

The above classification of Municipal Governments indicates that there is no uniform local government system in West Bengal as it so does in the western countries like France. The five cities selected for studies have also no uniform structure of urban governments. Howrah, Burdwan and Hooghly-Chinsura are governed by the Bengal Act XV of 1932 as modified as the Bengal Municipal Act 1932 after the independence.[3] Chandranagar is also governed by the Bengal Municipal Act 1932. But due to its historical antecedents there has been a special modification in the Bengal Municipal Act 1932, titled as Chandernagore Municipal Act 1955 (West Bengal Act XVIII of 1955).[4] Durgapur has been governed by the Bengal Municipal (Second Amendment) Act 1960 (West Bengal Act XXXV of 1960).

The above classification of the types of the municipal governments shows that there are five types of urban governments. Only the Municipal Corporation and Municipalities can be regarded as a full fledged urban government which are governed by the representatives of the residents of the cities, who are elected on a system of adult franchise. The Notified Area Authority, which *exists* at Durgapur, represents a stop-gap arrangement for such an area which does not fulfill the conditions for being constituted a municipality under the Bengal Municipal Act, 1932, is comprised in a newly developing town, and where new industries have been or are being established. The members of the Committee of this type of urban government are all nominated by the state governments which vest the committee with specific powers according to the Bengal Municipal Act, 1932 (Section 93A, 93B, 93C, 93D and 93E).

The Town Area Committees are set up for the small towns and entrusted with limited local functions. This type of urban governments are governed by no specific Act but to some extent West Bengal Panchayat Act 1956 (Section 93F, the Bengal Municipal Act 1932) is extended for such town committees. Here the members are usually nominated, or partly nominated and partly elected. None of our five cities are governed by Town Area Committees.

Similarly, we have no town governed by Contonment Boards, But, the contonment boards are governed by the Contonments Act, 1924, which is an Union Government Legislation. The Contonments are military stations that grew up during the British regime for historical reasons. Even today these are administered by the Central Ministry of Defence. In each contonment, there is a contonment board which is partly elected and partly nominated and its key officials such as the medical and engineering personnel are drawn from the army on ex-officio status.[5]

It should be interesting to review why so many different types of municipal governments exist in West Bengal. Each form of Municipal Government has been a product of a specific enactment. The history of such enactments begin long before the country attained independence. Some of the powers that the older municipalities enjoy have their antecedents, located even in the pre-British political systems. For example the kotwali system that we still have in the Hooghly-Chinsura Municipality has been derived from the days of the Mughals. Similarly the modern Octroi is functionally a derivative of the 'Chunghi' tax that the urban governments were allowed to charge on all transactions obtaining between the city and the country during the pre-Mughal days. In order to appreciate the antiquity of the tradition of municipal government one may have to look into the years long before the time when the existing municipal acts were instituted.

The origin of the modern Local-self government system as it exists to-day owes much to Sir Josia Child who obtained a Charter from James II to set up a Corporation at Madras in 1642.[6] The local institutions as they exist to-day does not represent a process of continuous growth but are the products of convenience which was found necessary by the British government in the interest of administration. The British regime had done away with the indigenous foundations. Yet a good deal of the rational of the ancient taxation systems continued to remain in the modern local financial arrangements. The "Chungi" of the Mughal rulers, the Sikh "Dharat", the "Muhtarafa" of the Maratha towns have a descendent in to-days Octroi. But from the structure aud procedure of earlier local institutions almost nothing has been incorporated into the modern local governments.[7]

It is only from the middle of the nineteenth century that the municipal governments emerged on after the other in a consistent manner. In every instance the municipal government owed its status from the specific grants of the government. This sometime leads people to believe that the British Raj in India was genuinely interested to spread examples of popular democracy within the Indian masses. But there is a good reason to believe that these grants came as an arrangements o f conveniences rather than in response to the rulers desires to institute popular democracy.

The history of Local-self Government in Bengal begins with the Royal Charter of 1727 which was passed for the administration of Calcutta and other presidency towns. The other towns were governed by different Municipal Acts. We need not go into the details of the acts on Calcutta, there being a large amount of research already available. Instead, we shall examine the characteristics of the other sets of Acts which deals with non-presidency towns in West Bengal and especially those which apply on our five cities under study.

The Act X of 1842 (Bengal Act X of 1842) was the first legislation enacted for permitting formations of municipal bodies in Bengal as far as towns other than Presidency town of Calcutta are concerned. It provided that if 2/3 of the house holders of any town within the Presidency of Bengal, desired to make better provision for repairing, cleaning, lighting, draining and watching public streets, roads, drains or tanks or any like local purposes, then on their application, the government could set up a committee for carrying out these purposes and to assess a tax on housing not exceeding 5% of the annual value by the Magistrate. The provision to involve 2/3 of the residents suggest that the institution was supposed to be founded on popular participation. However in the implementation of the provision, the participation of the people did not automatically follow. For example the Act was introduced in Sreerampore but, "the inhabitants when called upon to pay tax not only refused but prosecuted the collector for tresspass when he attempted to levy it".[8]

Due to its ineffective character, the '1842 Act' was replaced by a new Act in 1850 commonly known as 'Improvement of Town Act XXVI'. The Act provided for constitution of Town Committees and was empowered to levy certain indirect taxes. The substantive issue of this reform, as it can be seen, was to form the apparatus of town administration without necessary participation of the residents. The main function of these municipal committees were to make better provision fos making, repairing, cleaning, lighting or watching any public streets, roads, drains or tanks or for the prevention of nuisances or for improving the said town or suburb in any other manner. They were also empowered to raise monies necessary by house assessment or town duties. The provisions of the Act were to be put in force in any town or suburb on an application of the inhabitants of the town or suburb or by the Governor or Governor-General-in-Council or Lt. Governor.[9] This Act was more successful in setting up municipal governments than the Bengal Act of 1842.

The provision of indirect taxes also made the municipal governments more viable. The Act XX of 1856 is known as Town Police Act of 1856. The main object of this Act was to provide for the payments of Chowkidars (town police). For the first time, by this Act an assessment according to the circumstances and property was provided as an alternative rate on holdings. Thus, till 1856 there were altogether 3 Municipal Acts (Acts X of 1842, Act XXVI of 1850 and Act XX of 1856). Apart from these three Acts two special Acts XXI of 1857 (which was named as Howrah Offences Act) and Act XII of 1858 were passed to deal with the town of Howrah and the southern suburb of Calcutta. These two Acts mainly deals with the nuisance and thes anitary problem of Calcutta, Howrah Station and their suburb. All these Acts answered the contingent needs felt in specific situation in specific cities and towns in West Bengal.

It was only in 1864 that a more pervasive opportunity for the development of municipal Governments was laid in the soil of Bengal by passing the District Municipal Act (Act III of 1864). This Act served as the first step towards establishment of Local self-Government and dealt with most of the matters covered by subsequent municipal acts. The Act was more or less a follow up of Lord Lawrences' Resolutions in 1864 favouring the extension of the local-self government. The cost of maintaining law and order in the numerous towns which had grown up by then was heavily taxing the exchequer. The resolution itself was partly motivated by the needed relief to the Imperial Exchequer and partly by the finding of the Royal Army Sanitary Commissions in 1861 and the outbreak of epidemics in 1863.[10] It was therefore decided that the cost of the town police forces must in future be directly borne by the town folk themselves and the towns 'were to be permitted to enjoy municipal institutions' for civic improvement education and other local objects.[11]

The District Municipal Improvement, Act of 1864 consists of 88 sections. In its preamble it was stated that it is an Act to provide for the appointment of municipal commissioners in towns and places in the Provinces under the Lt. Governor of Bengal and to make better provision for the conservancy and watching thereof and for levying of rates and taxes therein. Under this Act three fold object had been given on which the municipality can spend its fund :[12] (a) maintenance of police (b) maintenance, repair and cleaning of roads, drains and tanks (c) conservancy services. This Act had given the power to the Local Government to appoint for a specific term a Municipal Body, consisting not less than seven residents of the town including the Divisional Commissioner. The Chief source of revenue was taxation which might extend upto 7½ on the annual value of the holdings other than arable lands. Carriages, horses and carts could also be taxed and offensive trades could be controlled and licensed and fee levied on them.

The small towns in Bengal Presidency however had to wait for municipalisation until the District Town Acts 1868 (Act VI of 1868) wes passed. This allowed the formation of town council, commonly of the District Magistrate as a Chairman and five other non-official members. Provision of election was also made under the Act. For the larger towns similar privilege was extended by the Bengal Act of 1873 (Act II of 1873). But the initial elections were held without much success in a few towns like Sreerampore, Burdwan and Krishnagar.[13]

After the passing of Municipal Improvement Act of 1864, a series of Acts affecting Municipal jurisdiction were passed. There are the Bengal Municipal (Slaughter House and MeatMarkets) Act (Act VII Bengal Council of 1865), Hackney Carriage Act (Act V Bengal Council of 1866) Bengal Cruelty to Animals Act (Act XXIV Bengal Council of 1874). Cattle Tresspass Act (Act IV B.C. of 1873). These acts, inter alia, enlarged the field of activities of the municipal councils.

By another special Act (Howrah Lighting Act, Act V of 1873) Howrah Municipality was empowered to levy a rate of 3% to meet the cost of lighting the street with gas.[14]

In 1872 there were four different legislations governing municipalities in Bengal. One town (Howrah) was placed under the Town Improvement Act of 1850, 68 towns came under the Town Police Act of 1856, 24 larger towns were governed by the Bengal Municipal Improvement Act of 1864 and 91 smaller towns functioned under the District Towns Act of 1868. The situation was decidedly confusing and no less confusing than what it is today.

In his Resolution No. 3334 dated 14th December 1870 Lord Mayo announced—"Local interest, supervision and care are necessary to the success in the management of funds devoted to Education, Sanitation, Medical Relief, and Local Public Works. The operation of this resolution, in its full meaning and integrity will afford opportunities for the development of self government, for strengthening municipal institution and for the associations of Natives and Europeans, to a greater extent than heretofore, in the administration of affairs."[15] Lord Mayo's Resolution was not merely a benevolent move, but it was intended to give relief to the Imperial finance as well. This resolution of Lord Mayo led to the issuance of Act No. II, 1873. In this Act it was stated that 2/3 of the Municipal Commissioners will be elected by the rate payers and also the Vice-Chairman, if government so permitted. An elected Commissioner was to hold office for 3 years, but 1/3 of them had to retire each year by rotation. It was Sreerampore Municipality which took the advantage of elective system in 1873. Burdwan and Krishnagar Municipalities followed in 1874.

Before 1876, as we have mentioned above, there were various Acts dealing with the municipal governments in Bengal. A single comprehensive Act was urgently required. Thus Act IV of Bengal Council of 1876 was passed and the four different Acts governing different towns and also the special Act of 1875 (Howrah Lighting Act) were replaced. Under this Act the towns which already enjoyed municipal government either under Act of 1864 or 1868 retained their respective privileges as First class or Second class municipalities. But for the new town to become a First or Second Class Municipality they were required to have atleast 3/4 of their male adult population as non-agriculturist. To become a First Class town a population of 15,000 with a density of 2,000 per square mile was necessary. For the first time the definition of a town emerged in Bengal within the framework of law.

The whole body of the Commissioners, until then as a rule, were required to be appointed by the government, unless the right of election had been extended to the municipality under the Act II of 1873. As regards First Class Municipalities the new Act fixed the number of commissioners as 30 and 7 respectively as maximum and minimum limits. In second class municipalities the number ranged between 20 and 4. The term of the office of the commissioners was 3 years and 1/3 of them were to retire every three years by rotation. The Chairman was appointed by the Government, but the Vice-Chairman was elected by the commissioners. If at least 1/3 of the rate payers desired an elective system, then the whole or any member of the appointed commissioners might be elected by the rate payers, if permitted by the government.

Part IV of the Act dealt with municipal taxation, provision for assessment and review. Under the Act the Commissioners might impose with the sanction of the Lt. Governor any one of the following taxes :

(a) a tax upon person occupying holdings within the municipality according to their circumstances and property. There was a provision that the amount assessed in respect of the occupation of any one holding should not be more than eighty-four rupees per annum or (b) a rate not exceeding seven and half per centum on the annual value of all holdings situated within the municipality. Apart from any other aforesaid taxes the commissioners at a meeting might also levy within the sanction of the Lt. Governor the following taxes, fee and tolls within the limit of the municipality :

(a) a tax on carriages, horses and other animals ;
(b) a fee on the registration of carts ;
(c) tolls on ferries, bridges and metalled roads.

In 1878 certain modifications were made in the Act of 1876. By this Act (Act VI Bengal Council of 1878) all the first class municipalities were empowered to impose a latrine rate for cleaning private privies and cesspools (night soil collections).

In 1882 Lord Ripon observed : "Considerable progress had been made since 1870. A large income from the local rates and cesses had been secured and in some provinces the management of income had been freely entrusted to local bodies. Municipalities had also increased in number and usefulness. But there was still need for greater degree of progress in different parts of the country. In many places services admirably adopted for local government were reserved in the hands of Central Government, while every where heavy charges were levied on municipalities in connection with police over which they had necessary no executive control."[16] So Lord Ripon bsought in further reforms in the municipal governments. Lord Ripon's historic Resolution on Local-Self Government of May 18, 1882 marks the beginning of a new chapter in the history of Local-Self Government in India as it paved the way for the foundations of the system which exists to-day. According to the Taxation Enquiry Commission "It was Lord Ripons Resolution of 1882 that paved the way for the development of Local Self Government specially in urban areas, with the accent on self-government."[17]

The period proceeding the reforms of Lord Ripons was marked by intense nationalist demand for obtaining self governance atleast at the local levels. Lord Ripon's Reforms came in the wake of such demands. The fundamental principles laid down in the resolution were as follows :

(a) Local Boards were to be developed not in the towns and cities but throughout the country ; and they were to be charged with definite duties and entrusted with definite funds. The area of jurisdiction allotted to each Board should in no case be too large. Over these Boards, District Boards were to be set up with certain controlling powers.

(b) In no case the official members were to be more than 1/3 of the whole.

(c) The non-official members should be selected on the system of election as widely as local circumstances may permit.

(d) Wherever practicable non-officials should be appointed Chairman of Local Boards—both rural and urban.

(e) It was recommended that the control over the Local Boards should be exercised from without rather than from within. The Government should revise a check upon the acts of Local Bodies not to dictate them.

(f) Local Bodies should have elastic and sufficient financial resources. They should have freedom to shape their own budget.

From the context of the Lord Ripons' Resolution, the Bengal Municipal Act, 1884 was passed. This act was a marked improvement over the earlier act of 1876, which provided for election of the 2/3 members of the board having a minimum of nine and maximum of thirty members. The Act consisted of 267 sections and six schedules. The main features of the Bengal Municipal Act, 1884 were as follows.[18]

(*i*) Election by the rate-payers of 2/3 of the municipal commissioners. The remaining 1/3 were nominated members.

(*ii*) Provision of elected Chairman, Vice-Chairman could be elected in all the municipalities.

(*iii*) Municipalities for the first time were relieved from maintaining 'Police charges' for the town.

(*iv*) In the Act the maximum and minimum number of commissioners (not less than 9 and not more than 30) had been clearly stated.

(*v*) The provision of ex-officio Commissioners, unlike the previous Act was abolished. Section 14 of the Act restricted the number of Commissioners holding salaried offices under the Government to 1/4th.

(*vi*) Unlike the previous Act (Act V of 1876) the new Act enlarged the powers of the Commissioners in regard to taxation. For the first time municipalities were allowed to impose water rate, light rate and fee for clearing the latrines under certain conditions. In regard to tax upon person, the provision was made clear and distinct.

(*vii*) Municipal Fund could be expended on the following heads :

(a) Construction and improvement of roads, tramways, bridges, gardens, drains, privies etc.

(b) The supply of water and the lighting ond watering of roads.

(c) The errection and maintenance of office and other buildings required for municipal purposes.

(d) Other works of public utility.

(e) Construction and repair of school houses and establishment and maintenance of schools wholly or partly with government-in-aid.

(f) The establishment and maintenance of hospitals and dispensaries.

(g) The promotion of vaccination.

(h) The maintenance of fire-brigade.

The Act of 1884 was amended from time to time. Act III, Bengal Council of 1886 provided for inspection of shops in case of municipalities where power to regulate sale of produce were extended. Act IV, Bengal Council, of 1894 provided for establishment of Sanitary Board to prepare and carry out schemes of water supply, drainage and fire-brigade and also power was given to the government to appoint Assessor to settle the disputes between neighbouring local bodies. Commissioners were given power to make Rule and Bylaws to revise building regulations and to control burial grounds and burning ghats. Act II of 1896 provided power to the municipalities to apply their fund for vaccinations, grants to schools, maintenance of hospitals etc. These Acts were followed by Act I of 1900 to make special provisions for the Hill municipality of Darjeeling and Act II of 1914 to empower Government to compel the appointment of Health and Sanitary Officers.

Apart from the various amendments, the Act of 1884 may be regarded as the foundation of the present municipal legislation in West Bengal. The 1884 Act also formed the basis on which most legislations in northern and eastern India was drafted. In 1923 Sir Surendra Nath Banerjee drafted a new Bengal Municipal Bill. The Bill could not be passed for almost a decade untill it was successfully pilotted by Sir Bijoy Prosad Singh Roy, the then minister of Local Self-Government, through the Bengal Legislative Council on 1st April, 1932 and the Act XV Bengal Council of 1932 was passed on 6th September 1932 and came into force from 1st December 1932. The Bengal Municipal Act of 1932 (Act XV of 1932) as amended from time to time, still governs municipal administr ation in West Bengal.

The 1932 Act made certain changes with regard to (a) municipal constitution, (b) control by the government, (c) municipal functions and (d) finance. The proportion of elected members was increased to 3/4 and in certain advanced municipalities this was raised to 4/5 of the total. In case of new municipality, however, government retained the power to nominate all the members for a period not exceeding one year. Women were given the right to vote, the educational qualification was lowered to matriculate and any rate payer and license was allowed to vote.[19]

Compared to the early Municipal Acts of this state the 1932 Act is both comprehensive and voluminous. The main features are as follows :—

(*a*) The principle of removing the internal control by the Government through the Divisional Commissioner over the affairs of the Municipalities and to limited it to mere external control of the Government was adopted in the Act. An attempt was also made to bring the municipalities directly in contact with the department of Local-Self Government to the extent possible. The three means of external control envisaged were dissolution, temporary taking over the management of the municipal department in respect of which there was a default and finally suppression.

(*b*) The priority items of expenditure included the obligations arising from any trust, payment to assessor or to other special officers.

(*c*) Wider powers were granted to the municipalities for improvement of conservancy, drainage and water supply, lighting and improvement of streets, building and slums.

(*d*) Establishment of municipal courts and works of public utilities were removed from the list of permissive functions, while provisions were made to restrain the spread of infection, for opening of municipal markets and slaughter houses, for taking steps for the supply of wholesome food, drugs and milk, registration of births and death etc.

(*e*) Where no education cess was levied, the government was empowered to prescribe a percentage of municipal income to be earmarked for primary education.

(*f*) The tax on persons was abolished as it was difficult to assess and could give a rise to complaints of unfair incidence.

(*g*) Another innovation in the sphere of municipal taxation was the provision for a panel of municipal assessors. The appeals against property tax assessment was to be placed before a committee consisting of Chairman, a member and person nominated by the Government.

(*h*) Reservation of seats (Commissioners) for the scheduled tribe was made.

In 1955 an amendment of the Act 1932 was made, which is known as Bengal Municipal (amendment) Act of 1955. The Act states that the Chairman can be removed by a simple majority vote with the approval of the Government, appointment of an Executive Officer by the Government and investing him with such powers as may contain in a notification, appointment of an Assessment Tribunal by the Government for hearing of assessment appeals, power to auditor to disallow an item of expenditure contrary to the law and surcharge the person authorising such expenditure, realisation of municipal dues by certificate procedure under the Public Demands Recovery Act.

The above short review of the legislative measures taken by the state government to institute the municipal governments in West Bengal permit us to observe three secular trends. In the first instance we must observe that the municipal government were created with a view to transfering the responsibility of goverenance over an emerging, but complex form of human settlement. There was a concordant theme wherein the cost of such goverenance was required to be met by taxing exclusively the people and economy of these emerging settlements. Yet the powers and authorities of thes instituted local governments were kept on a very restricted base. The tax base was made very specific and care was taken to exercise control from within through the ex-officio and nominated members. The desire to exercise such controls by the State Government has been a consistent obsession of recurring importance in the successive legislative amendments although the scope for popular participation was simultaneously created.

In the second instance we may observe that the desire to exercise control upon these institutions of local-self governments emerges from the fact that the need for supplementing the resources of these institutions from the State exchequer became a permanent feature. In the initial years the local resources could be gainfully utilized by the municipalities for laying basic civic infrastructure. But subsequently these institutions were charged with the responsibility of maintenance of these civic infrastructure over and above what would be required for enlarging service areas through capital investment. The gap in the resources had to be met from the resources of the State through Grant-in-aid. This may explain why the state government is so anxious to exercise restraining control upon the functions of the local self-governments. Such control the state has been exercising by requiring the municipal grants to attach themselves to the department of Local Self-Government of the state. By 1967 this demand had gone so deeply into the mechanism of governance that special cells of local self-government department were created within the district level administrative apparatus. The municipal governments are now required to keep these district cells posted with the copies of all resolutions in respective to whether these refer to policy decisions or administrative resolutions. In addition this cell enjoys the authority of final sanction of any developmental plan adopted and approved by the municipal governments.

The third phenomenon that should deserve our attention is the reluctance expressed by the people's representatives within the institutions of local self-governance to enhance their revenue. This is quite understandable in the context of retaining popularity within a framework of democratic electorate. One of the many different ways of overcoming such limitations could be the adoption of a procedure for involving local participation for augmenting revenue. But the current thinking in the government is to set up a special authority, outside the municipal governments, which will be entrusted to assess the valuation of property and other establishments for purpose of fixing enhanced municipal taxes. The desire to circumvent popular participant is indeed interesting. This matches with the ethos of the State Government as demonstrated by their repeated reference to the Act of 1932 and by recurring supersession of the municipal governments of the past. In 1974 almost all the municipal governments of West Bengal were being run after supersession by administrative officers deputed from the state government. This situation prevails even today.

These three secular trends indicate that the institutions of municipal governments has remained more or less as a symbol of convenience before the state political apparatus and the institutions so created has been allowed to operate on the norms of restrictive functions, where the State apparatus has exercised its rights to set such norms in a rather autonomous fashion. This should be kept in view while reviewing the role of the people as well as of the municipal governments vis-a-vis the emerging complexities of the urban-socio-economic life. We suspect that the two never got integrated as we shall see from the review of the powers of municipal governance, the role of the people and the management of urban infrastructure which has heen discussed in the following pages.

Powers of the municipal governance

While reviewing the powers of the Municipal Governments, we are required to see to what extent their autonomy is subordinate to that of the State Government. This will reveal how power interacts with assigned responsibilities.

According to the Bengal Municipal Act of 1932 the power of the Municipal Council can be divided into two parts ;

(a) Establishment or administrative power
(b) Legislative power or to make rule.

According to the section 66 of the Bengal Municipal Act 1932 the commissioners at a meeting may, subject to the provision of this Act and the rules made there under from time to time, determine what officers and servants are necessary for the municipality and may fix the salaries and allowances to be paid and granted to such officers and servants. This is the only authority that is not supervised over by the State Government.

All other powers are derived from the approval of the State Government. According to the same section of the Bengal Municipal Act 1932 the commissioners at a meeting specially convened for the purpose, by a resolution in favour of which not less than 2/3 of the commissioners present at such a meeting shall have voted, may subject to the approval of the State Government make rules :

(i) for the granting of pensions, gratuities and bonus out of the Municipal Fund ;
(ii) for granting of compassionate allowances and gratuities to the member of the family of deceased municipal officers and servants ;
(iii) for the creation and management of provident or annuity fund, for compelling contributions to such provident or annuity fund on the part of their officers and servants and for supplementing such contribution out of the Municipal Fund.

According to the Section 75 of the Bengal Municipal Act 1932 the commissioners at a meeting may subject to the sanction of the State Government make rules as to :

(i) the duties, appointment, leave, fining, suspensions and removal of the municipal officers and servants,
(ii) the nature and amount of security to be furnished by different classes of municipal officers or servants for the proper discharge of their duties,

Apart from these powers, Section 85 of the Bengal Municipal Act provides powers to the commissioners to check and inspect all the books and records of the municipality.

But in no way has these commissioners been assigned the responsibility to act as monitors or promoters of developmental works for their respective electorates. In other words, these representatives of the people have neither the power nor the responsibility to answer for their existence to their electorates, who need infrastructural development for their better participation in urban life. This is hardly commensurate with the nation's commitment to constitutional democracy or to urbanisation.[20]

It must be mentioned that the three municipalities (Howrah, Hooghly-Chinsura and Chandernagar) out of the five selected for study had been superseded by the West Bengal Government (Howrah in 1967, Hooghly-Chinsura in 1969 and Chandernagar in 1972) and all the power is vested in an executive officer appointed by the Government. Durgapur has a nominated Board with an Executive Officer. Only Burdwan has a board of elected commissioners.

Role of the people

The success of a local Self-Government or an urban government particularly in a country like India, which has adopted a democratic constitution with all power vested in the people, depends upon the consciousness of the urban dwellers toward their civic problems. The success of the urban government depends upon an enlightened and alert electorate, supporting a conscientious body of commissioners (Councillors in the case of Corporation). But from the field survey of the five cities selected for studies, it was known that the ordinary citizen is not showing any interest towards the urban government and towards the problems of their own city. The only exercise their franchises when called for to do so and feel that they have done their duty. This apathy of the citizen towards their civic government is a common feature of all the five cities under study. This apathy can be partly explained by the rootlessness of their elected representatives within the constitutional structure of Local Self-Government as described in the previous section.

But part of the apathy is certainly due to arising as it did from, the incapacity of the municipal governments to cope with the complexities of rapid population growth in recent years. Most of the civic conservancy services are being over-utilized or are not at all available to the newcomers to the cities.

Since independence there was a marked tendency to migrate from the rural areas toward the urban centres. The immigrants generally belong to the weaker sections of the rural community incapable of consuming good residential facilities. Housing became inadequate. Slums sprung up all around. The overcrowding of the city put great pressure upon the existing civic infrastructure. Yet the revenue of the City-government did not increase at the rate the population grew. The immigrants were poor. The gap between the resources and expenditure increased every year. Urban amenities and services started declining in their nature and standard. Water supply became inadequate, roads were not cleaned and maintained properly, garbage pilled up along the roadside, creating a hazard to public health.

All these together has made civic life unhappy. People lost faith in the urban government. The disgruntled electorate made civic government the places of political rivalries and group fighting,[21] who satisfied the electorate by not charging them. The percentage of the tax collected decreased by 25% to 30%, making the municipality bankrupt. Continuous strike and other events made the city life difficult. The confusion was thus confounded.

The other reason of non-participation of the citizen in the urban government affairs is the heterogenous character of the urban community. Human relations in the city are largely anonymous, superficial, and transitory. He has to concentrate on earning and laying aside as much as possible for the eventual and certain return to his "real" home.[22]

We have already seen how heterogenous the diverse social groups are in the five cities. The linguistic heterogeneity, it was observed from field survey, did not help the community to look upon their neighbourhoods as a place where they should 'belong'. Consequently their longing for a 'real' home remain nested in terms of the village or town from where they have emmigrated. The use the civic facilities without developing any commitment for those who provide such facilities. Similarly the municipal governments did not try to create any citizens' forum to educate the electorate otherwise. The unfulfilled satisfactions thus kept the citizens', the civic infrastructure and the municipal governments as an alien entities to each other. Such a socio-political ambience governs the urban life in West Bengal.

Some experience of management

In order to assess the results of the apathy of the citizens to these institution of governance and of the lack of autonomy of these institutions, it is necessary to examine the role played by the different municipal governments in the five cities under study. We shall examine these governments in so far as these have responded to the six basic functions of landuse control, water supply, conservancy, roads, health and sanitation and education. These six functions constitute the barest minimum required for sustaining any form of urban government.

Landuse control and advance planning

The cities selected for studies (except Durgapur) have grown without planning. The maps on the landuse of Howrah, Burdwan, Hooghly-Chinsura and Chandernagar clearly indicate how diverse landuse have produced mere amalgams within the cities. Residentials, shops, bazars, industries, bustees—all had clustered together forming very confused landuse patterns. This amalgam of landuse pattern are mainly due to the failure of the city government to apply any rational landuse control in the past.[23] Neither there is any conscious effort to remedy the ills in terms of future development. None of the five municipalities have any apparatus to evolve the principles of landuse control. These don't have any department of planning either. Through field investigation it revealed that neither the executives nor the past commissioners, councillors are of the need for setting up of any apparatus of planning or for exercising control on future landuse. The Howrah Municipality is now having the support of the Howrah Improvement Trust, an autonomous institution, who are prescribing the kinds of developmental—investments that the city should receive and not indicating how the required resources can be obtained by the municipal government. Similarly the Durgapur Development Authority is acting as autonomous institution, without the responsibility of mobilizing resources to support their development recommendation made on behalf of the Durgapur Notified Area Authority.

Water supply

One of the most important services maintained by the city government is the water supply. The five cities selected for study have provision of filtered water supply within their municipal boundary. But in the present state, due to rapid population growth, this service has deteriorated to a great extent. The water supply per head is at the rate of 12 to 18 gallons per day which is below the recommended standard of 20 gallons per head per day for Calcutta. During the summer the situation becomes more difficult.[24] Let us discuss the water supply situation of the five cities individually :

Howrah : The proposal of having a water supply system for the town was first mooted out in a resolution dated 20th June 1878. But only on 7th September 1882 the report was accepted by Mr. A.J. Hughes, Executive Engineer, Northern Drainage Embankment Division, for obtaining water from the neighbourhood of Rishra and to have their own waterworks to supply drinking water to the inhabitants of Howrah. The waterworks were completed in January 1896.[25] The total cost for the construction of the water works was Rs. 16,70,310.[26]

The Head Water works are on the Sreerampore bank of Hooghly some 12 miles upstream from Calcutta. This site was selected just to avoid the effects of salinity in the water arising from the tidal current of the river. Thus water supply plant was originally designed to supply 2.5 million gallons per day for a population of 1,25,000. The water works was expanded to 5 m.g.d. capacity in 1913 when the population exceeded 2,00,000. No further expansion in the capacity has taken place though the population has trippled now. To-day the supply of filter water is obviously inadequate.[27]

Water is supplied to the Howrah Municipal areas with the help of four Elevated Towers situated in Salkia, Panchanantola, Kaipukur and Cowies Ghat with a total capacity of

6,40,600 gallons and 93 miles of water distribution mains. The average water supply from the Sreerampore surface water sources is 7 gallon per head per day. So supplementary supply is being obtained by tapping the underground water resources. But per capita supply hardly reach 12 gallons a day. In addition to the Sreerampore water works there are 1,000 small diameter tubewells which have been sunk on the average of 200 feet deep to meet the water demand of the municipality. But in spite of such a large investment on water supply, the standard is very poor. Nearly 50% of the tubewells are out of commission. Interim water supply scheme undertaken by the Public Health Engineering Directorate is yet to be completed. Even if this plan comes into force nearly 1,00,000 people of Howrah will be without water because this scheme had been designed to supply water for 6,50,000 persons only. The population of Howrah according to 1971 census is 7,37,877.[28]

Durgapur : The Durgapur Notified Area Authority has no water system of its own. As Durgapur is a city of colonies and townships developed by the various industries, so these industries supply water to their respective colonies.

The Bhiringi-Benachiti area, the commercial hub of the city, has to depend upon Durgapur Project Ltd. and Durgapur Steel Ltd. for water supply and these two areas are under the direct control of D.N.A.A. for water. The requirement of these areas is 8 lakh gallons per day ; but D.N.A.A. can supply only 1 lakh gallons. The magnitude of the problem can be imagined by the existing gap of nearly 7 lakh gallons per day.[29] Apart from the colonies and various townships and Bhiringi-Benachiti area there are 35 villages within the boundary of D.N.A.A. where there is no filtered water supply.

Burdwan : Burdwan has a piped filter water supply system. Waterworks was constructed during the period 1884-85 at a cost of rupees 235,500[30] near Lakuddi village on the bank of Banka Nala some 2½ miles west from the centre of the town. The then Maharaja of Burdwan had contributed nearly 55,000 rupees. There has been no expansion in the water works since it was constructed. Four schemes worth 11 lakh rupees, for the improvement of water supply is pending before the Government of West Bengal for sanction since 1967-68.[31]

The present waterworks at Lakuddi has four engines, three boilers, one intake with a roughing filter, five high level settling tanks, two low levels settling tanks, five filter beds with a daily capacity of 8,75,000 gallons. This water works can supply water to 60,000 population. The present population of Burdwan is nearly 2,00,000. So the ratio of water-supply (filter) is 4.3 gallons per head per day. To meet the daily demand of the people the municipality had sunk 400 tubewells in the different parts of the municipal areas. The areas of Baburbagh, Tarabag, Golapbag, Kesabganj Chati. Gonda and the various neighbourhoods in Chhotonilpur. Baronilpur still have no proper municipal water supply system. In the summer days there is an acute crises of drinking water.

Hooghly-Chinsura : In Hooghly-Chinsura filtered water supply system was introduced in the year 1914. The water works is situated at Kamarpara (Bansberia). It has three settling tanks having a capacity of 7,00,000 gallons, 4 sand filter centres with a total area of 24,000 square feet and an underground reservoir with a capacity of 3,00,000 gallons.[32] There has been no extension in this water works. As the population has increased there has been an acute water shortage. So the municipal authority sunk 13 nos. deep tubewells and the whole municipal areas was divided into 13 zones. The deep tubewells are connected with 6 overhead towers which are located in different zones. But presently 6 nos. of deep tubewells are out of order making the problem of water supply difficult and uncertain.[33] The total water supplied to Hooghly Chinsura municipality is 1.5 million gallons which comes to average of 15 gallons per head per day.[34]

Chandernagar : As there is no water works in Chandernagar the water is supplied by deep tubewells. Before 1965 there were 7 deep tubewells, all located in the south and central Chandernagar. But to-day only 3 are functioning. Seeing the problem an Emergency Water Supply Scheme (first phase) prepared and executed by the Public Health Engineering Directorate at an estimated cost of over Rs. 34 lakhs could not produce the desired results due to the unusual delay in its execution. The lackadisical way of the PHE Directorate has carried much inconvenience to the residents. The two overhead tanks situated in the Laldighidhar and Moran Road areas are yet to be commissioned. The augmentation scheme (second phase) at an estimated cost of over Rs. 24 lakhs prepared by the PHED was not sanctioned by the government although similar schemes in neighbouring municipalities have already been executed.[35] This left the municipal authority to depend on their own sources. In two years (1973-75), 60 nos. of hand pump tubewells had been sunk in the different parts of the municipal areas. It had also sunk two deep tubewells at Boraichanditolla and at Hatkhola. The latter has not yet been commissioned due to unusual delay in getting the divisional Commissioner's sanction. The water supply was all the more critical due to the careless execution of sewerage scheme, causing frequent damage to the waterpipes mains. At present with all its sources Chandernagar Municipal Corporation is supplying nearly 1,18,000 gallons of water per day at the rate of 14 gallons per head per day.

Conservancy

These services can be regarded as the most improtant for the urban centres and the cities spend highest amount of rupees on these services. Mounting expenditure on these services has not yielded any fruitful result. The service conditions are deteriorating day by day as the drains are not cleaned, service latrines are not attended daily, garbage are piled up along the road side.

Howrah : Howrah is situated on a comparatively high land on the west of the river Hooghly. The general slope of the land and the consequent flow of drainage is away from the river with a natural fall towards west and north-west and south-west. There is a dividing line which runs along the G.T. Road north to south. Drainage on the east side of the line falls into the river Hooghly. That to the west of the road falls into low lying areas further west.[36]

The existing drainage system of Howrah is mostly through open channels and surface drains with the exception of Naskarpara Road interceptor, which empties in the Hooghly. Storm water run off is carried away to outfall points by a complex network of open drains. Drainage of the Salkia and Bali areas lying on the west of the G.T. Road passes under the Eastern Railway Tracks through a series of culverts to the Rani Jheel is carried through an outfall drain which runs upto Belgachia and Bhaga area of Howrah Municipality. The outfall joins with the other outfall drains coming from the Banaras Road culvert and meets the branch canal drainage, then passes through a series of culvert and empties into a branch canal of the Howrah Drainage Canal in Padmapukur Jala (Swamp).

The drainage system of Central Howrah to the south-west is through culverts under the Southeastern Railway line which empties into the branch channel in Padmapukur Jala and the Howrah Drainage Canal. Sluice gates on the Howrah Drainage Canal at Nazirgunj are operated during the monsoon to control discharge and to prevent flood water getting into the system.[37]

In the absence of an underground sewer system the night soil is removed from the latrines by tubs loaded in motor lorries and then carried to the trenching ground. After 1966-67 there has been no increase in the number of service latrines, because without a septic tank latrine the municipality is not sanctioning construction for new houses. Waste water and storm water are discharged into the same system of surface drains. As there is no suitable system of drainage outlet some portion of the city specially the central part become waterlogged during the monsoon. An elaborate sewerage plan is going on and it is hoped that it will be completed in next few years.

Durgapur : Due to the undulating type of land Durgapur has a natural drainage system. The residential areas are served by the Kunur Nala in the north and Tamla Nala and Damodar River in the South.

Except the Bhiringi-Benachiti areas all the townships and colonies have their own sewerage and conservancy system. So the Durgapur Notified Area Authority has no responsibility to provide these services. Only the garbage cleaning is in the hand of Durgapur Notified Area Authority which is done by 3 motor lorries and gang of mazdoors (labourers).

Burdwan : Due to the flat surface and old drains which are poorly laid, the drainage system of Burdwan is inadequate. Lack of fund is also a main problem in improving these. In spite of the various difficulties the municipality has reclaimed the town's main drainage channel more than two miles long, 15' ft. wide and 10' ft. deep in the year 1974. For years it was silted upto the ground level. Constructed by one of the Maharajas of Burdwan it is linked with the Banka river and now is capable of serving the 16 wards of the municipality.

There is no underground sewerage system. Thus the old system also prevails here. Night soil is carried by trailors and then carried by tractors to trenching ground. There are about 5,453 service latrines in the municipal areas which are attended on alternate days.[38]

Hooghly-Chinsura : Hooghly-Chinsura has no proper drainage system. The water is generally discharged in the Hooghly River. Unlined surface drains frequently overflow, making the environment unhealthy.

Hooghly-Chinsura has no underground sewerage system. The night soil is removed in old method. About 4,000 gallons of night soil are being removed with the help of 14 trailors with 2 tractors. There are 9,533 service latrines which are attended on alternate days.

Chandernagar : Due to ill maintenance of the drains the drainage system of Chandernagar has become inadequate. Drains are not cleaned properly in the compact residential units of the south and central Chandernagar.

The sewerage system of Chandernagar can be classified as an open surface drain. Night soils are removed with the help of hand trolley-carts and then tractors to the trenching ground. There are 3,668 water brone, 5,722 service latrines in Chandernagar. The ratio is 1 = 8.5 people (or one latrine is serving 8.5 people).

Thus the conservancy and sewerage system of all the cities selected for studies are inadequate.

Roads

Road is a symbol of motion which provides an easy means of communication to the urban dwellers from their residences to the place of work and other places. The five cities selected for study (except Durgapur) had no planned road system, which are creating traffic problems within the cities. In spite of the heavy expenditure, the roads of the cities are in poor condition.

Howarh : In Howarh the urban government had failed to provide a good street system. They are poorly laid out and have insufficient width for any volume of traffic. What streets they are, are required to fulfill non-traffic functions such as market sites, pedestrain ways of good storage areas.

The municipality possess about 123 metalled road having a ratio of 6,398 person to 1 mile of road. Only 4 miles of new road has been built since 1934. This is so startling a figure that its accuracy might be questioned ; but the point is nonetheless valid that laying of road rights-of-way has failed in all respects to keep pace with the increase in population and development.[39]

Durgapur : Durgapur Notified Area Authority has no such assignment as the other municipalities have in developing road system within their urban limit. The Durgapur Development Authority (DDA) makes all the detail programme for the construction of the road. Durgapur Notified Area Authority has the charge to keep them clean. But recently some morrum roads have been built by the Durgapur Notified Area Authority in the village areas in its boundary. The picture that Durgapur displays are quite different from the four other cities selected for studies.

Burdwan : The landuse map of Burdwan clearly indicates that there is no plan for the road system. The roads are poorly laid out. The compact residential areas of Barabazar, Mithapukur, Puratan Chack, Sarbamangala Para, Kalibazar areas, Tentultala area, Radhanagar south of G.T. Road have no efficient road system. The roads are very narrow and ill built. Burdwan Municipality claims that it has constructed 28.83 Km of metalled road, 4.85 unmetalled road since 1968.[40] Now it has 87 Km of roads in its jurisdiction. This gives the ratio of 1 Km road serving 1,609 people. Due to lack of fund the roads are not repaired properly.

Hooghly-Chinsura : In spite of being a Divisional Headquarters of Burdwan and also an old administrative centre, Hooghly-Chinsura roads are very ill built and poorly laid out. The Chari Mour and its adjoining areas which are the administrative and commercial centre of Hooghly-Chinsura, has no proper road system. The roads are very narrow and now they are not in a position to handle the traffic properly. Apart from this, the Municipal Authority had failed to construct any length of road since 1965. At present the municipality has 44.86 miles of metalled road and 32.0 miles of unmetalled roads. Thus 1 mile of road serves 1,367 persons.

Chandernagar : Except the down town area, which were laid by the French, Chandernagar presents the same picture as the other municipalities. Ill laid out, narrown ss and ill maintenance is the general characteristics of the roads of Chandernagar. Municipal authority did not pay attention to road till 1972-73 when the government granted money to improve 30 Km of road in Chandernagar. After this grant the road conditions of various colonies of south-west and north-west had improved. Presently Chandernagar has 73 Km of roads in which 52 Km are metalled and 20 Km are unmetalled. Thus 1 Km of road serves 1,046 persons.

Health and sanitation

All the five cities have a piped water supply system which is chemically treated. Except Burdwan and Hooghly-Chinsura the rest three urban governments have full-fledged Health Departments with medical officers to look after the health and sanitation problems of their respective cities. But the percentage of expenditure in the column of medical purpose in all the municipalities selected for studies varies from 4% to 6% of the total expenditure.

Howrah : Howrah being an industrial city clustered with labour colonies side by side of the industries has a severe health problem. The conditions of these labour colonies mainly known as bastees are very awful. There is no drainage system and no proper ventilation. The health department provides vaccinations and other medical facilities on a small scale to its people. General provisions of health services of the city (managed and aided by the Municipality) are :

1. Satyabala Devi Infections Diseases Hospitals
   Dispensaries managed by the Municipality :
   1. Salkia Charitable dispesnary at municipal own building at Bandhaghat.
   2. Charitable dispensary at 390, G.T. Road (N).

3. Bantra Charitable Dispensary at Narasingha Datta Road.
4. Charitable Dispensary at 14, Ananta Mukherjee Road.
5. Batore Charitable Dispensary, 223, Circular Road.
6. Ayurvedic Charitable Dispensary, 43 Jaliapara Lane.
7. X Ray Clinic at Municipal Office, Howrah.

Apart from these charitable dispensaries there are four state owned public hospitals with a total 315 beds having a ratio of 1 bed serving 2,498 persons.

Durgapur : The Durgapur Notified Area Authority has its health Department with a medical officer but it has no dispensary. Vaccination is administered in the main office of the Durgapur Notified Area Authority. There are three big hospitals controlled by Durgapur Steel Plant and Durgapur Project Ltd. with a total beds of 310. There is one state owned sub-divisional public hospital with 131 beds. Thus Durgapur has better health facility with one hospital bed serving 468 persons.

Burdwan : Burdwan Municipal Corporation has no hospital as well charitable dispensary of its own. It has a small maternity centre maintained by a single nurse. The service is inadequate. The health department provides vaccination and anti cholera inoculation. Apart from this, there is one state owned general hospital with nearly 350 beds, serving 408 persons per bed.

Hooghly-Chinsura : The health department of Hooghly-Chinsura is inadequate. It has practically no function except providing vaccination and anti cholera inoculation. There is one state owned general hospital with 185 beds serving 568 persons per bed.

Chandernagar : The health department of Chandernagar is looked after by a Medical Officer ; but the municipal corporation has no hospital of its own. There is one state owned hospital with 162 beds. Thus the ratio is 1 bed for 464 persons.

Education

The five municipal governments maintain primary school and sanction grant-in-aid to the many educa-

TABLE 8.1 : Number of Schools Maintained and Aided by the Municipalities

Municipalities/ Corporation	Maintained				Aided		
	Primary School	Jr. High School	High School	Tolls	Pr. Sch.	J.S.	H.S.
Howrah Municipality	26	x	x	37	38	1	9
Durgapur Notified Area Authority	x	x	x	x	x	x	x
Burdwan Municipal Corporation	11	x	x	x	x	x	x
Hooghly-Chinsura Municipality	11	x	x	x	x	x	x
Chandernagar Corporation	17	2	6	x	x	x	x

Source : Office of Municipalities and Corporation.

Note : Pr. = Primary, Jr. = Junior, H = High.

tional institutions. Chandernagar corporation is responsible for secondary education also. Education departments of Howrah Municipality and Chandernagar Corporation are looked after by their respective education officers. But due to increase in the cost of maintaining these primary schools, the municipalities are not willing to carry the responsibility any more.

CONCLUSION

The foregoing analysis of the status and performance of the municipal governments in general and those of the five cities under study leave us with no doubt that functional integration between the factors of urban growth, public consciousness, statutory devolution of powers of governance or management of the civic infrastructure has not taken place.

FOOTNOTES

1. Ministry of Works and Housing, New Delhi : Report of the Committee on Budgetary Reform in Municipal Administration, 1974 : pp. 9-10.
2. Bhattacharya, Mohit, Essays in Urban Government, The World Press Private Ltd., Calcutta, 1970 : p. 3.
3. Government of West Bengal, Legislative Department, Bengal Act XV of 1932, The Bengal Municipal Act 1932, West Bengal Government Press, 1967 : p. 1.
4. Government of West Bengal, Legislative Department, Bengal Act XV of 1932, The Bengal Municipal Act, West Bengal Press, 1970 : p. 53.
5. Bhattacharya, Mohit, Essays in Urban Government, The World Press Private Ltd., Calcutta, 1970 : p. 3.
6. Tinker, Hugh., *The Foundation of Local Self-Government of India, Pakistan and Burma*, Lalvani Publishing House, Culcutta, 1967 : p. 15.
7. Zakaria, Rafiq, Augmentation of Financial Resources of Urban Local Bodies, Report of the Committee of Ministers constituted by the Central Council of Local Self-Government, November, 1963 : p. 3.
8. The Imperial Gazetteer of India, Vol. IV, Clarendon Press, 1907 : p. 286.
9. The Bengal Government, Improvement of Town Act XXVI, Sec. II, 1850.

10. Datta, Abhijit, *Urban Government Finance and Development*, The World Press. Calcutta, 1970 : p. 139.
11. Argal R., *Municipal Government in India.* Allahabad, 1954 : p. 8.
12. District Municipal Act. 1864 : Section XV.
13. Datta, Abhijit, Urban Government Finance and Development, The World Press, Calcutta, 1970 : p. 140.
14. Banerjee, J., *Howrah Civil Companion*, Vol. I, Howrah Municipality, 1955 : p. 40.
15. Lord Mayo's Resolution on Provincial Finance, 1870 : p. 3. See also Augmentation of Financial Resources of urban local bodies, Delhi, 1963 : p. 4 & 5 and also Mukherjee, S.K. *Local Self-Government in West Bengal*, Dasgupta and Company (P) Ltd., Calcutta, 1974 : p. 125.
16. Zakaria, Rafiq, Augmentation of Financial Resources of urban local bodies, Report of the Committee of Minister by the Central Council of Local Self-Government, Delhi, 1963 : p. 5.
17. Zakaria, Rafiq, *Augmentation of Financial Resources of Urban Local Bodies* p,. 5.
18. Bengal Municipal Act 1884, Section 69.
19. Datta, Abhijit, *Urban Government Finance and Development*, The World Press, Calcutta 1970 : pp. 142-143.
20. Datta, Abhijit, *Urban Government Finance and Development*, The World Press, Calcutta, 1970 : pp 151-52.
21. The Calcutta, Way, *The Statesman*, Calcutta, October 25, 1975.
22. Nayak, P.R., The Challange of urban growth to Indian Local Government, '*India's Urban Future*, Ed. by Roy Turner, Oxford University Press, 1962 : pp. 368-69.
23. Chakraborty, S.C., Delineation of Planning Areas : An experimen on Calcutta 1961, *Geographical Review of India*, Calcutta, Vol. XXXIV, 1972 : No. 1, p. 5.
24. For Howrah : The Sunday Statesman, Calcutta, February 17, 1975 : p. 5 For *Durgapur Amrita Bazer Patrika*, April 26, 1975. For Hooghly-Chinsura : *Amrita Bazar Patrika*, May 29, 1975 and for Chandernagar : *The Statesman*, Tuesday, May 27, 1975.
25. Banerjee, J., *Howrah Civic Companion*, Vol. I, Howrah Municipality, 1955, p. 129.
26. O'Malley, L.S.S., and Chakraborty, M.M., *Bengal District Gazetteers*, Howrah, Bengal Secretariate Press, 1910 pp. : 61-62.
27. Howrah Area Development Plan, 1966-1986, Calcutta Metropolitan Planning Organisation, Government of West Bengal, 1967 : p. 28.
28. Ghose, Bhaskar, Census of India 1971 : *West Bengal Series* 22, Part XIIA, General Population Tables. p. 27.
29. District News. *Amrita Bazar Patrika*, Calcutta, 25 April 1975.
30. Peterson, J.C.K., *Bengal District Gazetteer*, Burdwan Bengal Secretariate Press, 1910, p. 169.

31. Annual Administrative Report of Burdwan Municipal Corporation for the Year 1974-75, Burdwan Municipality, p. 8.
32. Benerjee, Amiya Kumar, *West Bengal District Gazetteers,* Hooghly, October, 1972, p. 302.
33. Information collected from the Engineering Department, *Hooghly-Chinsura Municipal Office.*
34. *Amrita Bazar Patrika*, Culcutta, May 29, 1975.
35. Chandernagar in for water famine, *The Statesman*, Calcutta, Tuesday May, 27, 1975 and also see Purasree a Municipal Gazetteer in *Bengali of Chandernagar Municipal Corporation*, Vol. I, 14th April, 1973, pp. 2-3.
36. Benerjee, J., *Hawrah Civic Companion*, Vol. I, Howrah Municipality, 1955, p. 149.
37. Howrah Area Development Plan, 1966-1986. Calcutta Metropolitan Planning Organization, Government of West Bengal, 1967, p. 30.
38. Annual Administrative Report of Burdwan Municipal Corporation for the year 1974-75, p. 7.
39. Howroh Area Development Plan, 1966-1986, CMPO Government of West Bengal, 1967 : p. 13.
40. Annual Administrative Report of the Burdwan Municipal Corporation for the year 1974-75, p. 10.

REFERENCES

Bhardwaj, R.K., *The Municipal Administration in India*, Sterling Publishers (P) Ltd., Delhi, 1970, Chapters I & VI.

Buxton, R.J., *Local Government*, Penguin Books, 1970, pp. 17-86.

Carstairs, R., *A Plea for Better Local Government of Bengal*, London, 1904.

Jackson, R.M., *The Machinery of Local Government*, Macmillan, London 1967, pp. 1-39.

Lincberry, Robert L., and Sharkansky, Ira., *Urban Politics and Public Policy*, Harper & Row Publishers, London, 1971 : pp 109-44.

Redlich, Josef, and Hirst, Francis, W., *The History of Local Government in England*, Macmillan & Co. Ltd., London, 1958.

Sharma, M.P., *Local Self-Government in India*, Kitab Mahal Private Ltd., Allahabad, 1964.

Sharma, R.S., *Lolal Self-Government in* UP, Allahabad, 1951.

Singh, M.M., *Municipal Government in the Calcutta Metropolitan District : A Preliminary Survey*, Asia Publishing House, 1965, General Editor Leslis Green, Culcutta Research Studies, IPA, New York.

Weaver, Robert C., *The Urban Complex*, *Human Values in Urban Life*, Lyall Book Depot, Ludhiana, 1964.

Zakaria, Rafiq. Urban growth problems, Know Your States : 2, Maharashtra, *A Statesman Supplement*, Calcutta, December 30, 1975 ; p. 18 VII.

NINE

ARUN KUMAR SINGH

FINANCIAL MANAGEMENT OF MUNICIPAL GOVERNMENTS

A Case Study of Five Cities of West Bengal

IN RECENT times, perhaps because of international circulation of ideas, critique of squalor of the Indian urban scene has been forthcoming. The inadequacy of the urban infrastructure, the poor quality of urban services, the uncontrolled nature of growth of slums, and things in that order have attracted the attention of the scholars, the administrators and also the policy planners. Notwithstanding these attachment to the values of the cosmetic critical, demand for investment is commonly shared. In recent years, with the support of both the Union and provincial Governments, several urban development authorities have been set up to conduct investments in this regard. With or without the patronage of international funding agencies, considerable sum of money have been advanced to these diverse developmental authorities. However, as soon as the initial excitement was over on their success in obtaining such funds, questions are being asked whether the municipal governments, for whose benefit such investment are being made, would be able to maintain and repay back the charges so created. Such doubt clearly indicates that the financial position of the municipal government are in bad shape. Hence in every instances the administrative reports of the urban centres tries to identify the lack of financial resources as the main circumstances of inefficiency of civic operations. In a poor country like India scarcity of resources is a *sine-qua-non* of existence. But the situation of scarcity alone cannot explain the reality. In order to derive a better appreciation of the urban reality, it is necessary to examine the way municipal governments are managing their resources. This enquiry is carried by taking the case study of five cities of West Bengal. The samples are—Howrah, Durgapur, Burdwan, Hooghly-Chinsura and Chandernagar (Fig. 9.1). Howrah is located

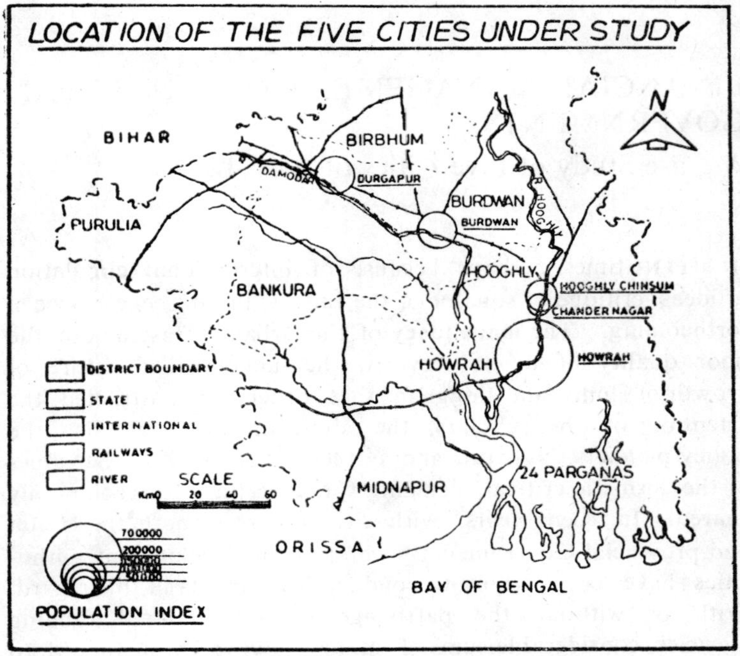

FIG 9.1 : *Location of the five cities under study*

on the river Hooghly opposite to Calcutta and is the second to it by population size. Historically Howrah has acted as an appendage to the city of Calcutta by housing the major railway terminal that connects it with the rest of the Indian economy, by quartering diverse industrial establishments with the associated working class slums—all in support to the metropolitan economy of Calcutta. Yet Howrah has its own municipal government district from that of Calcutta to take care of development as well as maintenance of its own urban infrastructure. In contrast Durgapur is a recently created new town, which came in the wave of a service of publicly decisions to set up a large number of industries backed up by norms of high quality of urban services. It has one form of municipal government which is known as Notified Area Authority. The third city, Burdwan, is a very old urban settlement of West Bengal, set within an entirely rural surroundings. Of course the agricultural economy around the city of Burdwan has always been remarkably productive. The Municipal government set up by the State Government had received the patronage of the local Raja (Raja of Burdwan) in addition. The fourth city, Hooghly-Chinsura, now located within the Calcutta Urban agglomeration, has a longer history of commerce than the private city itself. The municipal government however did not receive any patronage from any Raja. The last of the fifth city is Chandernagar, which is also located within the Calcutta urban agglomeration. It is also fairly old. While the cities of Howrah, Burdwan and Hooghly-Chinsura had their municipal governments formed within the policy of British India, Chandernagar was governed by the norms of the French imperial society. Although it had no industry and had little uninterupted interaction with any agricultural hinterland, it did thrive as a centre of commerce and distinct colonial government. In other words the five selected cities represent different histories of economy and polity and also have different orders of fiscal structure. We propose to begin this enquiry by examining the manner by which the municipal governments spend their resources. Such an examination of the accounts of expenditure will undoubtedly provide insights of the attitudes of the municipal governments regarding the real needs of the city. Interse priority allocated between different kinds of services as given by the city fathers reflect such attitudes in an understandable way.

One could argue that a better appreciation of the problem of financial management could be obtained through an enquiry into the sources of the municipal governments and then matched by an enquiry on the utilization of the resources through expenditure. We shall of course take up the enquiry on the income of municipalities. It would be sufficient to mention that by reversing the order of enquiry in the manner we have proposed above will permit us to ascertain the way the needs of the municipality emerged in their observed preference between diverse items of expenditure undertaken by the five municipal governments under enquiry. This provides a better appreciation of the municipal governments about their attitude to improve their resource status.

The organisation of the study undertaken in this chapter is simple enough to follow. This has been arranged not only to examine the attitude of the individual municipality regarding the relative importance of different service sectors but also appreciate the differences of such attitudes between the five municipal governments.

Trend of total expenditure

In Table 9.1 the gross expenditure as incurred by the five municipalities between 1964-65 and 1974-75 have been presented. In this context it is necessary to mention that such data on the city of Howrah are not available after the year 1968-69. It was also not possible to collect similar data on Hooghly-Chinsura municipality beyond 1973-74. To this extent our study related to comparison between these cities will be effected. It is however possible to claim that during this period the gross expenditure of all the municipal governments had increased.

In Table 9.2 we have converted the above data into an index number series by using the figures for 1964-65 as base (100). The same data have been plotted to construct a comparative temporal profile of annual expenditure. It is interesting to note that the total expenditure of the different municipalities have not increased at the same rate. On specific years, the rate of growth of expenditure of some municipalities compare to previous year have increased, while with others these may have decreased. In order to provide an overall estimate on the relative growth rates, a simple linear regression equation was fitted to the data as given in Table 9.1 for the individual cities.

In Table 9.3 the rate of growth of expenditure has been presented. In addition the computed expenditure during the initial period of observation has also been shown in this table.

TABLE 9.1 : **Total Annual Expenditure**

In Rupees

Name of the Municipal Governments	Years				
	1964-65	1965-66	1966-67	1967-68	1968-69
1	2	3	4	5	6
Howrah Municipality	13542697	13355622	13769769	14897458	15750229
Durgapur Notified Area Authority	1099304	429835	1579315	935167	646093
Burdwan Municipality	1502327	1570360	2470706	2040999	2132663
Hooghly-Chinsura Municipality	1256134	1585899	1161293	1211448	1357364
Chandernagar Corporation	1488575	1619195	1954749	2214333	2147312

(*Table 9.1 Contd.*)

TABLE 9.1 (*Contd.*)

Name of the Municipal Governments	Years 1969-70	1970-71	1971-72	1972-73	1973-74	1974-75
	7	8	9	10	11	12
Howrah Municipality	—	—	—			—
Durgapur Notified Area Authority	1221311	1174464	1681239	1819971	2662691	1595458
Burdwan Municipality	2414264	2788679	3216962	3177590	4068006	4578042
Hooghly-Chinsura Municipality	1333871	1848099	2567967	3356497	2537739	—
Chandernagar Corporation	2934549	3040311	5452467	4879625	4884417	5142110

Note : Annual Expenditure (1) General Administration and Collection Charges, (2) Public Safety, (3) Public Health and Convenience, (4) Public Instruction, (5) Contribution, (6) Miscellaneous & (7) Extraordinary and Debt.

Source : (1) Statistical Reports—Howrah, Durgapur, Hooghly-Chinsura—and Tables—Chandernagar.

(2) Annual Administrative Reports—Burdwan Municipality.

TABLE 9.2 : **Temporal Profile of Total Annual Expenditure**

(1964-65=100) in Rupees

Years	Name of the Municipality				
	Howrah Municipality	Durgapur Notified Area	Burdwan Municipality	Hooghly-Chinsura Municipality	Chandernagar Corporation
1964-65	100	100	100	100	100
1965-66	98.61	39.10	104.53	126.25	108.77
1966-67	101.67	143.66	164.50	92.44	131.31
1967-68	110.00	85.06	135.81	96.44	148.75
1968-69	116.30	58.77	142.00	108.05	144.25
1969-70	111.16	111.09	160.70	106.18	197.13
1970-71	—	106.83	185.62	147.17	204.24
1971-72	—	152.93	214.13	204.43	366.28
1972-73	—	165.55	211.51	267.20	327.80
1973-74	—	242.21	270.78	202.02	328.12
1974-75	—	145.13	304.73	—	345.43

(—) Data not available.

TABLE 9.3 : **Average expenditure and that per Rate payer**

Name of the Municipal Governments	Rate of Growth*	Expenditure** in the Initial Year	Remarks
Howrah Municipality	595690	130,71775	1964-65 to 1968-69
Durgapur Notified Area Authority	128679	7,06137	1964-65 to 1974-75
Burdwan Municipality	277252	13,37431	1964-65 to 1974-75
Hooghly-Chinsura Municipality	199072	9,25777	1964-65 to 1973-74
Chandernagar Corporation	431568	10,92855	1964-65 to 1974-75

Note : (*) Rate of growth is the b value of the education $Yc = a + bx$.
where x = time (Years).

(**) This is equal to a of the above equation $Yc = a + bx$.

(a) Initial Expenditure : Rate = +0.88.

(b) City size (Population (1971) : Initial Expenditure = + 0.16

(c) City size (Population 1971) : Rate of Growth = −0.08

Rank Correlation Coefficient $r = 1 \frac{6(\Sigma^2 D)}{N^3 - N}$

It can be easily seen that there is hardly any correlation between the size of expenditure incurred in the initial period of observation with the city size. In fact the rank correlation coefficient between them is as low as 0.16. In the same manner we can say that the relationship between rate of growth of expenditure and the city size is poor. The rank correlation coefficient is –0.08. Similar lack of relationship can also be seen to exist between the relative rate of growth of population of the cities and their rate of growth of exp nditure. The rank correlation coefficient is –0.32. However a high positive correlation (+0.88) is observable between initial expenditure and rate of growth of expenditure. This means that the cities which use to spend more money were also the cities which increased their expenditure at a high rate. Such a situation suggests that demand for increasing expenditure came as a matter of habit.

We have already mentioned that a large section of the population of each of these cities are not the rate payers. Since the rate payers are entitled to demand for services it is possible that the pattern of expenditure incurred by the individual municipalities tended to reflect the interest of the rate payers. In order to obtain a comparative picture in this regard we have prepared Table 9.4

TABLE 9.4 : **Average expenditure incurred per rate payer**

(*In Rupees*)

Name of the Municipal Governments	Average Annual Expenditure	Average No. of Rate Payer	Average Expenditure Incurred per Rate Payer
Howrah Municipality	14395026.33	45397	317.09
Durgapur Notified Area Authority	1349531.64	8337	161.87
Burdwan Municipality	2733690.73	21733	128.78
Hooghly-Chinsura Municipality	1821691.10	16291	111.82
Chandernagar Corporation	3250694.82	12835	253.27

In this table we have computed the average annual expenditure of each of the cities and have obtained the average expenditure incurred by these cities for each rate payer. In order to obtain this figure we have to divide the average annual expenditure by the average no. of rate payers for period under review.

It is interesting to notice that the relationship between the total population size of the cities and the average numbers of rate payers is poor. In fact the rank correlation coefficient is +0.28. The relationship between average expenditure incurred by the individual municipalities and their respective numbers of rate payers is however quite strong. The rank correlation coefficient is +0.64. The relationship between average expenditure incurred per rate payer and the total size of the population of individual cities is again poor. The rank correlation coefficient is +0.10. This means that the municipal governments in undertaking expenditure principally subserve the interests of the rate payers. However the rank correlation coeffiicent between average numbers of rate payers and average expenditure incurred per rate payer is hopelessly poor (+0.04). This means that the standard of services offered to the rate payers vaey greatly between the five cities.

Major categories of expenditure

In Table 9.5 the average annual expenditure incured by the

TABLE 9.5 : **Percentage of Average Total Expenditure**

(*In Rupees*)

Name of the Municipal Governments	Service	Establishment	Miscellaneous	Remarks
Howrah Municipality	79.69	12.46	7.85	100
Durgapur Notified Area Authority	64.22	15.44	20.34	100
Burdwan Municipality	83.55	12.55	3.90	100
Hooghly-Chinsura Municipality	85.06	10.32	4.62	100
Chandernagar Corporation	85.62	10.36	4.20	100

individual cities during the period under review has been computed by sub-dividing the accounts under the three categories of expenditure of services, establishment charge and miscellaneous items. It may be seen that the major part of the annual expenditure comesth rough the maintenance of services. While detailed analysis of the account of expenditure on the individual items of services will be undertaken in a subsequent section of this chapter, it is necessary to mention that the wages and salary bills of the personnel engaged in the services cannot be easily separated from the data given to us by the individual municipalities. If a separation of wages and salary cost from the cost of maintenance and material management of the services than a better appreciation of the reality could be obtained. The general view is that more than 80% of the expenditure under services arise from wages and salary bills. In a similar manner the major items under the miscellaneous accounts is the debts and related charges on servicing such debts. The establishment charges primary involve the cost of running the administrativc offiees, including salaries of the offlcers and clekrs The above limitations of the data do not help us to establish the general belief that the major expenditure incurred by the municipal governments could come under wages and salary accounts. Areliatively rmalı amount is spent on main tenance of the service infrastructure and replacement and development thereof.

Major categories of expenditure

This is however interesring, because it helps us to compare between the cities the relative apportionment of available resources between the major categories of expenditure. It is seen that with the exception of Durgapur, which is a newly developing city, all the older towns describe a similar bias between themselves in allocating their expenditure between the major categories. The proportions of the expenditure between the major categories for four cities of Howrah, Burdwan. Hooghly-Chinsura and Chandernagar are more or less similar. This means that the norms upheld in this regard are generally accepted by the municipal governments. Such an acceptance of the proportions in the allocation of respective budgets when reviewed against the objectively discernible differences in their respective urban economics, merely suggest that these norms are not necessarily integrated with the specific needs of their urban economic functions.

The deviation noted with regard to Durgapur can be explained by the fact that the Notified Area Authority has little servicing responsibilities to bear by themselves. The major residential areas are attached to major industrial establishments, which bear the responsibility of servicing their respective settlements. During this period the Notified Area Authority of Durgapur had received considerable amount of loan to undertake construction of their administrative building, integrated water supply system and also for developing some ancillary facilities for public transportation facilities. This explains the relatively high ration of apportionment on their budget on miscellaneous account head. The relatively high ratio on establishment can also be explained by the fact that a considerable portion of their middle and top level administrators are hired on lien from the state government. Therefore exceptionality of Durgapur as noted above does not indicat. that the municipal authority has discovered to integrate their expenditure with the urban economic needs of the city. In fact quite a major proportion of the real cost on servicing is not borne by the municipal authority directly. These emerge as direct cost of the creators as well as users of such facilities as it has been with the industrial residential pattern of development of the city.

In Table 9.6 we have presented data on average annual expenditure per rate payer for the individual cities. Here, as before, the different items of expenditure have been grouped under the three broad headings of service, establishment and miscellaneous. It can be seen that the per capita (rate payer) expenditure on services has been very much higher than that on miscellaneous and establishment charges. This table is however important to provide a comparative picture of expenditure under the three broad heads as incurred by the five cities.

It is seen that on service head the per capita expenditure

TABLE 9.6 : **Average annual expenditure per rate payer**

(*In Rupees*)

Name of the Municipal Governments	Service	Esta-blish-ment	Mis-cella-neous
Howrah Municipality	195.99	32.32	17.00
Durgapur Notified Area Authority	63.65	15.19	20.27
Burdwan Municipality	96.22	14.45	4.49
Hooghly-Chinsura Municipality	80.83	9.81	4.39
Chandernagar Corporation	203.99	24.76	8.62

is highest in Chandernagar, followed by Howrah, Burdwan, Hooghly-Chinsura and Durgapur. If we assume that the quality of services varied directly with the cost, than the above ordering of cities is an indicator of the problem of largeness of cities. We may recall that Chandernagar is the smallest city by population size, yet it incurs highest expenditure on services per rate payer. In fact the relationship between city size and, average expenditure per rate payer on services shows an inverse disposition. The rank correlation coefficient is —0.56.

Expenditure on establishment charges per rate payer is highest for Howrah, followed by Chandernagar, Durgapur, Burdwan and Hooghly-Chinsura. It can be seen that the population size of the city bears little relationship with expenditure on establishment per rate payer. The rank correlation coefficient is +0.28 However the relationship between expenditure on services and that on establishment is more apparent. The rank correlation coefficient is+0.52.

The above observation when read together lead us to conclude that the quality of services is inversely related to the population size of cities, wherein the charges on establishment bear no relationship with the population size of the cities. This means that the municipal governments have so far failed to relate the affairs of financial management with the growth of the cities.

In Table 9.7 the percentage share of the different types of services in the total expenses incurred on all services have been presented. It may be seen that conservancy takes away

TABLE 9.7 : **Average Expenditure of Various Services in % to Total Average Expenditure on Services**

(*In Rupees*)

Name of the Municipal Governments	Water Supply	Lighting	Conser-vancy	Health	Education	Others	Remarks
1	2	3	4	5	6	7	8
Howrah Municipality	13.22	2.67	55.06	7.47	5.46	16.14	100
Durgapur Notified Area Authority	16.48	8.56	36.10	13.08	2.11	23.64	100
Burdwan Municipality	11.10	9.45	43.95	4.02	9.25	22.23	100
Hooghly-Chinsura Municipality	16.07	6.24	51.14	0.92	7.09	18·49	100
Chandernagar Corporation	11.58	2.52	21.58	0.41	48.64	15.24	100

Other Expenditure : Market and slaughter houses, ponds, dak bungalow and other public works.

Miscellaneous expenditure : Extraordinary and Debts.

TABLE 9.8 : Percentage of Average Expenditure Under Major Heads

(Average Expenditure=100)

Major Heads	Name of the Municipal Governments				
	Howrah Municipality	Durgapur notified Area Authority	Burdwan Municipality	Hooghly-Chinsura Municipality	Chandernagar Corporation
Water Supply	20.77	10.64	17.83	16.49	9.64
Lighting	11.57	5.53	7.16	5.25	2.10
Conservancy	32.47	23.32	33.31	42.98	17.96
Health	4.41	8.45	3.03	.79	.34
Education	5.52	1.06	7.01	5.96	40.47
Others	9.52	15.00	16.85	15.54	12.69
Miscellaneous	5.32	20.00	3.57	4.32	3.40
Establishment	10.20	16.00	11.49	9.47	9.81
Remarks	100	100	100	100	100

the major chunk of the money allocated to services in four out of five cities. Chandernagar is the only exception where expenditure on education gets major preference. If we exclude the expenditure on miscellaneous items of services than we find that water supply accounts for the second major item of expenditure on services. The third expensive item of expenditure is health for Howrah and Durgapur, while it is lighting for Burdwan. This table in a way shows that the individual cities make subtle distinctions between the types of services they need or prefer. A better appreciation of these features can be obtained from Table 9.8

Types of services

In Table 9.8 the average expenditure per rate payer under different sub-heads of services for the five cities have been presented. This table confirms all the observations made with regard to Table 9.9 and in addition shows some relationship between the city size and the magnitude of expenditure incurred under different sub-heads.

TABLE 9.9 : **Bank Correlation between City-size and Magnitude of Expenditure Incurred under Different Sub-heads of Services**

Sub-heads of Services	Bank Correlation Coefficient
Wage Supply	—0.08
Lighting	−0.44
Conservancy	−0.20
Health	+0.88
Education	−0.56
Others	−0.56

In Table 9.9 the rank correlation coefficient between the city size and the magnitude of cost under different sub-heads of expenditure on services has been presented. It appears that expenditure on health alone is directly related to the size of the city. In every other instance the city size and magnitude of expenditure on different sub-heads of services are inversely related. The degree of correspondence is exceedingly low with water supply and conservancy. By reading Table 9.8 and Table 9.9 together we may conclude that while

TABLE 9.10 : **Total Receipt (Revenue) of Municipal Governments**

(In Rupees)

Years	Name of the Municipal Governments				
	Howrah Munici-pality	Durgapur Notified Area Authority	Burdwan Munici-pality	Hooghly-Chinsura Munici-pality	Chandernagar Corporation
1964-65	13426700	1243821	1488569	1123185	1884579
1965-66	13208523	675040	1588599	1424498	1494709
1966-67	13889472	2100481	1959531	1000079	1892160
1967-68	13774331	1037405	1919235	1240806	2113436
1968-69	15028548	743989	2145730	1063064	2191846
1969-70	—	1266084	2304380	1317934	3077526
1970-71		1237202	3200245	1317934	2751189
1971-72		1753866	2760573	1595810	3716250
1972-73		3797183	3141810	2670475	4825757
1973-74		2206229	3986388	2466141	4667735
1974-75		3543914	4575611	—	5034022

TABLE 9.11 : **Temporal Profile of Annual Receipt (Revenue) 1964-65=100**

(*In Rupees*)

Years	Name of the Municipal Governments				
	Howrah Muni-cipality	Durgapur Notified Area Authority	Burdwan Munici-pality	Hooghly-Chinsura Municipality	Chander-nagar Corporation
1964-65	13426700 =100	1243821 =100	1488569 =100	1123185 =100	1884579 =100
1965-66	98.375	54.271	106.719	126.826	79.312
1966-67	103.446	168.873	131.638	89.039	100.402
1967-68	102.181	83.404	128.931	110.472	112.143
1968-69	111.930	59.814	144.147	94.647	116.304
1969-70	—	101.789	154.805	117.338	163.300
1970-71	—	99.467	214.988	142.078	145.984
1971-72	—	141.006	185.451	237.759	197.193
1972-73	—	305.283	211.062	311.964	256.065
1973-74	—	177.375	267.800	219.566	247.680
1974-75	—	284.921	307.383	—	267.116

come per rate payer have been computed. It can be seen that the average income per rate payer is positively related to average total income of the municipalities. Their rank correlation coefficient is +0.88. However there is little correspondence between the size of the cities and their average total income. The rank correlation coefficient is +0.16. Similarly the relationship between average income per rate payer and the city size is poor. Here the rank correlation coefficient is +0.28.

Major sources of income

In Table 9.14 we have classified the different sources of income into three major categories, viz., income from economic base, income through grant-in-aid given by the State Government and income through extraordinary debts. The figures are average of the years under review.

In Table 9.15 these three major sources of income have been converted into ratios percentum of the total average annual income of the five cities under study. It can be seen

TABLE 9.15 : **Per Cent of Average Income on the Major Heads**

(*In Rupees*)

Name of the Municipal Governments	Income from Economic Base	Income through Grant-in-Aid	Income through Extra-ordinary Debt	Remarks
Howrah Municipality	54.03	17.03	28.93	100
Durgapur Notified Area Authority	70.44	12.59	16.95	
Burdwan Municipality	54.69	34.39	10.90	
Hooghly-Chinsura Municipality	45.99	40.74	13.26	
Chandernagar Corporation	41.69	51.39	6.91	

that with the exception of Chandernagar the income from the economic base accounts for the major chunk of income of all the cities.

It is necessary at this stage to mention the different sources of income which have been classified as income from economic base. There are taxes on property, service, economic transactional, following of professionals and similar other sources. We shall examine the relative importance of all this subheads of income in the next section of this chapter. For the present we may look back at Table 9.15.

The relationship between city size and the three categories of income and interse relationship between the categories of income can be best appreciated from Table 9.16.

TABLE 9.16 : **Some Interesting Relationship between Proportion of Income**

Variables	Rank Correlation Coefficient
City-size and Income from Economic Base	+0.7
City-size and Income through Grant-in-Aid	−0.9
City-size and Income through Extraordinary Debts	+0.9
Income from Economic Base and that from Grant-in-Aid	−0.9
Income from Economic Base and that from Extraordinary Debts	+0.5
Income from Grant-in-Aid and Extraordinary Debts	−0.8

Note : $r = \frac{1-6(\Sigma D^2)}{N^3-N}$.

This shows that income from economic base and also income through extraordinary and debts are directly related to the city size. But the proportion of the income derived from grant-in-aid from government bears a high inverse relationship with the city size. In the similar manner the relative disposition of the different sources of income have been computed.

By reading all these relationships together we find that the larger the city is the smaller is its relative dependence on grant-in-aid. This may give us an impression as if the governments' policy on grant-in-aid is consistent with the economic base of the cities. However such an impression will require serious revision in the light of Table 9.17.

TABLE 9.17 : **Average Annual Income per Rate Payer**

(*In Rupees*)

Name of the Municipal Governments/Major Heads	Income from Economic Base	Income through Grant-in-Aid	Income through Extraordinary Debts
Howrah Municipality	165.04	52.02	88.36
Durgapur Notified Area Authority	150.56	26.91	36.24
Burdwan Municipality	66.51	41.82	13.26
Hooghly-Chinsura Municipality	49.14	43.53	14.16
Chandernagar Corporation	99.37	122.48	16.47

In Table 9.17 the three major sources of income has been computed in terms of average rate payers. Here we find that the maximum amount of grant-in aid per rate payer is given to the smallest city whereas the second highest rate is associated with the biggest city. This clearly indicate that the state government's policy on the allocation of grant-in-aid is hardly consistent with either the city size or its income-base. This will be clearly visible from Table 9.18.

Table 9.18 shows that income from economic base per rate payer increased with the size of the cities. Similarly the debt burden is directly proportional to the income contributed by average rate payer. But the grant-in-aid per rate payer bears an inverse relationship either with the city size or with the amount contributed by average rate payer through the utilisation of city economic base. Undoubtedly the government policy on the administration of grant-in-aid is inconsistent with the urban reality.

TABLE 9.18 : **Some Interesting Relationship between Different Source of Income per Rate Payer**

Variables	Bank Correlation Coefficient
City Size & Income from Economic Base	+40.7
City Size & Income from Grant-in-Aid	—0.4
City Size & Income from Extraordinary and Debts	+0.6
Income from Economic Base & Grant-in-Aid	+0.1
Income from Economic Base & Extraordinary & Debts	+0.9
Grant-in-Aid and Extraordinary & Debts	+0.2

Note : $r = \frac{1-6(\Sigma D^2)}{N^3-N}$.

Income from economic base

In Table 9.19 the proportions of the major sub-heads which together constitute the economic base of municipal income have been shown. It can be seen that the tax from property constitute the major source of income in the two cities of Howrah and Durgapur. In the other three cities tax on services constitute the major source of such income. We have seen that no municipality has been found to have invested any capital for property development. Therefore the tax on property is basically a share that the municipal government claims on the rent of the land. Tax on services emerges as a claim because the municipalities are providing such utilities as conservancy, water supply, lighting etc. Both these taxes are related to the basic urban infrastructure. These do not directly refer to the urban economy that sustains itself from the utilization of the above mentioned infrastructure.

Transactional taxes and professional taxes are the two items of income which are directly related to the urban economy. The low proportion of the income coming from these two heads clearly indicate that the resource base of the municipalities are for all practical purpose unrelated to the urban economic activities. This is understandable. The tax on income is exclusively available to the Union Government of India. This is not available either to the State Government or the Munici-

TABLE 9.19 : **Income from the Economic Base of Cities**

=(100) Average Income of Economic Base

Name of the Municipal governments	Property Tax	Service Tax	Transactional Tax	Professional Tax	Other Tax	Miscellaneous Tax
Howrah Municipality	86.20	0.28	0.38	7.38	2.60	3.18
Durgapur Notified Area Authority	58.05	7.00	0.13	5.19	29.22	0.42
Burdwan Municipality	32.91	50.97	0.29	4.96	8.49	2.38
Hooghly-Chinsura Municipality	26.60	59.52	7.18	2.21	1.65	2.85
Chandernagar Corporation	20.16	33.72	19.10	4.09	17.50	5.42

TABLE 9.20 : **Average Income from Economic Base under Major Sub-heads per Rate Payer (Average Income on Major Sub-heads)**

(Average No. of Rate Payer)

Name of the Municipal Governments	Property Tax	Service Tax	Transactional Tax	Professional Tax	Other Tax	Miscellaneous Tax
Howrah Municipality	142.26	0.46	0.62	12.17	4.28	5.24
Durgapur Notified Area Authority	87.40	10.54	0.19	7.81	43.99	0.63
Burdwan Municipality	21.89	33.90	0.19	3.30	5.65	1.58
Hooghly Chinsura Municipality	13.07	29.25	3.53	1.08	0.81	1.40
Chandernagar Corporation	20.23	33.51	18.98	4.07	17.39	5.39

pal Governments. Therefore by the provisions of the constitution of India this component of the resources base is removed from the purview of municipal administration. Similarly all indirect taxes, e.g., tax on sales, excise duty, etc., are levied and collected by the State Government. These are not available to the municipal governments. Thus we may say the municipal government's resource base is basically removed from the urban economic activities that they support. Consequently the income from economic base is very much restricted or narrow.

Income from economic base

In Table 9.20 the average income from economic base under major sub-heads has been computed per rate payers. This table confirms all the observations that previous tables have produced. But, in addition, the present table permit us to compare between the relationship between city size and the different sub-heads of income from economic base.

In Table 9.21 some of the major correlations in this regard are presented.

TABLE 9.21 : **Some Interesting Relationship between City Size and Different Sub-heads of Income from Economic Base**

Variable	Bank Correlation Coefficient
City Size and Total Income from Economic Base	+0.9
City Size and Property Tax	+0.9
City Size and Professional Tax	+0.7
City Size and Miscellaneous Tax	+0.7
City Size and Other Tax	—0.0
City Size and Tax on Services	—0.7

Note : $r = \frac{1-6(\Sigma D^2)}{N^3-N}$.

As mentioned before the relationship between city size and total income from economic base is directly proportional. The rank correlation coefficient is +0.9. A similar correspondence (+0.9) is observable between property tax and city size. The relationship between professional tax and city size and also that between miscellaneous tax and city size are also directly proportionate. The rank correlation coefficient for in both instances is +0.7. However there is no relationship between other tax and the city size. Perhaps most interesting is the feature when we find the relationship between tax on services and city size being inversely related. The rank correlation coefficient is −0.7. The meaning of this inverse relationship is that the municipal governments increasingly find it difficult to upgrade their charges on services as the city grow in size. This is a sad testimony on the inconsistency of the attitude of the municipal governments. Since the municipalities are upholding the right to get a share in the temporal rise on the ground rent as reflected through property tax, their failure to similarly upgrade the charges on services is a lamentable comment on their financial management. On enquiry it has been found that none of the municipalities have tried to relate the service tax with the quantum of utility provided by them to the tax payers. There is no system of metering the water that the municipalities supply to the individual household, neither there is any variation in the charges on the amount of night soil or garbage cleared. We have noticed that the expenditure on these accounts are the heaviest and are increasing over time. Consequently a shortfall between income and expenditure is increasing.

TABLE 9.22 : **What Portion of Expenditure Coming from Grant-in-Aid**

(*Average Expenditure*=100)

Name of the Municipal Governments/Items	Economic Base	Grant-in-Aid	Extra ordinary & Debts	Remarks
Howrah Municipality	52.05	16.41	27.87	96.33
Durgapur Notified Area Authority	93.01	16.62	22.39	132.02
Burdwan Municipality	52.88	33.25	10.55	96.68
Hooghly-Chinsura Municipality	43.95	38.93	12.67	95.55
Chandernagar Corporation	39.24	48.36	6.51	94.11

In Table 9.22 we are presenting a set of interesting ratios between different items of income and total expenditure of five municipalities. Naturally we are working on the average annual figures for the period under review.

It may be seen that the income from the economic base never covers the total expenditure in any of the municipal governments. With the exception of Durgapur the municipal governments obtained 39% to 53% of the money required to undertake their total expenditure. The case of Durgapur is easily explainable. In the city, we have already mentioned, the major expenditure on conservance and water supply is not borne by the municipal government. These are met by the various public sector industries.

Under the circumstances the gap between the income from economic base and total expenditure has to be met from elsewhere. It is found that it comes from two sources. In the first instance a part of it comes from the State Government in the form of Grant-in-Aid. The second source is provided by the borrowing capacity of the municipal governments.

It can be seen that the Grant-in-Aid accounts for 16% to 48% of the total expenditure of these five municipalities. But what is more important to notice is that the expanded proportion of the total expenditure is Grant-in-Aid bear a very high inversely relationship with the city size. The rank correlation coefficient is—1.0. This means that the government is more keen to protect the conditions of the smaller towns in preference to that of the larger towns. Such a policy, is again a sad commentary on the State Government's appreciation of a proper urban policy. The ethical commitment to provide Grant-in-Aid can emerge only when the State Government recognize the fact that the municipal governments are divorced from the real urban economic base by the provisions of Indian Constitution. Since the Government of India provides similar grants to the State Governments as the tax from the income is not available latter, the State Government in terms accepts the responsibility to extend Grant-in-Aid to the municipal governments because the latter do not get any share of the tax granted through production and sale of commodities within the cities. Since the quantum of such taxes are directly proportion to such productions and sales of commodities and since production, and sales of such commodities are in turn related to the size of the cities, one could expect to see the Grant-in-Aid emerge in direct relationship with the city size. But in reality we find that this has been designed to produce an inverse relationship. Hence the policy is inconsistent.

It is true that the different Municipalities are permitted to incur loan. From Table 9.22 it can be seen that the proportion of expenditure covered by such loan vary between 7% to 28%. But what is more interesting to notice is that the relationship of such proportion to the city size is positive. The rank correlation coefficient is +0.9. This means that larger the city is the greater is the capacity to borrow. At least this has been formerly accepted by the State Government, because we know that no municipal government is permitted to borrow without explicit permission from the State Government. However we have already noticed that none of the municipalities has any source of unattached income that can be used to repay such borrowing. Consequently the municipalities are accumulating debts over the years. It is also true that the loan servicing charges are also gradually increasing over the years, which are steadily eating away the resources generated from the economic base of the city. Since the State Government cannot abnegate its responsibility regarding the municipal government, we can appreciate that the net results of such deficit financing will have to be accommodated one day or the other within the state budget itself. Therefore the policy on the municipal borrowings is irrational if reviewed against a long time perspective.

It is not however true that the municipalities are meeting their expenditure fully by putting together their income from economic base, the grant-in-aid that they received from the State Government and the borrowing that they are permitted by the State Government.

Relationship between income and expenditure

In Table 9.23 the average annual deficit between expenditure and income has been computed for the five cities under study. With the exception of Durgapur all the municipal governments are experiencing a shortfall between total expenditure,

The case of Durgapur is indeed interesting. It is a new town which has been created by the State Government through direct policy intervention. Consequently the State Government will have some extraordinary commitment for the development of the city. In Table 9.22 we have seen that the income from economic base accounts for 93.01% of its total expenditure. Yet it receives sizable amount of grant-in-aid and is also permitted to borrow. So the total expendable money available with Durgapur creates a situation of surplus. Such a situation can be justified if only the State Government has a policy which will require the Durgapur Notified Area Authority to undertake large scale investments for the development of urban infrastructure. However the actual policy of the State Government requires the Durgapur Development Authority, a separate institution, to undertake such developmental activities. Therefore the policy of the government on the financial management of the Durgapur Notified Area Authority cannot be explained rationally.

TABLE 9.23 : **Resource Gap between Average Expenditure and Average Income**

Name of the Municipal Governments	Items		
	Expenditure	Income	Deficit, Surplus
Howrah Municipality	14395026	13865515	—529511
Durgapur Notified Area Authority	1349532	1781771	+432239
Burdwan Municipality	2733691	2642788	—90903
Hooghly-Chinsura Municipality	1821691	1740593	—81098
Chandernagar Corporation	3250693	3059020	—191673

Note : — = Deficit
+ = Surpus

We may conclude this discussion on the inconsistencies in the management in the financial affairs of the municipalities by referring to the fact that the money available to the municipalities through grant-in-aid and sanctioned borrowing only in the last quarter of the financial year. Until then the individual municipalities are never sure of the quantum of money that they will be getting from these accounts. We can therefore easily appreciate why no desire for obtaining proper system of financial management has so far emerge from within the municipal governments. The inconsistencies on urban policies, the truncated resource base of the municipalities by the provision of the constitution and the consistencies in the flow of the financial assitance produce together a syndrome that afflicts the very perception of the municipal managers about their own role within such a reality.

REFERENCES

1. Banerjee, Tapan Kumar, April 1972, Resource Gap, A Case Study of the Calcutta Metropolitan Development Programme, Calcutta Metropolitan Planning Organisation.
2. Bhattacharyya, Mohit, 1970, Essays in Urban Government, Calcutta. The World Press Private Ltd.
3. Datta, Abhijit, Urban Government, Finance and Development. The World Press, Calcutta, 1970.
4. Datta, Abhijit and Ranneey, David C., Municipal Finances in the Calcutta Metropolitan District : A Preliminary Survey, Calcutta Research Studies, No. 3, Institute of Public Administration, New York.
5. The Report on the Finances and Adiministration of The Municipalities of the CMD. Calcutta Metropolitan Planning Organisation, Calcutta, October 1974.
6. Rationalisation of Grant-in-Aid and Shared Revenue for Municipal Governments of West Bengal, Calcutta Metropolitan Planning Organisation, July 1972.

Published Reports

1. Report on the Municipal Administration of Howrah for the year 1964-65.
2. Annual Administration Report of The Burdwan Municipal Corporation for the years, 1964-65, 1965-66 1966-67, 1967-69, 1968-69, 1969;70, 1970-71, 1971-1972, 1972-73, 1973-74, and 1974-75,

Unpublished Reports

1. Statistical Tables for compilation of forms I, II, III and Appendices A to K to be Incorporated in the Annual Government Resolution of the Working of Municipalities in West Bengal, Howrah, years : 1965-66, 1966-67, 1967-67, and 1968-69 for Hooghly Chinsura, years 1964-65, 1965-66, 1966-67, 1967-68, 1968-69, 1969-70, 1970-71, 1971-72, 1973-74, for Chandernagar for years 1964-65, 1965-66, 1966-67, 1967-68, 1968-69, 1969-70, 1970-71 1971-72, 1973-74, and 1974-75.

The results strongly support the hypothesis that the combined fiscal effect of service and nonproperty tax constraint mandates is stronger, and more negative, than their individual effects (H4). For example, 73 per cent of the cities on whom transportation mandates *and* heavy nonproperty tax constraints are imposed experienced a worsening of their financial condition between 1975 and 1979. In contrast, the fiscal condition of only 21 per cent of the cities with mandated public transportation responsibilities but without heavy constraints on their ability to raise revenue from sales and income taxes worsened. The difference between the two groups of cities (52 per cent) is greater than the difference between them when only the service mandate is taken into account (31 per cent) and when only the fiscal constraint mandate is taken into account (16 per cent). As the results indicate, each combination of education, leisure & recreation (with the exception of public library hour), and nonproperty tax constraint mandates increases the likelihood of municipal fiscal decline beyond that of mere imposition of the service or fiscal constraint mandates themselves.

Even in the case of public safety and public assistance mandates, a greater percentage of the cities with both service and nonproperty tax constraint mandates experienced fiscal decline than cities in which only one type of mandate was imposed. However, it is still the case that public safety and public assistance mandates are far less likely to be associated with municipal fiscal decline than other types of service mandates, even where heavy nonproperty tax constraints are imposed.

CONCLUSION

This study has shown that not all service mandates are associated with municipal fiscal decline. Transportation, leisure & recreation, and education mandates are linked to fiscal decline but most public safety and public assistance mandates are not. Neither reimbursement/external aid nor labor-intensive/unionization theories adequately explain the differences in the fiscal impact of state service mandates, indicating the need for further research in this area.

The study has also empirically confirmed what many local officials have felt for some time : that where *both* service mandates and fiscal constraint mandates (especially nonproperty tax constraints) are imposed on municipalities by their state government, the likelihood of fiscal decline increases.

This study demonstrates the urgent need for research which examines in more detail the effects of various combinations of state mandates, especially in light of the coming of state block grants. Only through such analyses can state policy makers determine whether a state's total "mandate package" produces desirable, and intended, policy outcomes.

FOOTNOTES

1 The specific mandates by category, are : Public Safety (Requirement to Provide Services—Police ; Level of Service—Police ; Requirement to Provide Services—Fire ; Level of Service—Fire ; Ambulance Operating Standards ; Jail Facilities Standards) ; Public Assistance (Local Share of Nonfederal AFDC Payment Costs ; Local Share of Nonfederal AFDC Administrative Costs ; Local Share of General Assistance or Relief Payment Costs ; Local Share of General Assistance Administrative Costs ; Local Share of Medicaid Program Costs' ; Local Share of Medicaid Administrative Costs) ; Leisure & Recreation (Public Library Hours ; Park and Recreational Programs) ; Transportation (Local Payment for Regional Public Transit System) ; Education (Special Education Programs ; Preschool Programs ; Pupil Transportation ; Mandatory Testing Program ; Bilingual Education).

2. Seventy per cent of all programmatic (service) mandates imposed between 1941 and 1978 were imposed prior to 1975. Fifty-six per cent were imposed between 1966-1975 (Lovell and Tobin 1981 : 322). And of the 43 cities (18 per cent) in states that imposed property tax limitations after 1976, only one (2.3 per cent) was located in a state that had no restrictions on municipal property taxing powers prior to its passage.

REFERENCES

Advisory Commission on Intergovernmental Relations (1978) : *State Mandating of Local Expenditures*. U.S. Government Printing Office, Washington, D.C.

Lovell, C.H. (1981) : Evolving Local Government Dependency. *Public Administration Review* 41, 189-202.

Lovell, C.H. ; Kneisel, R. ; Neiman, M. ; Rose, A.Z. ; Tobin, C.A. (1979) : *Federal and State Mandating on Local Governments : An Exploration of Issues and Impacts.* Graduate School of Administration, University of California at Riverside, Riverside.

Lovell, C.F. ; Tobin, C. (1981) : The Mandate Issue. *Public Administration Review* 41, 318-331.

MacManus, S.A. (1981) : The Impact of Functional Responsibility and State Legal Constraints on the 'Revenue-Debt' Packages of U.S. Central Cities. *International Journal of Public Administration* 3, 67-112.

Neiman, M. ; Lovell, C.H. (1980) : Federal and State Requirements : Impacts on Local Government. *The Urban Interest* 2, 45-51.

Zimmerman, J.F. (1976) : State-Local Relations : The State Mandate Irritant. *National Civic Review* 65, 548-552.

ELEVEN

HERMAN TURK AND LYNNE G. ZUCKER

LOCAL IMPLEMENTATION OF EXTERNAL POLICY

Effects of Majority and Minority Interests[1]

INTRODUCTION

APPLIED URBAN research has, in large measure, concerned itself either with identifying problems and evaluating corrective policies or with describing the distribution and activation of citizen interests. The papers in the present volume reflect these emphases. Our concern here is with a third, not as heavily investigated topic : *The means by which policy or activated interest is implemented.* Although drawing upon events surrounding California's recent "tax revolt", it is hardly our naive intention to expound on tax issues to nations whose local revenues might not even depend on property taxes. Rather, these events constituted for us a quasi-natural experiment in the interplay between external mandate and local interests.[2] The results permitted recent theoretical developments to be extended in ways that prove to be relevant to other nations.[3]

According to a view that has been prevalent, social movements rely on numbers of like-interested persons and do not require elaborate organizational and interorganizational structure for their success, especially when they address but a single issue (Piven and Cloward 1971, 1977 : passim. ; Garner 1977 : 12, 112, 118). More recent is the contesting view that movements require organization and outside links in order to succeed (Obershall 1973 ; Turk 1977b : 86-92 ; McCarthy and

Zald 1977 ; Jenkins and Perrow 1977). The present research report revises these broad assertions by showing that movements supported by the unorganized majority can be blunted through counter-movement by an organized minority, *provided* that the minority is aligned with external law. This may be summarized by the following two assertions, supported by our research :

1. Where local decision is subject to external mandate, it is affected more by an organized minority's accord with that mandate than it is by the unorganized majority.
2. But where local decision is not subject to external mandate, it is affected more by the unorganized majority than it is by an organized minority.

EFFECTS OF MANDATE AND NONMANDATE AND OF MOVEMENT AND COUNTER-MOVEMENT

Published nature and immediate consequences of the anti-tax initiative (*source* : Turk *1979*). In 1978 California's voters passed Proposition 13 by nearly a two-to-one majority (64.8 per cent). Reducing local revenues from property taxes by almost half, passage of the initiative was described by the press and by state and local officials as a clear demand for reduced government spending.

Yet the state legislation that implemented the vote included legal mandate which forbade—under threat of withdrawing state funds—any local budget reductions for police and fire protection or—of especial interest in this research—disproportionate reductions in health care for the poor. Unlike the other two, this last service is never shared between city and county, providing thereby comparability from one locality to the next. It also had identifiable sources of support and opposition. Disproportionately represented among the poor and fearing loss of public assistance, Blacks, for example, opposed Proposition 13 almost at the same rate as the majority favored it.

Thus, elected officials appeared to be responsive not only to the majority but also to minority interests among their constituents. It will be shown that such simultaneous catering was echoed at the local level during the months immediately following the initiative. The quasi-natural experiment not only allowed the effects of the majority to be assessed, among 43 California counties that funded hospitalization, on those internationally ubiquitous political documents called *local budgets*. It also enabled assessing the combined effect on these documents of central (state) mandate and accord with that mandate by a locally organized minority.

Mandated and nonmandated budget categories. Two county budget items were selected that—unlike any of their alternatives—allowed comparability of measurement but yielded variability in outcome from county to county. The first, already suggested above, is the extent to which budgeted expenditures were greater or less than those of the pre-Proposition 13 year (1977-1978) for delivery of hospital inpatient services to the poor. Though disproportionate reductions were prohibited by the state legislation which implemented the initiative, that mandate failed to be carried out in every county. The second budget item, constructed the same way,[4] is nonmandated budget increase or decrease in expenditure for the county government's main decision body, its board of supervisors. This expenditure was not subject to state legislation, and its reduction was indeed "in the spirit of Proposition 13."

That change in the inpatient budget is an indicator of conformity to mandate is supported by nearly perfect association between reduction of pre-Proposition 13 expenditures and whether or not the county was one of nine listed by the state government as facing legal action.[5] That reduction of the board of supervisors budget mirrored general reductions in nonmandated activities is supported by its explanation of 53 per cent of the variation[6] among counties of an indicator (developed by Turk, 1979) based on newspaper reports that listed *all* post-Proposition 13 cuts of programs, personnel, and service levels in every county. The level of association is high, considering that these reports appeared from two to four unstable months before the budgets were submitted. Moreover, no such association occurred in the case of the inpatient budget (direction insignificantly the reverse).

Overall effects of mandate and nonmandate. If the one

expenditure responded to mandate and the other did not, the amount budgeted for the county board of supervisors after the tax initiative should be less, relative to the amount spent during the year before, than in the case of money allocated to hospital care. The mean amount for inpatient services was reported to be $ 5.67 per county resident in the 1977-78 fiscal year and rose to a budgeted $ 6.59 in 1978-79. In contrast, the amount budgeted for boards of supervisors fell from a reported $ 3.69 per resident to a budgeted $ 3.08.[7] This change differs significantly from its inpatient counterpart. It would appear that law took precedence over sentiment or fiscal constraint in affecting budget retention, but that the latter ariables overshadowed immediate self-interest in making legally unrestricted political decisions.

Effects of movement and counter-movement. According to the previously prevalent view of social movements, the undifferentiated rate of favoring Proposition 13 *by the entire county* might be expected to have affected both kinds of budget reductions, the nonmandated one perhaps more strongly. Under the competing view, only the *organized preferences of interest groups* would have that effect, intensified in turn by links between interest groups and other organizations. The actual findings, to be described, support our own two assertions : The mandated inpatient budget was subject to the organized minority, but the board of supervisors budget was subject to the majority.

The counter-movement. Deprived groups were reported to have opposed Proposition 13 (Turk 1979). The political concentration of such opposition could be assessed. Each of the five members of the county board of supervisors is elected by one of five districts, into which each of the counties is divided. The greater the percentage opposing Proposition 13 *in the district least favorable,*[8] the greater the political concentration of opponents. That district's vote in opposition to the initiative was indeed associated with nonreduction in the inpatient budget (r = .46). More than this, however, the vote of the one district *fully accounted for the effect of the entire county's vote* (partial r = —.08, opposite direction).

This is taken to mean that a minority of one—here the

single county supervisor, reflecting his/her district's opposition to inpatient reductions—can prevail in the decision process, provided that the issue is conformity to law. Whether it is the threat of legal sanction or appeal to civic responsibility that enables this is moot. But irrespective of whether one or both mechanisms are responsible, an extension of interest group theory is suggested that accounts for the influence of lobbyists, special petitioners, or legislative minorities. It might also account for the survival of such legal structures as government itself in spite of mass discontent.

The movement. Mass preferences did, however, affect decisions not subject to mandate. Per cent favoring Proposition 13 in the entire county affected budgeted reductions for the board of supervisors ($r = .31$). And once this was taken into account, the district least favorable had no significantly independent effect (partial $r = -.16$, opposite direction).

Independent effects of movement and counter-movement in the face of other effects. Clearly factors other than citizen preferences or interest group mobilization affect political decisions. It was found, however, that both the effect of minority concentration on mandated decision and that of the majority on nonmandated decision remained when reexamined simultaneously (through multiple regression analysis) with all of these additional factors.

The county's urbanization (per cent residing in cities) is a global variable which is not only associated with poverty (negatively in California), but also signifies forms of social and political organization, distribution of responsibilities between city and county, county revenues and expenditures, and (inversely) the size and complexity of county government. Fiscal strain was measured by the magnitude, reduction, and uncertainty (latter, per cent of all revenues from what at the time was announced as a one-time "bailout" grant by the state) of each county's overall revenues after Proposition 13. Client demand for inpatient service within each county was measured by its poverty rate.[9] The results (just reported) that supported our two assertions remained undisturbed by these potentially confounding influences.

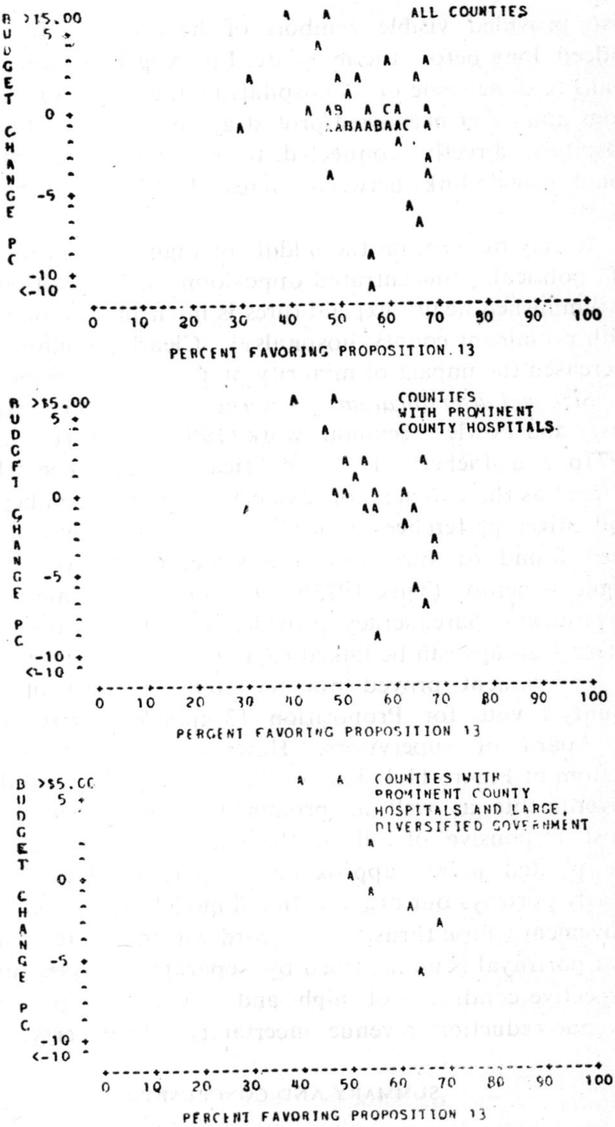

N = 4? COUNTIES, WITH A = 1 COUNTY, B = 2 COUNTIES, C = 3 COUNTIES, ETC.

FIG. 11.1 : *Increase in inpatient budget other the previous fiscal year, by voter support of proposition 13 in the least favorable district.*

been given to the sociopolitical processes by which plans are adopted, minority needs are satisfied, or social movements have an impact. Ours has been a modest attempt to provide some redress by modifying two basic models of such impact and applying them to those ubiquitous political documents called local budgets.

The effects of local interests and their organization are clear : In the absence of locally organized minority interests, the will of the majority sometimes prevailed ; and the external mandate was more likely to go unsupported. Budget decisions that were discretionary, however, were closely responsive to the overall local majority, the organized minority lacking here the external lever of "required by law".

One caveat is in order. In selecting budget items for which information was sufficiently detailed and comparable, we also have unavoidably chosen two extremes. County health has traditionally had vocal and organized interest groups to act in its behalf (though rather unsuccessfully before the mandate : Zucker 1979), while the board of supervisors was itself a visible symbol of the "big government" that Proposition 13 supporters tended to reject (Turk 1979), having few organized supporters other than itself. Regardless, the basic findings are likely to generalize to less extreme cases, simply because they are rooted in the differential power granted by external mandate. Organized groups which exert limited influence without mandate were transformed into effective pressure groups with legal or moral sanctions as their weapons.

The heretofore prevalent view of social movements appears to have applied to governmental decisions that were not subject to mandate. There the will of the majority appears to have prevailed without any elaborate organizational superstructure, and minority preferences appeared to have had no effect. But where conformity to mandate is at issue, the otherwise powerless minority can, it would seem, influence governmental decision, provided that it is politically represented through geographic concentration and that it can rally about and form links with an appropriate organization or have multiple links available to local government. This speaks to an organizational model of social movements, here a counter-movement.

of health care would have negative consequences for the county. In other words, a viable threat exists.

6. Unless explicitly stated otherwise all findings reported are statistically significant at atleast the .05 level adopted for this research. The findings designated not significant failed even to approach the .10 level.
7. See footnote 4 for data sources.
8. All election data were obtained from Eu (1978).
9. Sources : Per cent urban, U.S. Bureau of the Census (1977) ; revenues, comptroller's tapes (Note 4) and archives of the Office of the Legislative Analyst, California State Senate's Committee on Finance ; per cent of families with incomes less than 125% of the national poverty rate (California's cost of living is high), U.S. Bureau of the Census (1977). Reduction in overall revenues was computed by the residual method referred to in Footnote 4.
10. Source : A special publication in 1974 by the California Department of Health Services. Reliability is claimed on the basis of correlations of r = .99 with per capita number of county hospital beds and .73 with total number of county hospitals (14 of the 43 counties had none—i.e., awarded contracts to private or other non-county hospitals for health services to the poor).
11. The product moment coefficient, r, between voting against Proposition 13 increases from .32 (this differs from the .46 reported above that was based on variables which were transformed to remove the effects of assymetry and heteroscedasticity in multivariate analyses) to .52.
12. We approximated the measure used for large cities by Turk (1973b, 1977b) and Lincoln (1976), which is closely associated with Liebert's (1976) measure of governmental scope and has the same effects (unpublished manuscript) on the wide-ranging set of 30 urban variables from Turk's most recent book (1977b : 261-262.) All of California's 58 county governments were first dichotomized about the median according to relative size, their total numbers of employees per resident. The 58 governments were then ranked separately according to each of the following numbers of employees per resident : General administration, public protection, public ways and facilities, health and sanitation, public assistance, culture and recreation (source) : tapes published by the Comptroller's Office of California's State Department of Finance). The degree of similarity among these seven rankings (computed using the variance-related formula provided by Gibbs and Martin 1962) signifies how diversified the government is. The diversification score for California's 58 counties was also dichotomized about its median. The county governments above both medians—there are 13 among the present 43—are classified as large in scale and diversified to constitute a dummy variable (0,1).

It may be noted in passing that large city versions of this indicator either used or were closely associated with metropolitan expenditure levels (replacing numbers of employees). Anticipating the results reported in this volume by Aiken and his associates for Europe and by Newton for England and Wales by Newton, location in the urban hierarchy predicted municipal expenditures in the 130 largest United States cities (Turk 1970, 1977b : 33-65).

13. The .52 correlation is increased to .86. Indeed, when intensification by county hospital is introduced into multiple regression analysis, separately as well as with intensification by county government, the explained variation (Rsquare) increases by .17 over that obtained when just the simple vote of the least favorable district was employed. Moreover, the latter effect disappears once the two intensified effects are introduced. This last may be seen in what happens to the top graph on Figure 11.1 when the points that also appear on the center graph are ignored.

REFERENCES

Bohrnstedt, George W., "Observations on the measurement of change." In E.F. Borgatta (ed.), *Sociological Methodology.* San Francisco : Jossey-Bass. 1969.

California Department of Health, Health Care Costs and Services in California Counties. Sacramento. 1978.

Clark, Terry N., "Community structure, decision-making, budget expenditures, and urban renewal in 51 American communities." American Sociological Review 33 : 576-593. Slightly revised for C.M. Bonjean, T.N. Clark, and R.L. Lineberry (eds.), *Community Politics, A Behavioral Approach.* New York : Free Press. 1968.

Clark, Terry N. and Lorna C. Ferguson, Political Process and Urban Fiscal Strain. Draft manuscript, Chicago : University of Chicago. 1980.

Elling, R.H. and S. Halebsky, "Organizational differentiation and support." *Administrative Science Quarterly* 6 : 185-209. 1961.

Eu, March Fong, *Statement of Vote and Supplement : Primary Election,* June 6, 1978: Sacramento : Office of the Secretary of State. 1978.

Floderus, A., "Negotiating for development or change of urban land use." Presented at the European conference on Urban Research, *Essen, Germany,* October 2-5. 1981.

Galaskiewicz, Joseph, *Exchange Networks and Community Politics.* Beverly Hills, Cal. : Sage. 1979a.

——"Directions for an organizational analysis of cities." *Contemporary Sociology* 8 : 234-36. 1979b.

Garner, Roberta Ash, *Social Movements in America,* Chicago : Rand McNally. 1977.

Gibbs, Jack P. and Walter T. Martin, "Urbanization, technology, and the division of labor : international patterns." *American Sociological Review* 27 : 667-677. 1962.

Institute for Social Research, "Deepening distrust of political leaders is jarring public's faith in institutions." *ISR Newsletter* 7 : 4.5. 1979.

Janowitz, Morris, *The Last Half Century : Societal Change and Politics in America.* Chicago : University of Chicago Press. 1978.

Jenkins, J.C. and C. Perrow, "Insurgency of the powerless : farm worker movements (1946-1972)." *American Sociological Review* 42 : 249-268. 1977.

Laumann, Edward and Franz Pappi, "New directions in the study of community elites." *American Sociological Review* 38 : 212-230. 1973.

Laumann, Edward ; L. Verbrugge, and Franz Pappi, "Approach to the study of a community elite's influence structure." *American Sociological Review* 39 : 162-174. 1974.

Liebert. Roland, *Disintegration and Political Action : The Changing Functions of City Government in America.* New York : Academic Press. 1976.

Lincoln, James R., 'Power and mobilization in the urban community : reconsideration of the ecological approach." *American Sociological Review* 41 : 1-15. 1976.

Lineberry, R.L. and E.P. Fowler, "Reformism and public policies in American cities." *American Political Science Review* 61 : 701-716. 1967.

McCarthy, James D. and Mayer H. Zald, "Resource mobilization and social movements : A partial theory." *American Journal of Sociology* 82 : 1212-1241. 1977.

Miller, A.H., "Public policy and political cynicism : 1964-1970." In N.R. Luttbeg (ed.), *Public Opinion and Public Policy.* Homewood, II : Dorsey. 1974.

Oberschall, Anthony *Social Conflict and Social Movements.* Englewood Cliffs, N.J. : Prentice-Hall. 1973.

Piven, F.F. and R.A. Cloward *Regulating the Poor : The Function of Social Welfare.* New York : Pantheon. 1971.

——*Poor People's Movements : Why They Succeed, How They Fail.* New York : Pantheon. 1977.

Sayre, Wallace S. and Herbert Kaufman *Governing New York City : Politics in the Metropolis.* New York : Russell-Sage. 1960.

Turk, Herman, Interorganizational Activation in Urban Communities : Deduction from the Concept of System. Washington, D.C. : *Arnold and Caroline Rose Monograph Series of the American Sociological Association*, 1973.

——Organizations in Modern Life : Cities and Other Large Networks. San Francisco : Jossey-Bass. 1977.

——"Imageries of social control : On the publicized birth and early life of Proposition 13." *Urban Life (Special Issue on Social Control)* : 335-358. 1979.

U.S. Bureau of the Census, County and City Data Book. Washington, D.C. : U.S. Government Printing Office. 1977.

Warren, R.L. ; S.M. Rose and A.F. Bergunder. The Structure of Urban Reform. Lexington, Massachusettes : D.C. Heath. 1974.

Ziegler, H., "The effects of lobbying : comparative assessment" pp. 225-251 in N.R. Luttbeg (ed.), *Public Opinion and Public Policy.* Homewood, III : Dorsey. 1974.

Zeitlin, Maurice (ed.), *Classes, Class Conflict, and the State.* Cambridge, Mass. : Winthrop. 1980.

Zucker, Lynne G., *The impact of Proposition 13 on public funding and services for education and health in California.* Berkeley, Calif. : California Policy Seminar Monograph Series. 1981.

TWELVE

CARL E. VAN HORN AND PETER KOBRAK

INTEGRATING MANPOWER AND ECONOMIC DEVELOPMENT STRATEGIES

INTRODUCTION

DURING THE late sixties and seventies, a series of Federal initiatives evolved in the U.S. relating to manpower and economic and community development. Unfortunately, however, these efforts remained uncoordinated and lacking in sufficient resources individually to achieve a significant impact on the employment and other economic needs of disadvantaged individuals residing in aging central cities and rural poverty areas.

Such problems were found to exist even after many of the categorical program constraints were removed in the early 1970s through subsequent Federal block grants, such as the Comprehensive Employment and Training Act (CETA) and the Community Development Block Grant (CDBG). A report issued by the Department of Housing and Urban Development (HUD) in 1976 thus noted that "coordination between Community Development and Manpower was least evident..." in the sixteen cities where the research team conducted case studies (HUD 1976). This report also described low levels of cooperation between employment and training programs and other private economic development efforts. One of the major constraints to linking employment and training programs with economic development was Federal grant requirements and funding cycles. A host of local, historical impediments to cooperation were also listed. Yet, this study noted that

Paper presented at the "European Meeting on Applied Urban Research", Essen, Oct. 2-4, 1981.

positive signs of coordinated economic, community, and manpower development were evident in a number of communities where local government agencies had learned to work together and to respond to private sector needs.

On March 27, 1978 President Jimmy Carter announced a comprehensive national urban policy and called for a "*New Partnership* involving all levels of government, the private sector, and neighborhood and voluntary organizations in a major effort to make America's cities better places in which to live and work." Emerging out of this policy, which had been developed over a period of a year by numerous Federal agencies and outside experts and organizatons, were three central principles : coordinated Federal assistance at the local level, employment through the private sector, and jobs and business opportunities for minorities and the economically disadvantaged. These principles provided the grounding for the subsequent Targeted Jobs Demonstration Program (TJDP).

TJDP represents an innovative effort of link the private jobs created by the Federal government through various economic and community development programs, mass transit projects, and other Federal investments with manpower programs for the economically disadvantaged. Through a variety of approaches to be decided largely at the local level, employment training programs should be coordinated with Federal economic, community, and transportation projects so that the "miximum feasible" number of jobs created by the projects go to the economically disadvantaged and so that the "maximum feasible" number of spinoff business opportunities go to small or minority businesses.

TJDP is being operated under an interagency agreement among the Departments of Housing and Urban Development (as the lead agency), Labor, Transportation, and Commerce, Small Business Administration, and Community Services Administration that provided grants of between $ 100,000 and $ 200,000 to 13 communities and an Indian tribe. The Communities are Lynn, Massachusetts ; Philadelphia, Pennsylvania ; Wilmington, Delaware ; Portland, Maine ; New York City ; Portand, Oregon, Genesee County, Michigan ; Paterson, New Jersey ; Seattle, Washington ; San Antonio, Texas ; Milwaukee,

Wisconsin ; Buffalo, New York ; The Blackfeet Tribe (Browning, Montana) ; and Metcalfe, Mississippi. Most of the grants began in April 1980 and are scheduled to terminate in April 1982.

Though the direct expenditures on TJDP are relatively small, the demonstration is highly significant because the activities undertaken with demonstration funds are aimed at affecting contract provisions relating to huge sums of Federal assistance in the communities where the demonstrations operate. The demonstrations are also important because they provide a valuable opportunity to identify effective institutional arrangements, planning procedures, client referral processes, employment project techniques, and marketing strategies for increasing the likelihood that the economically disadvantaged and minorities will realize employment and business opportunities when substantial Federal investments in local projects are implemented.

In this paper we will seek to achieve three objectives. First, we will lay out the type of research design that in our view is needed to describe and analyze the implementation of an innovative, intergovernmental program that by its nature must assume markedly different forms at the various sites. This model of intergovernmental policy implementation utilizes both impact analysis and a process approach, because we believe that either failure to measure social program results quantitatively or failure to take account of policy standards, the local policy environment, and the national policy environment will inevitably result in unbalanced description and misleading analysis. The evaluation proposed in this paper is, therefore, designed to capture the essential experiences of those demonstrations, to describe the extent to which program goals have been achieved, to examine the social, economic, and political factors that hindered or aided the projects, and to detail the specific techniques and strategies of program implementation used in the demonstration sites. Second, we will present our preliminary findings on the extent to which TJDP is succeeding in providing jobs for the economically disadvantaged and business opportunities for small and minority businesses and achieving changes in institutional structures and procedures for coordinating manpower and economic development programs at the local level. Finally we will conclude the paper with some observations on the implications of our TJDP findings for urban economic development policy.

THE EVALUATION STRATEGY

When examining social programs, almost inevitably, a major challenge is to develop an evaluation strategy to measure performance in attaining program goals comparatively and within each community. The purpose of the evaluation is to determine *what* usable information about strategies, techniques, and program models may be "exported" to other communities—and to explain *why* particular program components worked. These goals for the evaluation pose a challenge to the researcher because project performance must be assessed, while at the same time the effective implementation strategies that can be replicated by other communities are isolated.

During the last decade a methodology suitable for this purpose has been developed by a number of social scientists, but primarily by political scientist interested in the study of program implementation. The methodology requires that the effects of program performance—the dependent variable here —be measured, and that the influence of environmental variables, or contextual variables, be differentiated from the influence of "process" variables. This strategy allows the analysts to separate those factors that are not subject to manipulation or control, such as national and local economic conditions, from factors that can be manipulated, such as agency structure or procedures. Figure 12.1 presents a "model" of what will be examined in this evaluation. The boxes in the diagram suggest the major variable clusters requiring study, and the arrow suggests what variables are expected to influence other variables. This model of intergovernmental program implementation is firmly grounded in the empirical and theoretical work of the last several years (See for example, Van Horn 1979 ; Ripley 1977 ; Palumbo and Harder 1981).

The evaluation of the Targeted Jobs Demonstration

Program (TJDP) involves two stages. First, program performance for each demonstration must be determined. Then, broad explanations for those program outcomes can be derived by examining the series of intervening events and conditions posited by the model of policy implementation in Figure 12.1. Though no model can completely capture reality, it helps to structure our understanding of the implementation process by grouping a number of complex attitudes, relationships, and conditions into general sets of factors that influence program performance. Each of these general variable clusters is considered in our analysis of TJDP.

The Targeted Jobs Demonstration Program and its evaluation can be viewed as having four different objectives in mind. First, TJDP is intended to alter the distribution of benefits within a community emanating from federally funded economic, community, and mass transportation projects. For TJDP to be successful, using this criterion, it must facilitate a redistribution of resources to the economically disadantaged (CETA-eligible individuals), and to small and minority businesses and Community Development Corporations (CDCs). Given that a federal economic development project will yield a certain number of job opportunities and a certain number of business opportunities, TJDP should result in *relatively more* of those opportunities flowing to the targeted groups and businesses. TJDP intervenes in an on-going pattern of distribution within each community and should alter the normal distribution in desirable ways.

Second, TJDP is intended to promote changes in institutional structures and procedures that will lead to better coordination between the economic and community development, and employment and training sectors of the local jurisdiction. Viewed from this perspective TJDP should, once again, alter the normal methods of carrying out federally assisted economic and community development projects. It should create and nurture structures, procedures, and relationships that will endure beyond the demonstration and have applicability to other communities.

A third, even more important, objective is the testing of procedures and strategies in a variety of settings so that national and local policy and practice may be transformed as a result of this experience. The problems identified by the demonstration are, of course, long standing ones. TJDP is another attempt to fund some communities which can give serious attention to these issues. From their efforts to cope with the problems of coordination, job development and business targeting it is hoped that broadly applicable lessons will be learned.

Finally, the TJDP evaluation's more limited purpose is to assess the performance of 14 communities against their stated objectives. Each community has, in its proposal, outlined a set of specific goals and the tasks deemed necessary for achieving them. This requires measuring and assessing their performance in relation to their stated goals.

Because it has various purposes, TJDP requires an evaluation strategy that is precise enough to make objective statements about program performance, and, where possible, to compare that performance with both the "normal" distribution of jobs and business opportunities and with the proposal's targeted goals. It also requires an evaluation strategy that is sensitive to unanticipated consequences within each research site and that fully captures local behavior in relation to TJDP's broader objectives so that other communities can learn from the grantees' experiences. At the same time, quantitative precision must be sought in documenting the number and types of job and business opportunities that go to targeted groups. Performance on these measures will be compared with the grantee's plan, with pre-TJDP performance, and with other non-TJDP sites. Comparisons of specific TJDP components is also made across sites. Qualitative assessments are also offered to describe and explain the TJDP experience in each community and uncover the common issues.

Finally, although the proposed evaluation strategy represents the general approach used for all communities, each community has required a sufficiently flexible analysis to reflect those areas where the grantees place *their emphasis*. For example, a grantee might concentrate on targeting jobs rather than methods and techniques to assist small or minority business.

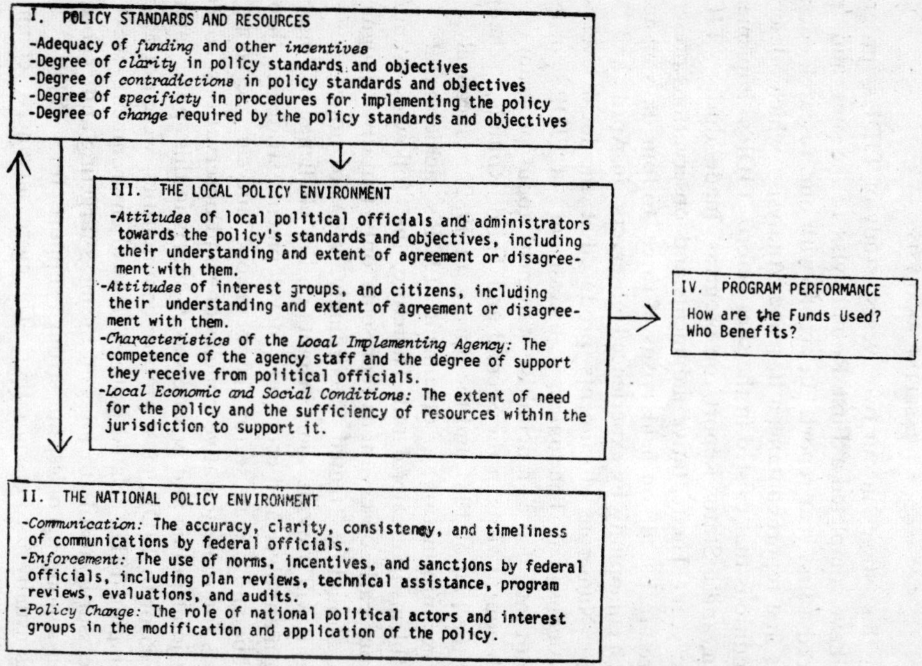

FIG. 12.1 : *A model of intergovernmental Policy inplementation*

BASELINE ANALYSIS

At this stage in our two years study of TJDP's progress, we have completed a First Round visit to the sites and produced a first year report. In accord with our research design, this first report contains a Baseline Analysis, which describes conditions that existed in the sites before TJDP's implementation, and a Status Report on progress made during TJDP's first year. The tentative judgments and observations presented here are based on field visits of three to four days made to each community by experienced observers in April and May 1981. Numerous documents produced at the local level were also consulted. The summary assessment of TJDP's progress is not intended as a definitive statement about program results. Subsequent visits in the Second and Third Rounds, scheduled for the Fall of 1981 and the Spring of 1982 respectively, will gather information to document TJDP's achievements and problems in greater detail. Therefore, the following summary of our early observations represents only tentative judgments, and should be treated accordingly. We do hope, however, that it will provide some insights on the challenge of integrating manpower and economic development strategies through public and private sector cooperation, and can serve as the basis for some tentative conclusions and observations concerning joint public and private sector efforts in this policy arena.

Prior to TJDP, most grantee communities were not actively pursuing TJDP-related goals. The local environment was not necessarily hostile to job and business targeting and coordination among agencies, but strong support for TJDP's goals was usually not present either. The more advanced communities had experimented with job and business targeting programs, but none had established workable procedures before TJDP.

Job opportunities prior to TJDP

I. Efforts to target jobs from economic development projects prior to TJDP were minimal. Eight of the 14 sites made no attempt ; six made limited attempts and failed to institutionalize procedures for capturing job opportunities for the economically disadvantaged.

II. Little or no information exists on the actual number of jobs that economically disadvantaged people obtained from Federal economic development projects prior to TJDP. The absence of data reflects the low priority afforded to job targeting before TJDP. It also creates serious obstacles for meaningful comparisons with performance during the TJDP period.

III. Local actors believe that low-income people obtained very few jobs from federally-funded economic development investments. Explanations for this pattern can be found in the nature of Federal projects, which create construction jobs that seldom employ disadvantaged workers ; the low-skill levels of the CETA-eligible individual ; the absence of job targeting policies in local governments ; the resistance of private sector firms to CETA-eligible individuals ; and the reluctance of economic development agencies to promote CETA clientele to there private sector clients.

Business opportunities prior to TJDP

I. Few communities attempted to capture spin-off business opportunities from federally-funded economic development projects for small and minority businesses prior to TJDP. Four communities tried to obtain federal contract opportunities directly for minority firms ; four established minority set-aside policies for city contracts ; and four communities tried to assist minority contractors. Business development services were offered in most communities but not predominately for small or minority firms.

II. Low levels of business opportunities and services for small and minority firms were attributed to several factors, including the absence of local policies endorsing the "set-aside" concept ; the lack of an institutional mechanism for identifying business opportunities and referring appropriate firms ; the weak minority business requirements ; the difficulty of tracking economic development projects ; and, the marginal nature of many small and minority firms.

Coordination among agencies prior to TJDP

I. Informal information sharing about economic development projects had occurred in many of the communities, but more meaningful efforts to coordinate programs and services were missing in most communities.

II. Five of the twelve active TJDP communities had experimented with various coordinating mechanisms prior to TJDP, but no systems for regular consultation between employment and training, and economic development agencies had been implemented.

III. Bureaucratic inertia, agency goal conflicts, and rapidly changing and full agendas combined to keep agencies from working with one another.

STATUS REPORT ON TJDP'S FIRST YEAR AS OF MAY 1981

Job opportunities under TJDP

I. TJDP grants have brought about changes in several communities' policies and procedures for economic development, and employment and training assistance. Tentative linkages, begun in four communities before TJDP, have been strengthened. New linkages have been developed in five others. Little or no change has occurred in four communities.

II. Eight sites are focusing their efforts on obtaining jobs generated through publicly-assisted economic development projects. These sites are classified as the "targeting" communities because they embrace TJDP's central tenet—that the economically disadvantaged should benefit from jobs created by specific public investments in economic development.

III. Four sites are attempting to place unemployed, low-income individuals with employers, regardless of whether the firm has obtained economic development assistance or not. These sites are classified as "non-targeting" communities because they are not attempting to link the provision of specific economic development assistance with employment benefits for low-income people.

IV. Within the targeting communities, TJDP staff hold varying expectations for the response of private sector firms. In one community, legally enforceable agreements are negotiated which specify the number and type of jobs that the private firm will provide to CETA-eligibles. In several others non-legally binding agreements, whereby the employer promises to make a good faith effort to hire the economically disadvantaged are pursued. In all the targeting communities, employment and training clients, and programs are linked with the provision of economic development assistance.

V. The more demanding the expectations of the local government, the more complex and lengthy the process required to effectively target jobs. Several procedures and policies must be established if legally enforceable agreements are used, including (1) a policy on job targeting ; (2) direct negotiations between the city and the employer during the application or early stage of the economic development project ; (3) timely referral of trained applications or other employees to the employer ; (4) monitoring of the hiring process at the firm ; and (5) the establishment of an enforcement mechanism. If non-legally binding agreements are negotiated, the community's process can be simpler and need not include public policies on job targeting and enforcement mechanisms.

VI. The four non-targeting communities, because they do not require or expect private firms receiving economic development aid to hire CETA-eligibles, have taken on a task which is less complex and time-consuming.

VII. Progress is evaluated in terms of the communities' willingness and ability to establish a process for targeting and then channeling jobs from economic development projects to the economically disadvantaged and the extent to which they obtain actual and planned placements. According to these criteria, four TJDP sites have made significant progress during the first year. Five communities have made limited progress. Naturally, the two communities that had not yet begun their projects had made no progress (as of May 1981).

VIII. Several conditions help to explain the differences among the grantees and the rate of progress within each TJDP community. Some of these conditions are directly or indirectly under the control of local governmental officials ; others are not. Few, if any, of the important conditions can be manipulated by TJDP staff alone.

IX. TJDP seems to have made the most progress in communities where a local policy supports TJDP's goals ; when local objectives can be linked with Federal job targeting policies ; and when continuing political support is provided by elected officials. Support from key senior and middle level managers and a stable administrative environment also seem to be important to TJDP progress as is the location of TJDP staff so that they have access to policy makers and information. Because TJDP requires demanding and delicate tasks, experienced staff to serve as skilled negotiators and brokers are needed. Finally, TJDP requires a workable process so that timely negotiations with employers may take place, referrals may be made by CETA agencies, and hiring by private firms may be monitored.

X. Several factors outside the control of the local government can contribute to program delay or failure. These include private sector attitudes towards hiring CETA-eligible persons and local economic conditions. Many private employers resist hiring economically disadvantaged employees and hold negative attitudes about CETA agencies. Generally depressed economic conditions, evident in most of the TJDP sites, also make job targeting more difficult by reducing the number of desirable employers, delaying projects, eliminating large numbers of construction jobs, and convincing some TJDP staff and their supervisors that attempts to target jobs are pointless or counterproductive.

Business development opportunities and services under TJDP

I. Seven of the twelve active TJDP sites are involved in the small and minority business assistance goals of TJDP. The other communities have eschewed this goal.

II. Only two of the TJDP communities are directly engaged in the procurement of business contracts for small and minority business. The others are involved in the provision of business development services to small and minority businesses. Their activities, however, are not targeted specifically to businesses which receive or will receive governmental contracts.

III. Community Development Corporations are almost wholly ignored under TJDP, in part because few exist in the demonstration sites.

IV. Those TJDP's that became involved in providing spin-off business opportunities and business services shared the following characteristics : (1) a commitment was made in their proposals ; (2) federal grants are an important component of their local economic development efforts ; and (3) services of this nature were lacking prior to TJDP.

V. Five factors seem to explain why one-half of the active TJDP sites are giving little attention to the business opportunities goal : (1) the weak emphasis in the original grantee proposals ; (2) TJDP's administrative location in CETA-agencies that are not interested or experienced in business development services ; (3) the availability of other business development services in the community ; (4) the absence of political support for this concept ; and (5) the reluctance of TJDP staff to negotiate agressively with investors to pursue this goal.

Coordination among agencies under TJDP

I. Coordination between economic development, and employment and training sectors has been positively affected by TJDP in almost all communities. All sites have increased informal information exchange for job and business targeting decisions. Identifiable systems of regular communication developed in several communities, where slight or sporadic consultation took place before TJDP.

II. In about half the TJDP sites, there is a willingness on the part of at least one economic development agency and one employment and training agency to share control over resources for joint program implementation.

III. Several conditions seem to contribute to increased coordination between employment and training, and economic development sectors when it occurs. These include : (1) support from community leadership ; (2) support from economic development agencies ; (3) co-location of staff in the same organization and building ; (4) general economic health of the communities ; (5) experienced staff and stable organizations ; and (6) memoranda of understanding between agencies. While these conditions were not simultaneously present in any one site, they were more likely to occur in communities that made the most progress in coordination.

OBTAINING EFFICIENCY AND EQUITY BENEFITS FROM URBAN ECONOMIC DEVELOPMENT PROGRAMS

The Targeted Jobs Demonstration Program addresses an important set of policy issues about the mix of public and private sector strategies to foster urban revitalization. At the heart of this policy question is the search for the appropriate mix of concessions and incentives to private firms, on the one hand, and requirements and sanctions placed on the firm, on the other. Specifically, TJDP and similar policies raise the question : What can/should government demand from private firms in return for public assistance for urban economic development ? To what extent should policy-makers emphasize efficiency concerns over equity concerns in fashioning urban revitalization policies ?

Traditionally, U.S. government policy-makers have segmented programs aimed at stimulating private sector investments in urban areas from programs aimed at directly fostering the employment of low-income people. Consequently, the typical urban economic development program doesn't demand equity benefits from the private firm.

Federal, state, and local economic development agencies have adopted a pro-business and anti-government posture. Their principal concern has been to provide financial assistance so that businesses can expand in or move into particular political jurisdictions. Economic development agencies have also tried to lessen government intervention into businesses by eliminating red-tape and by reducing the "strings" on public assistance that businesses find objectionable.

However, programs of low-interest loans, grants, tax abatements, guaranteed loans and the like are sold to legislators and executives and justified to the public on the grounds that they will not only benefit private investors but also benefit the community. It is argued that such programs which lower the costs of conducting business in urban settings should help stabilize declining urban areas, increase tax ratables, halt physical deterioration, and most importantly provide jobs. In practice, however, economic development agencies have largely ignored the rhetoric about job creation and have not focused systematically on the equity benefits that might accrue from public investments in private firms. Following their pro-business advocacy role, these agencies tend to concentrate on the efficiency of the investment. They are concerned with how much money the public investment will generate or salvage for the community.

Equity concerns are indirectly addressed by nearly all urban economic development policies. Public assistance is often limited to companies located in or moving to distressed communities (measured in a variety of ways). Public investments are tied to a policy agenda that goes beyond efficiency considerations, but, the equity benefits that might be derived from urban economic development aid are considered as secondary and indirect outcomes rather than primary and direct result of the government intervention.

Inter-state and inter-city competition has also dampened the demands that policy makers in any one jurisdiction are willing to place on private sector firms. Economic development programs at the state and local level are usually designed to lure companies from one location to their community or at minimum to stem outmigration. Consequently, lawmakers have designed packages of financial assistance that make their jurisdiction more attractive than other locations. In the bidding war that ensues, policies that require the firm to behave according to government prescription are naturally viewed with skepticism, if not alarm.

Finally, concerns over employment benefits have rarely been imported into the economic development process at the local level because the agencies responsible for implementing federal, state, and local urban aid programs operate independently of one another. Economic development and employment and training agencies, having been created by an independent funding source, tend not to interact with one another or understand each other's missions and responsibilities. They tend to recruit people with different orientations and goals and seldom are forced to examine how they might work together. The bureaucratic and political incentives run in the opposite direction ; coordination is irrational.

While economic development programs have been focused in the capital market, federal manpower programs have concentrated on the functioning of the labor market by attempting to upgrade the ability of chronically unemployed people to compete for jobs. In contrast to economic development programs, manpower programs have been justified almost entirely on equity grounds. It is argued that such programs will stimulate increased employment for certain groups, such as low-income people and minorities, who otherwise face significant barriers to employment, even when the economy is relatively healthy. Manpower programs are also justified in party by their contribution to efficiency (a more highly trained workforce is more productive) and by their contribution to lowering income transfer payments.

Since their inception in the United States in the early 1960s manpower programs for the structurally unemployed have extracted a mild quid pro quo from private firms. They offer moderate financial incentives, usually in the form of reduced wages or specialized training, in order to induce the private firm to hire unemployed and low-income people. Policymakers assume, therefore, that the private employers are altering their behavior by employing someone whom they would not normally hire. Whether this assumption is correct or not, the programs were designed to produce a public benefit—hiring the chronically unemployed—in return for a public investment.

Recently, the federal government added a new wrinkle to employment and training programs by creating the so-called Private Sector Initiative Program (PSIP). This program is similar to previous manpower programs in all respects except one : it is the first time that manpower agencies have specifically adopted a pro-business posture. Each political jurisdiction receiving PSIP funds is expected to appoint a Private Industry Council with majority representation from the private sector. This group in turn is expected to advocate a pro-business position to the employment and training community and elected officials and spend its funds in such a way as to benefit the business community. Businesses hiring individuals from PSIP programs are still required to take those that have low-incomes and histories of chronic unemployment.

Within the last few years a growing number of federal, state, and local policymakers have begun to challenge the traditional isolation of equity and efficiency concerns in urban economic development. The willingness to place demands on the private sector in return for public assistance has increased, but it is still not widespread. What has brought about this movement and change ?

There is a growing dissatisfaction or unease among long-time supporters of urban economic development programs that they don't produce many jobs in relation to the investment. Federal, state, and local elected officials have been asking some tough questions about economic development projects, such as whether economic development assistance is a windfall or a necessary incentive. Moreover, various studies commissioned by the federal government have demonstrated that the job generating outcomes of economic development assistance are much lower than claimed by the applicants for aid. One study based on field evaluations of economic development projects concluded that applicants overestimated the jobs created through economic developmen aid by a factor of seven to one (Shaikh and Salinas 1978). One way to demonstrate that economic development aid is worthwhile is to tie it with other public purposes, such as hiring unemployed city residents.

Local officials are also becoming more sophisticated, or perhaps more cynical, about the economic development process. They are beginning to question the assumption that a modest provision of tax incentives and low-cost expansion decisions are very complex and governmental inducements may be marginally important. Much more salient are such factors as the availability of suitable labor and access to markets to which the firm can sell their product or service. Government decision-makers are gaining more knowledge about how to intervene in the economic development process and what they can reasonably expect from businesses in return for public support.

A set of policy initiatives have also contributed to changing attitudes and practices regarding urban economic development assistance. During the Carter Administration, federal officials initiated several program demonstrations and promulgated policy statements supporting the concept of obtaining jobs for the structurally unemployed from economic development aid. The only one of these initiatives to reach maturity was the

Targeted Jobs Demonstration Program, but the widespread discussion and promotion of job targeting has influenced the thinking of policymakers at state and local levels. According to one recent study of twenty-five cities, eighteen cities targeted their economic development projects to either a specific resident population subgroup such as minorities, women, or youth, or to the structurally unemployed (Hartford Policy Center 1980).

More recently, bipartisan support has been growing for an Urban Enterprise Zone concept which would provide substantial tax relief and other assistance to companies locating in distressed urban areas. Nearly all the proposals for such special zones contain provisions to encourage the hiring of the structurally unemployed residents of the "enterprise zone".

Finally, the impact of scarce federal resources has helped renew emphasis on inter-agency coordination and program consolidation. Federal, state, and local officials are looking at the range of programs in their jurisdictions and trying to devise ways to achieve public benefits with less money. As resources shrink, strategies that might guarantee higher returns on investments become more attractive. A program that ties job benefits to economic development assistance thus becomes more appealing to hard pressed administrators and elected officials.

Given the increasing in job targeting policies and practice, the Targeted Jobs Demonstration Program bears careful examination. The task of targeting jobs from economic development projects for low-income and long-term unemployed residents is very difficult. Local officials must support jobs and business targeting. Two and probably more agencies must cooperate with each other by sharing information and resources in a timely manner. Procedures for tracking economic development projects must be established and implemented. Private employers must be receptive to hiring the structurally unemployed. The local economy must remain vital enough to sustain the private firms who obtain public assistance. Despite the obstacles to effective job targeting an increasing number of local officials are finding it an attractive strategy for gaining direct public benefits from economic development programs.

REFERENCES

Hartford Policy Center, "Employment Leveraging Strategies for Cities : Working Draft," prepared for the U.S. Department of Commerce, Economic Development Administration, 1980 (Mimeo).

Palumbo, Dennis J. and Marvin Harder (eds.), *Emplementing Public Policy* (Lexington, MA : D.C. Heath and Co., 1981).

Ripley, Randall B. et al., *The Implemantation of CETA in Ohio*, R & D Monograph No. 44, Employment and Training Administration, U.S. Department of Labor (Washington, D.C. : Government Printing Office, 1977).

Shaikh , Abdul Q.J. and Patricia Salinas, "Evaluating Economic Development Programs," prepared for the U.S. Department of Commerce, Economic Development Administration, 1978 (Mimeo).

Van Horn, Carl E., *Policy Implementation in the Federal System* (Lexington, MA : D.C. Heath and Co., 1979).

U.S. Department of Housing and Urban Development, *Community, Economic, and Manpower Development Linkages, Section 1. Summary and Analysis*, processed, 1971.

THIRTEEN

K. NEWTON

PUBLIC SERVICES IN CITIES AND COUNTIES

INTRODUCTION

CONVENTIONAL attempts to explain the variations in public expenditure on the part of local authorities in the western world have not proved particularly successful. By and large, the research has major problems; first, it lacks theoretical coherence, and second, it has not resulted in particularly good empirical results. On the first problem, an excellent overview and summary of the literature has concluded that "Rather than a comparative theory of performance, we seem to be laying the foundations for another monument to 'adhockery'."[1] And in what is one of the best studies of local spending carried out in Britain and elsewhere, Danziger writes: "The broadest criticism of the approach has argued persuasively that it lacks any theory of linkages which explicates the relationships between policy outputs and characteristics of the environment."[2]

Lack of theory to explain interesting results would be a severe failing, but unfortunately, interesting results are few and far between. Danziger concludes that his own work provides a weak and generally unsatisfactory explanation for the variation in country borough resource allocation...the demographic approach has minimal explanatory power for most allocation measures.[3] Danziger's poor results were repeated in our own work.

Consequently, it was decided to go back to the simplest

Paper Presented at the "European Meeting on Applied Urban Research", Essen, Oct. 2-4, 1981.

of string-and-sealing-wax methods which entailed nothing more complicated than ranking authorities from the highest to the lowest per capita spenders on their full range of main services, and inspecting the resulting league tables in the hope that they would tell us something of general interest. The work reported here deals with the top tier of the local government system of England and Wales, which includes urban (county boroughs) and more rural (counties) authorities. The financial years 1960/1 and 1972/3 were chosen for study in order to (1) reduce the possibility of trying to generalise from an odd or unusual year, and (2) to examine stability or changes over time. The paper will examine each service in turn, and then suggest some generalisations at the end.

Parks

Although parks consume a small proportion of the local authority budget, they are as good a place as any to start because this item has firmly resisted satisfactory analyses in the past. The hypothesis that wealthier authorities spend more on parks, in the absence of the most pressing demands for other services, is barely supported by the British evidence, but nothing else of any significance materialises in regression analysis, and most of the variance (80-90 %) is unexplained.

When authorities are ranked from the highest to the lowest, however, two explanations for high expenditure jump out of the league table. At the top of the table in 190/61 come a group of seaside resorts—Eastbourne, Great Yarmouth, Bournemouth, and Brighton—and not far behind them come the remaining resorts of Southend, Blackpool, and Hastings. After 1968 the newly created Torbay joins this select group. The reasons for high parks expenditure in these cases scarcely needs comment—the economic success of a resort partly depends upon beautiful and extensive public parks.

At the same time, there is another, but completely different group of cities, which also spend heavily on parks. These are the capitals of large urban agglomerations, including Manchester, Birmingham, Liverpool, Bolton, Sheffield and Newcastle. It seems that these cities spend relatively heavily because they are surrounded by large urban areas, and have great need of their parks. In contrast, the smaller county towns which have rural surroundings spend little.

Systematic evidence for these relationships is presented in Table 13.1. The first part of the table demonstrates the differences between urban and rural authorities. The 83 county boroughs were divided into four groups, as follows :

1. *Conurbation authorities*—those which are at least 75% surrounded by other authorities with a population density of at least five people per acre.
3. *Semi-urban authorities*—those which are mainly (75%) surrounded by other authorities with a population density of more than three but less than five people per acre.
3. *Semi-rural authorities*—those which are mainly (75%) surrounded by other authorities with a population density of less than three but more than one person per acre.
4. *Rural authorities*—those which are mainly (75%) surrounded by authorities with a population density of less than one person per acre.

As the figures show there is a fairly strong relationship between high spending and an urban or semi-urban environment. If the seaside resorts are removed from the rural category, the relationship is stronger.

The relationship holds irrespective of the social populations.

Two general points emerge from these findings. First, when looking for factors which might explain expenditure variations it is not enough to deal only with the characteristic of resident populations. Most studies collect detailed, census-type data about such things as population size and change, age, density, housing conditions, wealth, voting turnout, etc., and little or nothing else. Table 13.1 shows that factors which are not simply aggregates of individual characteristics can be much more important—in this case, the economic function of the city (the seaside resorts), and the nature of the city's physical environment (in the case of conurbation and rural places).

TABLE 13.1 : **Per Capita Parks Expenditure (£), by Type of Authority, Country Boroughs, 1960/61 and 1972/3**

Type of Authority	1960/1	(n)	1972/3	(n)
Conurbation	0.956	(17)	1.881	(14)
Semi-urban	0.834	(18)	1.882	(18)
Semi-rural	0.826	(22)	1.838	(23)
Rural	0 797	(26)	1.699	(28)
Seaside resorts	1.167	(8)	2.240	(9)
County towns	0.661	(12)	1.510	(12)
Suburbs	1.135	(2)	1.615	(2)
County Borough Mean	0.846	(83)	1.795	(83)

TABLE 13.2 : **Per Capita Parks Expenditure, by Social Class and Urban Rural Dictonomies, County Boroughs, 1960/61**

	Urban	Rural
Middle Class	Croydon 1.555	Ipswich 0.502
	Wallasey 1.059	York 0.556
Working Class	Salford 1.201	Burton 0.505
	Oldham 1.003	Barrow 0.605

Second, it is clear that different kinds of cities can spend similar amounts on a given service but for different reasons, and vice versa. This greatly complicates the picture and, quite possibly, is what fools the computer and its complicated cluster and factor analysis programmes. It is not enough to be multi-variate ; analysis must be multi-variate and multi-dimensional.

Sewage

Sewage expenditure is another which resists satisfactory analysis in conventional demographic studies. It correlates weakly with only a few social and economic variables, and no political ones, and regression explains no more than twenty per cent of its variance. However, a casual inspection of the county league table of high and low spenders shows that a crucial factor is the geographical location of the authority ;

very simply, those on the coast spend less than inland authorities. Of the twenty-five at the bottom of the table in 1972/3 seventeen were coastal cities, and of the twenty-five at the top, twenty-one were inland.

Among the coastal cities, the seaside resorts are notable for their relatively high spending, in spite of their predominantly rural surroundings—whereas the coastal cities had a per capita average of £ 2.247, the seaside resorts averaged £ 2.523.

TABLE 13.3 : **Per Capita Sewage Expenditures (£), by Coastal and Inland Cities, County Boroughs, 1960/1 and 1972/3**

Type of Authority	1960/1	(n)	1972/3	(n)
Inland	0.971	(57)	3.183	(56)
Coastal	0.619	(26)	2.247	(27)
Seaside Resorts	0.667	(8)	2.523	(9)
Others	0.597	(18)	2.109	(18)
County Borough Average	0.801	(83)	2.878	(83)

Refuse

Common sense and a little knowledge suggest that, like parks expenditure, refuse costs may be determined to a greater extent by the physical setting of a city, than by its population chracteristics. That is, authorities which are in the middle of large conurbations are likely to have to transport refuse long distance to rubbish tips, or else invest in expensive capital equipment for burning or crushing rubbish. Conversely, the costs of rural and free-standing authorities are likely to be lower. Transport costs are a high proportion of refuse expenditure.

The validity of this explanation may be judged by the figures in Table 13.4 which show that urban authorities do, indeed, spend more than rural and free-standing ones. It is notable that some of the seaside resorts are also high spenders, presumably because they go to special trouble to attract tourists by being clean and hygienic.

TABLE 13.4 : **Per Capita Refuse Expenditures (£), by Urban and Rural Authorities, County Boroughs 1960/1 and 1972/3**

Type of Authority	1960/1	(n)	1972/3	(n)
Conurbation	0.810	(17)	2.909	(14)
Semi-urban	0.843	(18)	2.740	(18)
Semi-rural	0.759	(22)	2.324	(23)
Rural	0.730	(26)	2.270	(28)
County Borough Average	0.779	(83)	2.495	(83)

Note : Authorites are classified in the same way as in Table 13.1.

These figures suggest that it is not population size and diseconomies of scale which cause high refuse expenditure, but rather the scale of urban society in England and Wales which causes the high spending of authorities which are embedded at the centres of the largest urban areas.

Housing

Housing is the first divisible service discussed so far, and it is also the first which is well explained by the demographic approach. The size of the rate fund contribution to the housing revenue account of county boroughs correlates strongly with a wide range of social, economic, and political variables.

Together these variables explain 70.2 per cent of the variance in 1960/1. A slightly different combination of variables are included in the regression for 1972/3, but basically the results are similar, in that they show that housing expenditure is basically a function of Labour control in authorities with poor housing, a poor population, and a relatively small school aged population.

Libraries, museums, and art galleries

In the majority of authorities, expenditure on libraries is included with museums and art galleries, but for the sake of brevity all three will be called library expenditure. As with other indivisible services, library spending has resisted explanation, although it does correlate with statistical (but not much substantial) significance with wealth and class measures which explain about a third of the variance. A ranking of county boroughs, however, shows that the biggest and most important conurbation capitals have rather high figures. Liverpool is right at the top of the table. At the other extreme, many of the smaller, industrial cities which exist in the shadow of the major capitals, spend the least on libraries.

This raises the distinct possibility that library expenditure is closely connected not with size or nature of the resident population of a city, but with the size and nature of the population for which that city is a regional capital. Fortunately, we have a study which grades cities in terms of their importance as metropolitan or regional capitals, so we can put this proposition to a rough-and-ready test. The geographer Carruthers has ranked and grouped cities in England and Wales (excluding London) according to their importance as service centres, and the average library expenditure for each group in the hierarchy shows clearly enough that spending does decline as the importance of the city as a service centre declines (Table 13.5).

TABLE 13.5 : **Per Capita Library Expenditure (£), by Importance of Service Centres, County Boroughs, 1960/1 and 1972/3**

City Rank[1]	Examples	1960/1	1972/3	(n)
Group 2B	Manchester	0.667	2.424	(5)
Group 2C	Cardiff	0.590	1.703	(4)
Groups 3A/3a	Bradford	0.530	1.777	(31)
Groups 3B/3b	Halifax	0.472	1.493	(27)
Groups 3C/3c	Burton	0.421	1.427	(72)
County Borough Mean		0.503	1.672	(74)[2]

Notes 1. The ranking is that of I. Carruthers, 'Major shopping centres in England and Wales', *Regional Studies*, Vol 1, 1967, 56-81. For some details of this study see Appendix 3.

2. The total number of observations is 74 because Carruthers does not classify all county boroughs and because, for comparative reasons, the analysis is limited to boroughs which existed in both 1960/1 and 1972/3.

This approach does not lend itself to the counties, but a league table of high and low spenders reveals that the former consists mainly of the wealthier, larger, and rather more urban authorities, while the latter includes mainly poorer, smaller, more remote, and rural counties. Four of the top ten are not only large, but also wealthy, and fairly urban. Seven of the top ten are fairly large and densely populated by county standards. The average population of the top ten is slightly more than a million, compared with that of the bottom ten which is 400,000. The low spenders also include some of the smallest and most sparsely populated counties.

Town and county planning

Planning expenditure constitutes a small part of local authority budgets (less than half a per cent), and, of course, a good deal can be done without spending much money. Yet the league tables show up something of interest, for it is clear that cities which suffered from heavy bombing during the war are grouped at the top. In fact, of the twelve county boroughs listed as having had major air attacks and at least 150 tons of high explosives dropped on them, ten are in the top twenty in 1960/1 for planning expenditure. If one adds to these the cities of Exeter, Greath Yarmouth, Hastings, Southend, Eastbourne, and Birkenhead, because they were also attacked by air at least fifty times and suffered great damage, then there are few county boroughs among the twenty highest spenders which did not suffer from extensive wartime damage.[5] The position is not drastically changed by 1972/3, when Portsmouth, Newcastle, Manchester, Exeter, Coventry, Plymouth, Hull, Birkenhead, Sheffield, and Birmingham are all in the top twenty. It seems that cities which had to set to work planning and rebuilding on a large scale in 1945 were still spending relatively heavily on planning twenty-five years later. By comparison places such as Chester, Carlisle, Blackpool, Solihull, Southport, and Bournemouth, which received no more than the odd stray bomb, spend well below the national average.

Besides the heavily bombed cities, a group of historic county towns also spend relatively heavily on planning. Bath, Worcester, Norwich, Oxford, Canterbury, and Glucester all spend considerably above the average. Once again, not all historic, county towns spend a lot (Chester and Ipswich, for example), but the majority are on or above the average.

Turning from county towns to the counties themselves, it is clear that war destruction does not account for their planning expenditure. Few of the counties which were the targets for flying bombs and rockets are notable for high spending ; on the contrary, the counties which took the brunt of the action more usually appear at the bottom of the table.[6] Nor is there much evidence that the poorer and more industrial counties spend the least ; on the contrary, some of the wealthiest counties do so (Kent, Buckingham, Berkshire, Essex, Hunts, and Peterborough, and Kent).[7] Beyond this, however, little sense can be made of the league table, and planning expenditure among the counties remains much of a mystery.

Police

A study of police expenditure is complicated by the amalgamation of many counties and county boroughs to form a smaller number of police districts.[8]

The league tables reveal that the conurbation capitals (Liverpool, Manchester, Newcastle, and Leeds) spend the most, followed by slightly less important centres, like Hull, Bristol, Nottingham, and Salford. Bottom of the list comes a group of small, industrial cities which are overshadowed by the more important urban capitals. It looks as if police expenditure may be strongly influenced by the importance of a city as a regional or metropolitan centre. Cutting across this trend, however, are the seaside resorts which, though not centres of great importance, spend relatively heavily on police services. Hastings and Eastbourne spent more than Birmingham, and Great Yarmouth, Southend, and Southport only slightly less in 1960/1.

It seaside resorts are removed—as special cases—from the list of county boroughs, and if the remainder are grouped, as they were in Table 13.5, according to the Carruthers urban hierarchy, it can be seen that police spending is associated with the importance of a city as a service centre. Table 13.6 shows that the most important provincial capitals have the highest figures, and that these gradually decline as one goes down the hierarchy, although the curve turns up again at the very bottom. Nevertheless, police and library spending appears to follow the same general pattern.[9]

TABLE 13.6 : Per Capita Police Expenditure (£), by Importance of Service Centre, County Boroughs, 1960/1 and 1972/3

City Rank	Examples	1960/1	1972/3	(n)
Group 2B	Manchester	3.12	10.856	(5)
Group 2C	Cardiff	2.34	8.102	(4)
Groups 3A/3a	Gloucester	2.103	7.493	(27)
Groups 3B/3b	Rochdale	2.148	7.016	(24)
Groups 3C/3c	Merthyr Tydfil	2.198	7.920	(6)
County Borough Average		2.271	7.715	(66)

Note : The total number of observations is 66, because the seaside resorts have not been included, because Carruthers does not classify all county boroughs, and because for comparative reasons, the analysis is limited to authorities which existed in both 1960/1 and 1972/3.

Fire

Fire and police services are often grouped together, and yet correlation analysis suggests they have rather little in common.[10] Fire service expenditure is influenced by Home Office standards of fire cover, which are based on four categories of fire risk.[11]

Class A. Includes concentrations of factories in towns, shopping and business centres in large cities and towns, docks and shipbuilding yards in congested areas.

Class B. Model factory estates, shopping and business centres in smaller cities and towns, old timbered property in medium sized towns, and large seaside holiday resorts.

Class C. Built up areas not falling in Class A or B.

Class D. All other areas.

Given these risk categories one would expect higher spending authorities to have large industrial and commercial areas, and ports and shipyards. The league table for fire expenditure shows this to be the case, in general. Ten ports are in the top twenty-five, and only four are in the bottom twenty-five. Of the remaining fifteen high spenders, most are small industrial county boroughs. In addition, the seaside resorts have higher than average expenditures, and five are in the top twenty-five.

It is difficult to categorise the low spenders, since these cover a fairly wide range of cities, including some of the small industrial authorities, some ports, and some seaside resorts. Consequently a distribution of high and low risk fire areas in only part of the explanation.

The counties show a distinct but different pattern. In the first place, nine of the ten Welsh fire authorities appear in the top twenty, and with an average per capita expenditure of £ 2.026, they are well above the county average. In the second place, of the remaining eleven non-Welsh authorities in the top twenty, seven have above average densities of more than one person per acre (their average is 2.38). Compared with this, fourteen of the bottom twenty have below average densities (their average is 0.49 persons per acre). Low density counties not only have less risk of fire starting and spreading, but it is also more difficult and more expensive to provide them with more than a fairly minimal cover. Sparsely populated counties tend to have a fairly high proportion of part-time and volunteer firemen. For example, in 1972/3, the most sparsely populated county (Westmorland) employed whole to part-time staff in the ratio of 1 : 6, but the most densely populated (Lancashire), had a ratio of 1.6 : 1. It should be noted that most of the high spending Welsh counties have a low density, so that density, as such, will not show up as a significant demographic correlation.

TABLE 13.7 : **Per Capita Fire Expenditures (£), by Fire Risk and Population Density, Among English County Boroughs with Highest and Lowest Expenditures, 1972/73**

	High Density		Low Density	
High Risk	1.643	(8)	1.385	(2)
Low Risk	1.597	(3)	1.387	(9)

1. Note that the classification is approximate since fire risk figures in 1972/3 are estimated from those available for 1977/8.

Highways

The demographic approach explains with a modest degree of success the per capita highways expenditures of the county boroughs, but the league tables suggest ways of improving upon this. The metropolitan capitals are notably heavy spenders, as are the seaside resorts. Presumably the major capitals spend heavily because of their particularly high traffic densities, whereas the seaside resorts do so partly because of their heavy summer traffic, but also because they provide wide and well maintained road to attract tourists and minimise traffic congestion. Casual observation of seaside resorts suggests that they often have exceptionally good roads.

Cities spending the least on highways include many of the smaller, industrial boroughs of the major conurbations, and also some of the smaller free-standing industrial boroughs. The suspicion that the small industrial cities spend relatively little is strengthened by the fact that the smaller residential cities spend an average or above average amount. As simple relationship between an industrial tax base and low highways expenditure, however, is disturbed by the seaside resorts, at one extreme, and by the major capitals at the other.[12]

The demographic approach works rather better in the counties, where spending is highest in the smaller, more rural, and more sparsely populated authorities. In fact, one indicator or another of these variables, plus a high voting turnout, explains 80 per cent of the variance in both 1960/1 and 1972/3. The tables also show a strong regional effect, with nine of the thirteen Welsh counties in the top thirteen spenders in both years.

Public health

Like planning, public health accounts for only a small proportion of total local expenditure (little more than 2%), and like planning it is firmly resistant to the attempts of conventional output studies to pin down the causes of variation, particularly in the county boroughs. An examination of the high and low spenders reveals some regularities, although they are faint and indistinct. The seaside resorts stand out, once again, for their high spending, no doubt in order to maintain a high service quality. The two wealthy suburban authorities of Wallasey and Croydon also spend heavily. The ports are also notable for having an average of £0.60 in 1960/1 compared with a county boroughs average of £0.44. What is also clear, is that public health spending is consistently associated with Labour strength, or an absence of Conservative strength, these being among the few significant variables which oppear in the regression equations.

Politics does not seem to matter as far as public health spending in the counties is concerned where the smaller, more rural, and/or poorer seem to spend the most. Cornwall, Norfolk, Suffolk and Lincolnshire all appear in the top fifteen, as do seven of the thirteen Welsh counties. Only three of the Welsh counties are among the lowest twenty. The latter consists largely, but not exclusively, of the wealthier and/or more urban counties. There are quite a few exceptions to the general pattern, however, and a good deal of the variation remains to be explained in other ways.

Personal health services

One would expect personal health costs to be higher in the poorer, more urban, and more industrial authorities, and so it is in both the counties and the county boroughs, although the association is not strong. In the boroughs, indicators of poverty, poor housing and an aging population are the more powerful, but even they account for no more than 20 per cent of the variance. Nevertheless, Rotherham, Salford, Barnsley, Newcastle, West Ham, Oldham, Smethwick, Bradford, and Gateshead are in the top twenty, compared with more affluent and commerical/residential cities such as the seaside resorts and the county towns, which make up the majority of the bottom twenty. The association between poverty and high spending is not strong, however, because boroughs like Tynemouth, Bootle, Walsall, St. Helens, Barrow, and Dudley also appear in the bottom twenty. As with public health, it is not clear what distinguishes them from similar but high spending boroughs.

Once again, the Welsh counties stand out, with eight of

also high spending, while some English counties with a low density also spend rather little. Besides, if the Welsh counties are excluded, the high spending authorities have a higher population density (0.95 per acre) than the low spending (0.84).

Children's welfare, and social services

The regression equations of the demographic approach have a mixed success with spending on welfare and on children per child, but rather little when the two were amalgamated to form social services. This is to be expected since different types of city spend heavily on the two services, and this cancels out any simple, linear relationships. Taking the children per child figures first, the high spenders are the major urban capitals, and the industrial satellites. At the other extreme the low spenders are primarily the more affluent seaside resorts and county towns, such as Southport, Blackpool, Canterbury, Eastbourne, Ipswich, Gloucester, and Bath.

This pattern is partly reversed for welfare spending, where the high spenders are the more affluent commercial and residential towns, plus a fairly large number of the smallest and poorest industrial boroughs. What confuses this simple pattern, however, is the appearance of some of the small, industrial boroughs among the low spenders on welfare. And in addition there are quite a few boroughs which spend little on both children and welfare. This is quite a mixed them appearing in the top fifteen (they fill the first four places in 1960/1) and only one in the bottom twenty. Many of the remaining high spenders are the more urbanised or industrial counties. In contrast, a clear majority of low spenders are the most rural of the English counties. The exceptional high spending of the rural and sparsely populated Welsh counties obscures the tendency for their English equivalents to spend rather little.

Education

The results of an analysis of education expenditure depends on whether one takes per capita or per pupil figures. So far, expenditures have been analysed on a per capita basis, either because they are community-wide services (e.g. parks or libraries), or because there are no appropriate figures for the target population (e.g. those in need of public housing). But in the case of education, the school age population is known, and the more interesting figure is what is spent on each pupil, rather than what is spent on education per capita of total population.[13] It is worth noting that the greater proportion of pupils in an authority, the higher its per capita education expenditure, but the lower its per pupil spending.

The pupil expenditures are also less well explained by the regression equations of the demographic approach than are per capita figures, although the results are better for the

bag of places, and includes Blackpool, Birkenhead, Bury, St. Helens, Carlisle, Wallasey, and Darlington.

However, something of value emerges from the league tables for they show two fairly strong tendencies which contribute to an explanation :

1. Children's spending is generally highest in the smallest and poorest industrial boroughs, which often have a large proportion of children and bad housing and social conditions.
2. Welfare spending is high in some of the industrial boroughs with high children's spending, but it is generally even higher in the small but affluent commercial and residential boroughs—particularly the seaside resorts and some of the county towns. Whereas poverty and a relatively large old population explains the former, the sheer weight of retired people, though many of them are well off, explains the latter.

Lastly, politics matter to a significant degree for the social services. In both the county and the county borough regressions, the percentage of Labour members of the council is significantly associated with high social services spending, and a political variable of one kind or another is included in three of the four regressions for children's and welfare spending. While it is the low turnout, Labour authorities which spend most on children, it is the high turnout and more affluent authorities which spend most on welfare.

Total expenditure

Total spending is, of course, heavily determined by the major spending services, which are education, housing, highways, police, and social services, and authorities spending more than the average on most or all of these are likely to emerge at the top of the league table for total expenditure. These are likely to be authorities which combine a relatively heavy need for local services (a large working class and school aged population, poor housing and social conditions, and a large hinterland population making demands upon libraries, police, fire, and highways), a relatively good tax base of commercial and industrial property, and a disposition to tax and spend relatively heavily (a large Labour group on the council). The great majority of the top spenders in 1972/3 fit this profile : four are the major conurbation capitals, and fifteen are the smaller, industrial boroughs.

At the other extreme are the predominantly commercial and residential cities which are Conservative controlled, and which have relatively little the seaside resorts, both of the middle class suburbs of Solihull and Wallasey, and an assortment of county towns and commercial centres. The pattern is not perfect, by any means, however, for the low spenders also include some small, industrial boroughs just as some of the league leaders include the county towns.

Because the Welsh counties are so regularly league leaders on a wide range of services, it is no surprise that they also emerge at the top of the table for total expenditure. In fact, twelve of the thirteen are in the top twenty (Flint alone has a low figure, and it is in the bottom twenty in 1972/3), and the Welsh average of £ 102 compares with the English average of £ 80-27.5 per cent higher. The top six counties are Welsh, as are eight of the top ten.

Of the English counties in the top twenty, most are rural but relatively wealthy (Buckinghamshire, Hertfordshire, Gloucestershire, Herefordshire), while many of those at the bottom of the table are urban and/or relatively industrial, but relatively wealthy—Essex, Surrey, West Yorkshire, Lancashire, Nottingham, Derbyshire, and Kent. There are enough exceptions to this general tendency, however, to suggest that further analysis is necessary, and it may well be that the exceptional nature of the Welsh figures has obscured general trends and tendencies among the English counties.

Conclusion

This paper has worked its way through a great mass of data, and although only a small fraction of the statistical material has been presented, there is still far too much wood obscuring the trees. It is possible to draw out some generalisations, however, and these will serve as a basis for more incomes, and taxable capacity', *Public Administration*, 55 (Spring 1977), pl. 38-39.

8. In 1972-73 there were forty-four police authorities in England and Wales and although a large majority covered one or more counties and/or county boroughs, this makes the statistical analysis much less precise, but still enables a rough and ready analysis to be carried out.
9. On sparsity and police expenditure see I.M.T.A., *Local Expenditure and Exchequer Grants*, p. 115
10. The correlations between per capita police and fire expenditure in the counties and county boroughs are not higher than 36 and of not much substantial significance.
11. See, Fire Service Actual Statistics 1977-78, London, C.I.P.F.A., 1978, p. 20.
12. It is important to note that the wealth of a city's resident population may not be a good indicator of the wealth of the local authority. This is because the size of the local authority tax base is primarily dependent upon offices, shops and industrial, rather than domestic property. Therefore it is important to distinguish between the wealth of an authority's resident population, and the wealth of the authority itself. It is perfectly possible for an authority with quite severe social problems to have a relatively good tax base, and this is generally the case in the largest cities, although generally the wealthiest urban authorities are those which combine a wealthy resident population with a large commercial tax base, particularly among the commercial cities, the seaside resorts, and some of the county towns.
13. Per pupil and per capita education expenditures are reasonably strongly correlated in the counties (0.78 and 0.67 in 1960-61 and 1972-73), but not in the county boroughs, where the figures are 0.35 and 0.18.

FOURTEEN

JOHN A. SCHOFIELD

DETERMINANTS OF URBAN SERVICES EXPENDITURES
Fire and Social Services

INTRODUCTION

INVESTIGATION of the determinants of expenditures on local public services (as reviewed, for example, in Wilensky [1970]) has enjoyed an active tradition since the seminal work of (Fabricant [1952]). The thrust of research has frequently been directed to the question of whether scale effects exist in the provision of municipal services and to the related question of optimum city size from the point of view of efficiency in service provision. Size has been alternatively defined in terms of population numbers (e.g. Gabler [1969, 1971] ; Popp and Sebold [1972] ; Weicher and Emerine [1973]), population density (e.g. Gabler [1969, 1971]), Weicher [1970], Walzer [1972]) and geographic area (e.g. Walzer [1972] ; Hufbauer and Severn [1975]). Interest has also been directed to the influence of housing conditions and other socio-economic factors on the level of service provision (e.g. Gabler [1971] ; Weicher [1970, 1972] ; Weicher and Emerine [1973]), as well as to the influence of political factors (Davies [1968], Davies *et al.* [1971a, 1971b, 1972]).

Despite its relevance for purposes of planning public service developments, very little work along these lines has been undertaken in the U.K. Davies *et al.* have sought to explain variations in standards of provision of local services for the aged (Davies [1968], Davies *et al.* [1971a, 1971b), education

(Davies [1968]) and children (Davies [1968], Davies *et al.* [1972]). Detailed as these studies are, their use of factor analysis for defining needs variables obscures the effects on provision of specific influences with which decision-makers might be concerned. Studies providing evidence on the separate effects of specific expenditure determinants appear to be limited to the analysis sponsored by the Royal Commission on Local Government regarding economies of scale in local housing, health and highways (Gupta and Hutton [1968]) and an examination of education expenditure in county councils (Storey [1975]).

The current paper explores the separate influences of selected socio-economic, geographic and political factors on the supply of and demand for municipal fire and social services.* The analysis is applied to what were the non-London boroughs of England and Wales in 1971-72. While the data are thus some few years old, they are the most recent available so far as required census series are concerned. And while local government reorganization has occurred in the meantime, lessons can be provided for current practice.

In the next section of the paper, the estimating model is developed. In the third section, results are presented and in the fourth section, conclusions drawn. Details of definitions and sources of variables are given in Appendix I.

MODEL

Dependent variables in the analysis are fire and social services expenditures met from the rates and rate support grant per 1,000 population. Minor items of income are therefore netted out. It might have been useful to separate operating and capital expenditures, although the lumpiness of most capital expenditures does not create a significant problem of distortion in average total expenditures for any given year since these expenditures are annualized as capital changes.

Independent variables are factors expected to influence the supply of and demand for fire and social services. On the supply side are included :

*Local authority social services have since 1971 comprised care of mothers and young children, child care, services for the physically handicapped, the mentally ill and handicapped, the aged and infirm, and 'problem' families.

Fiscal capacity (FISC)
Scale effect variables
—Population size (POP)
—Population density (DEN)
—Local authority area (AREA)
Political factors (POL)

On the demand side are included factors reflecting need for service :

Demographic conditions
—Population change (POP△)
—Population density (DEN)
—Class composition of the population (CLASS)
—Proportion of the population permanently ill (ILL)
—Age composition of the population (AGE)
—Geographical origin of the population (MIG)
Industrial structure (IND)
Housing conditions (HOUS)
Employment conditions (EMP)

It is not expected that each one of the influences on the demand side will play a role in the determination of expenditure in each type of service. For example, neither ILL nor AGE are expected to affect fire service expenditures (except conceivably as proxies for more fundamental influences). It should further be said that a variety of additional factors specific to particular circumstances will also influence service expenditures in any year. Examples may cover local public issues affecting any municipal function (social, fire or other service), historical tradition, even the relative strength of executive personalities ; and results are to be seen in light of the fact that these influences are not measured.

In the remainder of this section, the expected influence of each supply-and demand-side factor is discussed in terms of specific hypotheses to be tested.

Factors influencing supply of services

Although the rate support grant to local authorities ensures a minimum level of financial resources (equal to the average product of the penny rate standardized for population size), authorities enjoying a greater than 'standard' product of the penny rate retain a financial advantage. Local authority fiscal capacity (FISC) is, therefore, expected to have a positive influence on service expenditures per 1,000 population.

The possibility of scale effects in service provision is also explored on the supply side. In the absence of clearly-defined measures of output in fire and social services, independent variables used to test for scale effects include alternatively population size (POP), population density (DEN) and local authority geographical area (AREA). Scale effects, if they exist, are therefore to be interpreted as relating to these variables rather than to output *per se*. The approximate nature of scale estimates is also to be emphasized since expenditure per 1,000 population as the dependent variable is obviously not a very exact proxy for per unit costs.* Signs on coefficients, of course, cannot be predicted *a priori*.

As a final supply side factor, the influence of the party political balance in local councils (POL) is investigated as it is likely to affect supplier preferences regarding absolute levels of public service as well as preferences for one service as against another. It is expected that the proportion of Labour party representation on local councils will exert a positive impact on expenditures especially in social services. Given the lesser opportunity for the exercise of discretion in the supply of fire services, the impact of political preferences may be lower in that area. Likely collinearity between party political balance and other expenditure determinants on the demand side (for example, class structure) is recognized, and dealt with in the Parameter Estimates Section of the paper.

Factors influencing demand for services

On the demand side, need for services will depend, *inter alia*, on various demographic conditions. The rate of change of population (POP△) over a period prior to the date of sampling may reflect the pressure of demand in either of two ways. On the one hand, the rate of change of population may exert a positive influence on per 1,000 expenditures (at least in social services) if strains on the social fabric of urban centres vary

*The justification for its use rests on both data constraints and precedent from other work (cited earlier).

directly with the rate of growth of population. On the other hand, to the extent that population loss is associated with physical and social deterioration of city environments, a negative influence on per 1,000 expenditures (in both services) would be expected. Density of population (DEN) as it affects the quality of the physical and social environment may also influence the need for both fire and social services. The expected positive effect will interact with the possible supply side effect as discussed earlier.

The class structure of the population (CLASS) may also be expected to influence expenditures, the greater the proportion of the population in lower income groups the higher the expected expenditure per 1,000 population. In the case of fire services, CLASS should reflect the impact of such influences as social mores and the state of the building stock.

Other population characteristics (the proportion of the population permanently ill (ILL,) the age composition (AGE) and the immigrant structure (MIG)) are likely of themselves to influence only the need for social services. The greater the proportion of the population permanently ill and in very young and very old age groups, the higher is expected to be per 1,000 expenditure. A direct effect of the immigrant structure of boroughs on the need for social services may be felt because immigrant communities rely to a greater or lesser extent on state support than indigenous communities.

In addition to the influence of population characteristics, the propensity to use either fire or social services may be affected by the industrial structure (IND) of a local authority area. This is expected to be the case in so far as risks of fire and social casualty vary with economic activity. It is reasonable, too, to hypothesize as elsewhere (e.g. Weicher [1970, 1972] ; Weicher and Emerine [1973]) that housing conditions (HOUS) may influence the need for both fire and social services. The better are housing conditions, the lower are expected to be the levels of per 1,000 expenditure in both services. Here as with the variable (CLASS), the analysis tests for the prevalence of selected slum-generated social costs in which cost-benefit analysts have been so interested (e.g. Mao [1966], Messner [1968]).

TABLE 14.1 : Social Services : Estimated Coefficients

	1	2	3	4	5
Constant	8354.069†	16655.639†	3994.754†	3496.585†	2181.094
	(5.543)	(3.339)	(2.977)	(2.284)	(1.292)
ᵃFISC	2432.153†	1963.290	2049.332	1989.826	3255.788†
	(2.318)	(1.813)	(1.836)	(1.766)	(2.825)
DEN					
POP△	—6281.871†	—6830.780†	—7945.599†	—7419.315†	—6973.145†
	(—4.002)	(—4.139)	(—4.721)	(—4.509)	(—4.194)
HOUS	—5911.826				
	(—3.681)				
ᵇEMP		—13207.110†			
		(—2.423)			
ᶜPOL			1123.683		
			(1.719)		
CLASS				3918.973	
				(1.702)	
ILL					75620.717†
					(2.317)
ᵈAGE^{-3}	—9.195†	—11.599†	—13.083†	—13.646†	—96.428
	(—2.523)	(—3.103)	(—3.366)	(—35.465)	(—1.525)
ᵉMIG	10079.70	16945.853†	16985.42†	12217.082†	15645.011†
	(1.931)	(2.962)	(2.948)	(2.210)	(2.695)
R^2	.466	.415	.402	.392	.369
R^{-2}	.430	.375	.360	.351	.324

TABLE 14.1 (*Contd.*)

	6	7	8	9	10	11
Constant	8879.540†	20070.461†	2828.101	2264.453	119.432	16773.893†
	(5.276)	(3.650)	(1.905)	(1.369)	(0.601)	(2.972)
[a]FISC	236.519†	1793.918	2017.891	1934.401	3350.536†	2215.089
	(2.052)	(1.521)	(1.689)	(1.590)	(2.671)	(18.83)
DEN	45.800	51.439	91.230†	72.452†	56.013†	67.012†
	(1.700)	(1.793)	(3.265)	(2.640)	(2.010)	(2.294)
POP△						
HOUS	—7147.692†					
	(—4.149)					
[b]EMP		—17307.569†				—14725.240†
		(—2.922)				(—2.473
[c]POL			2065.144†			1290.26
			(2.924)			(1.980)
CLASS				6123.429†		
				(2.550)		
ILL					98456.869†	
					(2.826)	
[d]AGE−3	—9.738†	—12.749†	—15.940†	—16.386†	—102.668	—14.343†
	(—2.411)	(—3.086)	(—3.763)	(—3.831)	(—1.491)	(—3.472)
[e]MIG	9857.306	18622.053†	18227.996†	12258.709†	17118.893†	20111.709†
	(1.745)	(2.995)	(2.962)	(2.054)	(2.718)	(3.273)
R^2	.375	.309	.316	.292	.254	.344
$\bar{R}^2$	.332	.262	.267	244	.201	.290

n = 80 (76 for equations including POL)

t-values in parentheses : † = significant at the 5 per cent level at least

(a) FISC = $FISC_3$ (Appendix I) b) EMP = EMP_2 (Appendix I) c) POL = POL_1 (Appendix I) d) AGE = AGE_2 (Appendix I) e) MIG = MIG_2 (Appendix I)

TABLE 14.2 : **Fire Services : Estimated Coefficients**

	1	2	3	4	5	6	7
Constant	8266.441† (4.406)	2167.252† (17.212)	1624.404† (6.392)	8931.157† (4.433)	1738.850† (9.259)	1240.713† (4.643)	1428.618† (2.514)
POP	—0.002† (—3.498)	—0.002† (—3.254)	—0.001† (—3.084)	—0.003† (—3.603)	—0.003† (—3.349)	—0.003† (—3.049)	—0.003† (—3.731)
POP2	0.002† (2.510)	0.002† (2.429)	0.002† (2.232)	0.002† (2.838)	0.003† (2.960)	0.002† (2.654)	0.003 (2.978)
FISC							275.197 (0.579)
DEN				17.488 (1.491)	32.323† (2.714)	24.040† (2.081)	33.095† (2.748)
POP△	—2042.404† (—3.114)	—2453.009† (—2.457)	—2224.029† (—3.346)				
EMP	—6445.228† (—3.321)			—7359.034† (—3.497)			
POL			238.486 (0.967)		491.308 (1.934)		543.963† (2 007)
CLASS				2107.330† (2.599)		2540,707† (3.019)	
R^2	.360	.271	.328	.995	.227	.267	.231
$\overline{R^2}$	.324	.228	.291	.255	.181	.226	.173

n = 77 (73 for equations including POL)

t-values in parentheses : † = significant at the 5 per cent level at least

Data definitions as in Table 14.1

Social services

The significance or near-significance (at the 5 per cent level) of the coefficient on the variable FISC provides some evidence that the better-off municipalities retain an advantage in service provision despite the purpose of the resources element of the rate support grant to introduce a measure of equality into the financial resources of local authorties. This of course is because, while authorities with below average resources are brought up to average, authorities with above average resources are not reduced to average.

Unreported tests revealed that when the variables DEN and POP△ were used together, DEN was persistently insignificant. Yet without POP△, DEN is significant or nearly so (at the 5 per cent level at least). It is therefore apparent that these variables capture very similar influences on service provision, reflecting the correlation between urban crowding and population loss, or flight to the suburbs (see the matrix of correlation coefficients in Appendix II). The greater the degree of density or loss, the higher the level of social services expenditure per 1,000 population, presumably in large part the effect of the state of the social environment in towns and cities.

It is also possible that the findings for DEN (and also POP△ as a result of collinearity between the two variables) could incorporate effects of scale in the provision of services, although it is not possible to separate these out from the influence of urban social conditions. Given what would be conflicting implications for scale, however, such effects, if any, would not be more important than social conditions ; and tests on other scale variables provided no evidence of significance. The variables POP and AREA were highly insignificant in all forms tested and are not included in reported results.*

Except for using EMP and POL together in only one formulation (equation 11), the variables HOUS, EMP, POL, CLASS and ILL are included separately in recognition of the fairly high degree of collinearity between them (Appendix II).

---

*Among several forms tried, scale variables were tested in quadratic form for evidence of U-shaped cost functions.

As anticipated, the better are housing conditions, the lower is expenditure per 1,000 on social services. This provides some evidence regarding one form of slum-generated social costs. It also reflects the effects of class structure on social services use, effects reflected directly in the findings for CLASS. The greater the proportion of the urban workforce who are unskilled or semi-skilled, the greater the level of social services expenditure per 1,000 population. Also as anticipated, the higher the level of employment, the lower the degree of support.

Results for the variable POL provide some evidence that the higher the proportion of council seats held by the Labour party, the higher the per 1,000 level of social service expenditure. While this finding may indicate something about party political preferences, it also reflects the collinearity between party structure and underlying social/class conditions.

Results for the variable ILL are significant with the expected sign. The higher the proportion of the population (over age 15) permanently sick, the higher is per 1,000 expenditure on social services.

The variable AGE enters into equations in highly significant non-linear form, the coefficient indicating, as expected, that the greater the proportion of the population who are very young or very old, the greater the per 1,000 expenditure on social services. The proportion of immigrants in the population (MIG) also appears to have a generally significant positive influence on expenditures. It is important, however, to interpret this finding with care. It may indicate merely that the underlying socio-economic conditions which account for high social services expenditures are the same conditions which attract immigrant workers to urban centres.

It is to be noted, finally, that IND, the proportion of the workforce in manufacturing, was insignificant in all tests conducted and is accordingly excluded from final formulations reported.

Fire services

The findings for fire services reveal strong evidence of the existence of a U-shaped relation between expenditures per 1,000 and population. In terms of scale effects (approximately measured) it is suggested that economies are derived up to a population size of at least around 500,000 above which diseconomies set in. Coefficients are stable and highly significant across all equations.

The variables DEN and POP△ again serve as alternative explanatory variables, POP△ remaining the more powerful of the two. The higher is urban population density or the greater the outflow of population (over the preceding five years), the higher is per 1,000 expenditure. Presumably these findings reflect the effect of the general condition of the urban environment upon fire risk. The more densely-populated urban areas will clearly be the more built-up boroughs and will typically also be those with a more debilitated building stock. These are likely also to be the boroughs from which population is leaving, either voluntarily or under the impetus of urban renewal.

The hypotheses appear to be confirmed that CLASS and EMP would exercise an influence on fire expenditures, presumably because these factors reflect social conditions and the state of the building stock. Per 1,000 expenditures vary significantly with the proportion of the workforce in lower socio-economic groups (positively) and with the proportion of the workforce employed (inversely). The variable HOUS would be expected to have captured the same sorts of influence, but it proved to be insignificant though negative as anticipated in sign.

There is some evidence that the higher the proportion of council seats held by the Labour party, the higher the level of fire expenditures per 1,000. However, the influence of POL is neither so clear nor so strong as in the case of social services, a finding anticipated in light of the generally greater discretionary element attaching to social services expenditures, as well as Labour preferences expected to favour services for the disadvantaged.

Finally, fiscal capacity (FISC), industrial structure (IND) and geographical area (AREA) appear not to exert a significant influence on fire expenditures. In the case of the FISC, the sign was positive as expected in all tests, the insignificance of the coefficient testifying to the presumed low degree of discretion in fire service expenditure decisions. While insignificant, the coefficient on IND was always negative, and in some cases only barely insignificant at the 5 per cent level. The coefficient on AREA was both highly insignificant and unstable.

SUMMARY AND CONCLUSIONS

While it has clearly not been possible to measure all the many influences on social and fire services expenditures, results confirm a number of *a priori* hypotheses connected with the supply of and demand for these services (in non-London boroughs 1971-72). Collinearity between explanatory variables (see Appendix II) is dealt with by fitting alternative formulations which avoid the severest intercorrelations.

On the supply side, excess of fiscal capacity over average in municipalities has a positive impact on expenditures per 1,000 population, but is statistically significant only for social services. This finding confirms the expectation that financial resources in excess of average are channelled more readily into areas allowing substantial discretion in spending decisions such as social services than into services such as fire where an adequate standard of provision is probably achieved, whatever the strength of the local fiscal base.

The evidence on scale effects in service provision has to be seen in light of measures used. Results suggest that economies (measured in terms of expenditure per 1,000) are achieved in fire services up to a population size of at least around 500,000 and that thereafter diseconomies set in, a finding of some interest in light of the creation of larger local government units in 1974. In social services, there is no clear evidence of the existence of scale effects. Geographic area as a measure of scale does not appear to have any significant effect on expenditures in either service, and if density of population exerts an effect it remains inseparable from the variable's impact on the demand side.

Finally on the supply side, there is evidence that the higher the proportion of council seats held by the Labour party, the higher is expenditure per 1,000 in both services. This reflects expected supplier preferences for government spending. The evidence is also somewhat stronger and the effect greater in the case of social services. This reflects expected preferences as between services.

On the demand side, crowding and population decline exert a positive influence on spending in both services, findings which probably reflect in large part the impact of the quality of the urban environment on social casualty and fire risk.

The state of the housing stock also reflects the degree to which the urban environment is in decay and results indicate that the lower the standard of housing, the greater the expenditure on social services. Housing conditions show no impact, by contrast, on fire service expenditures. Information of this kind relating to slum-generated social costs may provide a basis for estimating some of the benefits of urban renewal.

Results for class structure and employment conditions, factors closely correlated with housing conditions, show an influence on expenditure in both services. The greater the proportion of the workforce in lower socio-economic groups and the lower the proportion employed, the higher the per 1,000 expenditure in both social and fire services.

Three other demand side influences, the proportion of the population permanently sick, the age structure of the population and the proportion of immigrants in the population, affect only social services expenditure. The greater the proportion of the population (over age 15) permanently sick, the greater the proportion of the population under the age of 5 and over the age of 65, and the greater the proportion of immigrants in the population, the higher is per 1,000 expenditure. This last result is to be interpreted with particular care as it may simply be the case that the underlying socio-economic conditions which influence social services expenditures are also those which influence immigrant settlement.

Lastly, there is no evidence that the industrial structure of urban centres (as measured by the proportion of the workforce in manufacturing) has any significant effect on expenditures in either fire or social services. This is an area which would bear further research.

So far as policy making is concerned, the method of analysis outlined here would appear to be relevant in the following ways. First, similar models covering all services could be used in the on-going search for an improved rate support grant formula which would bring the needs and spending abilities of widely different authorities into balance. Second, judgements regarding expenditure levels in different authorities would be more soundly based if built upon recognition of the range of factors affecting needs for and capabilities to provide services, rather than, as is so often the case, on the simple criterion of divergence from an average level, unstandardized for various expenditure influences. Third, investigation of scale effects in individual services is clearly relevant to the continuing debate concerning local government structure. And finally, information regarding the impact on service expenditure of variables over which policy-makers can exert some control (e.g., crowding, housing conditions, industrial structure) should assist in the formulation of policies at the local level.

ACKNOWLEDGEMENT

The author is grateful for comments on this paper from an anonymous referee.

REFERENCES

Davies, B. (1968), *Social Needs and Resources in Local Services*, London, Michael Joseph Ltd.

Davies, B., Barton, A., McMillian, I. and V. Williamson (1971a), *Variations in Services for the Aged : A Causal Analysis*, London, G. Bell and Sons.

Davies, B., Barton, A. and I. McMillan (1971b), "Variations in the Provision of Local Authority Health and Welfare Services for the Elderly : A Comparison between Counties and County Boroughs", *Soc. Econ. Admin.*, 5, pp. 100–124.

Davies, B., Barton, A. and I. McMillan (1972), *Variations in Children's Services among British Urban Authorities: A Causal Analysis*, London, G. Bell and Sons.

Department of Environment and Welsh Office (1973), *Rates and Rateable Values in England and Wales*, London, HMSO.

Fabricant, S., (1952), *The Trend of Government Activity in the US Since 1900*, New York, NBER.

Gabler, L.R. (1969), "Economies and Diseconomies of Scale in Urban Public Sectors", *Land Econ.*, 45. pp. 425–434.

Gabler, L.R. (1971), "Population Size as a Determinant of City Expenditures and Employment—Some Further Evidence", *Land Econ.* 47, pp 130–138.

Gupta, S.P. and J.P. Hutton (1968), *Economies of Scale in Local Government Services,* Royal Commission on Local Government in England, Research Studies No. 3.

Hufbauer, G.C. and B.W. Severn (1975), "Municipal Costs and Urban Area", *J. Urb. Econ.*, 2, pp. 199–211.

Institute of Municipal Treasurers and Accountants (1967), *Fire Services Statistics, 1966–67*, London, IMTA Society of County Treasurers.

Institute of Municipal Treasurers and Accountants (1972), *Fire Services Statistics, 1971–72*, London, IMTA Society of County Treasurers.

Institute of Municipal Treasurers and Accountants (1973), *Local Health and Social Services Statistics, 1971–72*, London, IMTA Society of County Treasurers.

Mao, J.C.T. (1966), "Efficiency in Public Urban Renewal Expenditures through Benefit-Cost Analysis", *J. Am. Inst. Planners*, 32 pp. 95–107.

Messner, S.D. (1968), "Urban Re-development in Indianapolis: A Benefit-Cost Analysis," *J. Reg. Sci.*, 8, pp. 145--158.

Municipal Journals Ltd. (1971), *Municipal Yearbook*, London, Municipal Journals Ltd.

Office of Population and Census Surveys (1966), *Sample Census*, London, HMSO.

Office of Population and Census Surveys (1071), *Census*, London, HMSO.

Popp, D.O. and F.D. Sebold (1972), "Quasi Returns to Scale in the Provision of Police Service", *Pub. Fin.*, XXVII, pp. 46–61.

Storey, D.J. (1975), "Statistical Analysis of Education Expenditure in County Councils", *Loc. Gov. Stud.*, 1, pp. 39–57.

Walzer, N. (1972), "Economies of Scale and Municipal Police Services: The Illinois Experience", *R. Econ. Stat.*, LIV, pp. 431–438.

Weicher, J.C. (1972), "The Effect of Central City Expenditures: Some Overlooked Factors and Problems", *Nat. Tax. J.*, XXIII, pp. 379–396.

Weicher, J.C. (1972), "The Effect of Urban Renewal on Municipal Service Expenditures", *J. Pol. Econ.*, 80, pp. 86–101.

Weicher, J.C. and R.J. Emerine (1973), "Econometric Analysis of State and Local Aggregate Expenditure Functions", *Pub. Fin.*, XXVIII, pp. 69–83.

Wilensky, G. (1970), Determinants of Local Government Expenditure", in Crecine, J.P. (ed.), *Financing the Metropolis*, Beverly Hills, Sage Publications.

APPENDIX—I

DATA DEFINITIONS (AND SOURCES)*

Dependent Variables :

Fire and social service expenditures met from rates and rate support grant per 1,000 population (IMTAa, IMTAb).

Independent Variables (showing alternative definitions where used) :

$FISC_1$ = rateable value per capita (DEWO, Table 7 ; IMTAb)

$FISC_2$ = penny rate product per capita (IMTAb)

$FISC_3$ = adjusted penny rate product standard penny rate product (IMTAb)**

POP = population size (000s) (IMTAb)

DEN = population per acre (000s) (IMTAb)

AREA = acreage (IMTAb)

LOP_1 = proportion of council seats held by Labour (MJ)

POL_2 = labour control dummy (unity for Labour control ; zero otherwise) (MJ)

POL_3 = labour majority dummy (unity for Labour majority ; zero otherwise) (MJ)

POP△ = proportionate change in population 1966—71 (IMTAa ; IMTAb)

CLASS = proportion of work force in socio-economic groups 7, 10 11, 15 (OPCSa, County Leaflets, Table 4)***

AGE_1 = proportion of the population over age 65 (IMTAc)

AGE_2 = proportion of the population under age 5 and over age 65 (IMTAc)

MIG_1 = proportion of the population born outside UK (OPCSb, County Reports, Part I, Table 13)

MIG_2 = proportion of the population born in new Commonwealth countries (OPCSb, County Reports Part I Table 13)

ILL = proportion of the population over age 15 permanently sick (OPCSb, County Reports, Part I, table 18)

IND = proportion of work force in manufacturing (OPCSa, Country Leaflets, Table 3)***

HOUS = proportion of households having exclusive use of hot

water, fixed bath, inside WC (OPCSb, County Reports-Part III, Table 25)

EMP_1 = proportion of the economically active population in employment (OPCSb, County Reports, Part I, Table 18)

EMP_2 = proportion of economically active males in employment (OPCSb, County Reports, Part I, Table 18)

---

*IMTAa = Institute of Municipal Treasurers and Accountants (1967)

IMTAb = Institute of Municipal Treasurers and Accountants (1972)

IMTAc = Institute of Municipal Treasurers and Accountants (1973)

DEWO = Department of Environment and Welsh Office (1973)

MJ = Municipal Yearbook (1971)

OPCSa = Office of Population and Census Surveys (1966)

OPCSb = Office of Population and Census Surveys 1971)

** In cases where the penny rate product was less than standard it was adjusted to equality with standard in order to reflect the effect of the rate support grant in guaranteeing all boroughs a fiscal base at least equal to the standard.

*** There is an assumption in using this series that proportionsdid not alter significantly between 1966 and 1971.

APPENDIX II

MATRIX OF CORRELATION COEFFICIENTS

	POP	POP^2	AREA	FISC	DEN^2	POP △	CLASS	HOUS	EMP	ILL	POL	AGE	MIG	IND
POP		.93	.90	−.02	.40	−.23	.02	−0.6	−.11	−.04	−.03	.14	.24	.08
POP^2	.93		.80	−.04	.32	.24	.05	−.05	−.13	−.00	−.02	,08	.15	.10
AREA	.90	.80		−.02	.04	−.07	−.03	.01	−.02	−.03	.07	.15	.23	.15
FISC	−.02	−.04	−.02		−.05	.09	−.33	.23	.20	−.34	−.32	.11	.04	−.28
DEN	.40	.32	.04	−.05		−.41	·15	−.26	−.28	.03	−.16	.03	.05	−.15
POP △	−.23	−·24	−.07	.09	−.41		−.29	.31	.38	−.25	−.15	.07	−.02	−,08
CLASS	.02	.05	−.03	−.33	.15	−.29		−.51	−.54	.47	.57	−0.5	.04	.22
HOUS	−.06	−.05	.01	.23	−.26	.31	−.51		.47	.59	−.29	.26	−.10	−.17
EMP	−.11	−.13	−.02	.20	−.28	.38	−.54	.47		−.57	−.31	.35	.27	.24
ILL	−.04	−.00	−.00	−.34	.03	−.25	.47	−.59	−.57		.46	.23	−.23	−.07
POL	−.03	−.02	.07	−.32	−.16	−.15	.57	−.29	−.31	.46		−.13	−.23	−.14
AGE	.14	.08	.15	.11	.03	.07	−.05	.26	.36	−.23	−.13		.05	.06
MIG	.24	.15	.23	.04	.05	−.02	.04	−.10	.27	−.23	−.23	0.5		.48
IND	.08	.10	.15	−.28	−.15	−.08	.22	−.17	.24	−.07	.14	.06	.48	

Coefficient for POL based on reduced sample (see earlier).

PART TWO

CITIZEN PARTICIPATION

FIFTEEN

PETER C. DIENEL

NEW OPTIONS FOR PARTICIPATORY DEMOCRACY

THE discussion on the necessity of enlarged citizen participation has more or less reached a point of general consensus. Controversial, however, is the question of how to install the necessary participation into the different processes of decision making.

The classic instruments of parliamentary democracy as well as the commonly used techniques of citizen participation are of limited capacity. They cannot be enlarged without negative side effects for the situation involved and for society as a whole. We are forced to look for new ways if we want to increase opportunities of participation.

There are countless situations in which millions of people get dissatisfied by being regulated from above. A new technique of participation, therefore, must provide a base that is replicable, i.e. it must offer chances for a great number of people. To be useful as an additional mode of citizen participation, a model, moreover, has to take into account certain requirements. Among these are :

— *information*. Democracy should not develop in the direction where more and more people decide more and more often on more and more issues about which they do not know enough. New models of participation have to provide the chance for the ordinary

Paper presented at the "European meeting on Applied Urban Research, Essen", Oct. 2-4, 1981.

citizen to catch up with the information advantage held by experts and administration.

— *time*. To select, understand, and apply the necessary information requires time. People making public decisions generally get the time they need in their jobs as civil servants, planners, judges, etc. The citizen, however, is expected to use his leisure time to work through the necessary information. New modes of participation should set the citizen free from the stress of his ordinary job and should grant him sufficient time to carry out his participatory responsibility.

— *equal opportunity*. The social gadget we look for should be unbiassed. It should recruit its members from all the social strata of the affected area.

— *seriousness of the situation*. The sought for technique must present problems which cannot be misunderstood by those participating as simulation games or ordinary adult education. Participants should be aware that their taking part is not a game but serious business. The findings of the participation scheme should not remain on paper. They should be channeled formally into the mandated planning procedures and, thus, have real influence.

— *neutral organizational structure*. To take part in a public decision should not mean to strive at the same time for your own career or reelection. Moreover, the needed participation technique should create as little self-interest as possible, which organizations customarily produce. By limiting participation to one case and to a certain period of time, the intensity of such interests could be curbed, if not reduced entirely.

Characteristics of the model

Keeping in mind these requirements, it would seem that the so-called Planning Cell which is to be presented here, is one way to bring about additional participation opportunities.[1]

The Planning Cell is a group of people (ages 18 to 68), selected at random. It exists for a limited period of time during which the participants work full-time on the problem at hand. In order to compensate for their lost earnings, they are remunerated out of public funds.

Since the Planning Cell is designed to tackle clearly defined problems, it cannot choose its own tasks. The task is determined by the responsible authorities and the institution in charge of running the Planning Cells. Not every problem is suited to be coped with by a Planning Cell.[2] On the other hand, since the issues are chosen, it is possible to assign to the groups disadvantaged, disliked, or demanding problems. Information relevant to the specific case under consideration is made available to the participating citizens. Besides the necessary technical information, the views of various interest groups have to be presented. This means, that the sources of the crucial information have to be tied into the Planning Cell process. This can be done through assessment sessions, outdoor inspections, or (this is what we have done most often) through hearings, where those affected, the consumers and experts, give their points of view. Officials of the administration concerned are available for any additional information which may be requested. A 'process escort' aides the group, presenting it with schedule and helping to organize its work.

The results from the Planning Cells will be brought into the institutionalized planning process. For this reason, they must be summarized in some presentable form. One way to do this is through what we call a 'Citizens 'Report'.

To keep this technique replicable, the size of the ground should be standardized. It seems favorable to have around 25 persons in each Planning Cell. This allows for some internal division of labour while ensuring a group situation small enough to be rewarding.

Some characteristics did not manifest themselves until the experimental phase began. The model is suited to have the same set of issues considered by several groups either simultaneously or in sequence. In addition, the Planning Cell should be able to secure a motivation to participate and access to necessary information, independently of whether one is directly affected or not in any given case. This would mean that Planning Cells could be assigned to non-neighborhood problems, such as those at the state or federal level. Test runs have already proven that people from non-affected areas are able to cooperate in Planning Cells as deeply committed to produce reasonable results as affected participants are.

Outputs

Every technique of participation has to be ultimately judged by what it achieves. The Planning Cell is capable of accomplishing factual results which are applicable to different processes of planning, evaluating, or regulating. For these processes, the 'Citizens' Report' of the Planning Cell provides more solid results than those of some other participation techniques. Data are qualified by the way they are generated :

— task-oriented,
— heterogeneous with respect to values,
— sufficiently informed,
— rational,
— assessing not only present, but also future needs,
— and relatively independent of special interests.

If subjects are chosen where a more rational approach is helpful, the Cell's results will facilitate the implementation of the planned measures, even if they seem to be controversial. The output of the Planning Cell proves to have a highly legitimizing effect.

As true for all types of citizen participation, the Planning Cell has its side effects in addition to the intended planning output. This 'spill-over' from the Planning Cell, however, seems to be considerably functional for society, for the group, and the individual. Although this topic has been discussed at length already,[3] I should like to mention some side effects here.

— The participation techniques that we know of strengthen the positions of the established social strata. Compared with this, the Planning Cell offers fresh possibilities. The test runs were undertaken with a large portion of participants from low income groups, foreign labor, or from all the silent majorities which until now have acted like minorities in relation to the respective decision processes.

— Organized interests dominate in many respects. One is tempted to speak of a silent exploitation of the non-organized by the organized. I do not refer here to definite groups of people. We all are involved in different issues on one side or the other. However, there are areas in life, personal or public, which are structurally disadvantaged.

In the Planning Cell those areas have a better chance. Here the members meet each other and work together in the absence of the representatives, leaders, and supervisors of organized interests. Compared with the situation in other opinion 'markets', the organized interests will not enjoy their favourable terrain in the Planning Cell.

— In the areas of 'administration' and 'politics',[4] the number of given positions is comparatively limited. The nucleus of people taking part in the making of political decisions is relatively small. Today, the vast part of the population remains within the area of the 'audience'. Considering this, the Planning Cell offers new roles which are able to multiply themselves with time. This would mean a tendency toward a redistribution of positions within the political subsystem. The actors in these roles are recruited out of areas where only audience-roles had been available. Yet, the functions these people now fulfill in their limited task are located in the central area of the decision making system.

— Countries, where segregated social positions build up latent conflicts, try to implement integration by having people of different backgrounds meet in task-oriented, small-group situations. In the Planning Cell, too, very diverse social positions are present, since its members are picked at random. The experience of having accomplished a meaningful task together has an impact on the extent prejudice sprouts between social groups and classes. Though evaluation is difficult, the willingness to work in heterogeneous settings and the acceptance of arguments from the other side in the Planning Cells already signal a change of attitudes.

— Massive doubts concerning parliamentary democracy are growing—and not only in Germany. The Planning Cell technique may help to overcome some of this distrust. If one sees a planning procedure that is fair, competent, and efficient, one will be inclined to transfer one's positive attitude not only to other cases solved in a similar way, but also to the decision making machinery as such. Operating successfully, the Planning Cell frees parliamentary and governmental institutions from the burdens of false expectations.

— Becoming senator does something to a man. A person taking part in a Planning Cell, exercising evaluation processes, finds himself being used as an expert in a short, but rewarding situation. This person will tend to remember this experience. The most fundamental 'spill-over' of the Planning Cell is its effects on the individual. Here everybody taking part gets a chance to gain self-esteem, self-identity, and a new identification as a citizen.

Test runs

During recent years the Planning Cell model has been tested in several trial runs. To reduce the risk always connected with innovations, we started off with small scale experiments in towns not too big for ourpr ecarious beginings and without informing the press. The size of the experiments can be measured (see table 15.1) in the number of full-time workdays the participants served in the groups. The first test runs were financed through research funds, e.g. the Volkswagen Foundation or the Minister of the Interior of Northrhine-Westfalia. The later ones got part of their necessary funds from the cooperating cities as well.

The Planning Cells up to now have dealt with urban renewal issues (see table : issues of planning). This is the field in which citizen participation in Germany is thought to be urgently needed. Therefore, the funds and interest available in this area combined to give us a starting point here. This however, does not mean the Planning Cell technique is limited to this specific area.

Every attempt to make an innovation work meets with resistance. At the beginning of each test run there have been those who felt threatened by the model one way or the other. Generally speaking, an implementation of the Planning Cell technique has to reckon with 'irritation' within a least four discernible groups. Their uneasiness finds expression in various ways :

— *Administration* : Officeholders feel reluctant to give citizens access to the responsibilities they have been entrusted with. "There is enough impediment to decision making with pressure from special interests already." Besides, citizens are not thought to be able to contribute anything new to the process.
— *Elected bodies* : Representatives feel they do not get enough money themselves for the necessary improvements in their working capacity. "We need secretaries and assistants, and not paid citizens".
— *Political parties* : They are afraid that new forms of citizen participation will ultimately minimize their function as opinion leaders.
— *Public volunteers* : Confronted with the Planning Cell model, people volunteering in public service areas feel potentially degraded in their important functions within the community. They are deeply convinced of the necessity and dignity of a volunteer's devotion to the common good. "Drafted people are no substitute for us". The truth is that society will never be able to do without these kinds of people. Yet, with respect to the Planning Cell, these arguments resemble those in history where the attitude was prevalent that the installation of a social security system was equivalent to an asault upon the charity ball.

TABLE 15.1 : **Test Runs of the Planning Cell Model in Germany**

Date	Project area (population)	Implementation of the model: number of groups	Implementation of the model: groups with identical programs	Implementation of the model: full-time workdays served in planning cells	Issue of planning	Output for the mandated planning processes: reaction of the public (press)	Output for the mandated planning processes: editing a Citizens Report (CR)	Output for the mandated planning processes: communication of results	Output for the mandated planning processes: acceptance
1972-73	*Schwelm* (34,000)	3	—	91	garbage disposal	—	—	mayor listens to the discussions	—
1974-75	*Haspe Valley* (Hagen) (33,000)	8	yes	381	urban renewal	+	—	oral presentation to the city administration	+
1978-79	*Solingen* (175,000)	8	yes	414	design of a recreation park (former Barenloch dumping area)	++	yes	CR presented to the city parliament (Rat der Stadt)	+ +
1979	*Cologne* (980,000	10	yes	964	rebuilding of the historic Town Hall area	++ ++	yes	CR presented to the city parliament (Rat der Stadt)	++

The fact that Planning Cells were formed despite such fears, indicates the need for additional means of participation. As the Planning Cells commenced their work, the afore mentioned apprehension usually proved unfounded. People, having a chance to work with a Planning Cell, seem less and less moved to resist. The output of the participants' groups has proven to be reasonable and advantageous even to those affected. The reaction of the local press has been positive and the acceptance of the results (see table) remarkably high.

The results of the test runs were documented on two levels. Observation records and minutes taken according to sociological standards were condensed to papers describing certain elements of the experiments. The evaluation and decisions of the citizen planners were also documented through different media (e.g. maps, drawings, questionaires, models).

After the Solingen test run, more than 150 maps had to be analyzed ; after the Cologne test run 50 models of the area in question had to be data-processed (see Figure 15.1). The collected data accumulated went into recommendations contained in the 'Citizens Reports'[5]) which were then presented to the administrative body in charge.

Perspectives

Right now we are starting new test pro jects. They will not so much concentrate on communal problems, but rather focus on regional or even national ones, like highway routing, assessment of energy systems or third world trade issues. With these topics, we are still running zero performances. Considering the possibilities the designed technique is making available to us, the Planning Cell model stands at the very beginning of its development.

In the Wuppertal Research Unit, we already calculate theoretical designs for planning systems of high capacity. Such systems could institutionalize a fresh access to participation for millions of citizens. These people will have the chance to work in a task-oriented manner, remunerated and deeply engaged for a limited period of time. They should be incorporated into the 'goals programs', identifying future priorities for the state (*Land*) and at the federal level. They should be used in all

Fig. 15.1 : Some of the models turned in by the 50 task groups of the Cologne Planning Cell

fields where specifically non-affected people bring about solutions to some of the unpopular problems of our times through participating. Remuneration on such a scale will be a heavy public investment in citizenship—a most worthwhile one.

The selected citizens generally accept the invitation to take part, enjoy their group work with their unknown counterparts, like to concentrate on the long-term aspects of our society, and do labor their way towards possible solutions. This could be observed e.g. in the hard work performed by the ten Planning Cells in the Cologne project during their plenary sessions and 400 task group meetings.

The Planning Cell technique requires a relatively large amount of time and effort. In particular, the preparation of a definite project, i.e. the recruiting of the participants at random as well as collecting the necessary information and making it available, is rather time-consuming. Evaluating and editing the results during the follow up phases requires much effort, also.

For the next couple of years, the problems the groups are offered to work on have to be carefully selected. Not every problem we have is suited to be handled in this manner. We will have to find out what works and does not work.

Communication always brings with it chances for manipulation. Within the citizen groups this danger is already reduced by providing information from different interest groups. However, additional safety devices against manipulation ought to be developed.

People functioning in parties, interest groups, parliaments, or in public administrations are tied to the vested interests of those organizational entities. We know of certain problems which could be solved better and earlier if such organizational interests could be counterbalanced more effectively by the long-term common interest expressed by ordinary people. Moreover, people functioning in parties, interest groups, parliaments, or in public administrations monopolize the opportunity to identify themselves with the common good and to develop a special sense of obligation. This opportunity has to be disseminated among more people. Every adult citizen deserves the chance to deliberate on public interest issues seriously. How else can be identify himself with the common goals of his city, of Europe, or of mankind ?

The new participation technique of the Planning Cell is highly formalized and not inexpensive, yet, it produces useful results, and it opens new options for participatory democracy.

FOOTNOTES

1. P.C. Dienel : Die Planungszelle. Eine Alternative zur Establishment-Demokratie. Westdeutscher Verlag. Opladen 1978.
2. The proposed model is limited to a certain range a problems. This is discussed in *Die Planungszelle*, pp. 160-165.
3. See : *Die Planungszelle*. pp, 173-224.
4. Luhmann distinguishes three different sectors in the political subsystem : the administration, the politicians, and the audience. See : Niklas Luhmann : *Soziologische Aufklarunig*, Opladen 1970, p. 163..
5. As a recent example of a 'Citizens' Report' see : City of Cologne (edit.): *Burgergutachten Bereich Rathaus-Gurzenich*. Koln 1980.

SIXTEEN

DAN FERRAND-BECHMANN

'BE A GOOD NEIGHBOUR"

"LES Marguerites" at Meylan :

The study of a neighbourhood cooperation network.

The question is what form can cooperation take among neighbours, friends and members of the same family ?

Our aim is a better understanding of the alternatives to social work, i.e. the different forms of social work which operate within institutional systems, for example day nurseries, youth clubs, etc., in fact, because we have chanced upon a system to deal with a neighbourhood cooperation network at its purest, little by little we came to think mainly about neighbourhood cooperation, and not only on forms of solidarity which social work may have otherwise taken charge of, but also of material and verbal exchanges.

STRATEGY

Our question stems from previous studies. On the one hand in the area of voluntary and professional social work, on the other hand in the field of informal cooperation which appears as an alternative to social work.

It may seem strange to speak of mutual assistance as an alternative to social work.

Originally Social work/Social workers, specialised educa-

Paper presented at the "European Meeting on Applied Urban Research", Essen, Oct. 2-4, 1981.

tors, community workers, the staff of public services catering for the minding out entertainment of children and old people, formed the bulk of the professionally qualified population of social workers.

But in some areas social work tends to assume functions formerly taken up by friends, neighbours and the family.

Having had to study mainly social work, we were under the impression that mutual assistance network had gradually been superseded by social work.

We had noticed the dysfunctions of social work.

As mutual assistance became institutionalised, friends, neighbours and kins tended to abandon to the social worker services which they had rendered a few years earlier.

But comparisons with some foreign countries and participation to some team work caused us to steer our thinking in a new direction.

The Grenoble area in general and the Meylan area in particular are appropriate for our purpose. This is a fast expanding area as far as social action is concerned and it is run politically by a socialist inspired team. Thanks to various studies on child-minding (in day-nurseries or with child-minders) and on the cost of social action two questions were raised :

1. The dysfunction of social work.
2. The means used by those whose problems are not solved through social work.

The dysfunctions are the new—or false needs which day nurseries bring with them : the network of childminding or self help nursery would disappear.

The second question stems from the discrepancy between the number of children whose mothers work and the number of places available in day nurseries and with child-minders. How do those mothers manage to have their children looked after ?

And what do children do between the time they leave school and the time their parents get home ? The questions are many, they are about the manifold problems of daily life, problems which the individual and more precisely families can't solve on their own. In this study we are only interested in answers found outside the field of social work. We have chosen to study further a few of our mutual hypotheses through some empirical work, and shall present those in a paragraph devoted to methodology.

Les Marguerites consist of a series of houses surrounded by a small garden. The houses in the modern style are spacious and wide open to day light. They look onto greens. One cannot see inside the house from the street. The fronts looking on the street have a garage. The streets are in fact private roads on the estate and there is for this reason a peaceful atmosphere. Traffic is low.

That setting is important to understand the nature of mutual cooperation.

We could list 13 items :

1. Joint ownership (legal solidarity) and common maintenance ;
2. The lending of tools, cars, casual financial help ;
3. Objects jointly owned, like freezers ;
4. Borrowing stuff (salt, eggs...) ;
5. Help in the case of an accident (a storm causing damage) ;
6. Help in case of death, sickness, emergency ;
7. Lending the house (in summer to invite friends) ;
8. Small presents, such as plants ;
9. Mutual surveillance, keeping the keys of the house ;
10. Children : games, child-minding, transport, sickness, sport ......;
11. Welcoming newcomers ;
12. Entertainments, cups of coffee, mechouis ;
13. Speaking, listening......

Why cooperation ?

1. The lay-out and architecture of the house ;
2. *Les Marguerites* is separated from the rest of Meylan district ;
3. *Les Marguerites* is far from public service ;
4. Reciprocity ;
5. The framework of joint ownership ;

6. The age of children ;
7. Social homogeneity ;
8. The intermingling of generation ;
9. The lay out of the estate ;
10. The ideology ;
11. The residents moving in all at the same time ;
12. Women going to work.

This is our personal interpretation of the various elements gathered.

Many interview stressed the fact that mutual cooperation differs widely when talking flats or houses.

Reciprocity is the first cause of solidarity. Everyone knows he or she might need his or her neighbour's help some day. We help first of all because we want to be able to ask for help. Nobody will explicitly admit that he or she assesses and keeps an account of the help received or given but some of us would rather not ask too much for fear of having to give back too much and because of their work or of the size of their family, resort to a system of fee paying baby-sitting. Most of the times nobody keeps an account, that's the apparent norm. But we have also been told "we don't need it any more ; our children are too old", nobody asks us anything or that is exceptional.

So, it is a matter of exchange.

We have also heard people talk of service in a way which was definitely an implicit condemnation of those who don't play the game fairly.

Reciprocity appears under its most crystallised norm. MAUSS defined it very well in the title of his famous pages : an essay on the gift and the necessity to give back :

"You know, if you have a friend
whom you can trust
and if you want to obtain good results,
you will have to mingle your soul with his
and exchange gifts
and visit him often."

"Those processes of offering and returning gifts are entered, into a fairly voluntary basis, in the way of presents, gifts, although they are really compulsory, failing that private or public wars break out."

Later on, in his conclusion, MAUSS writes :

"Society wants to return the social cell. It wraps the individual in a strange mood in which the notion he has of his rights and other, purer feelings mingle : charity, service, cooperation. The theme of gift giving, of freedom and obligation in the giving, the feeling of generosity and of the interest that we have to give, come back to us, just us too long forgotten a motif would."

CONCLUSION

Neighbourhood is a group ranging from a plain juxtaposition to an exchange of goods and services in a more or less intensive non monetary circuit.

A system in which the whole is more than the whole and in which the whole is less than the whole, and in which there are potentialities. A permanent system, but undergoing processes of transformation and regeneration. In other words, it is impossible to describe one valuable method without describing them all. The periphery of the ones comes and influences the others'. The architecture of the houses is modulated by the spatial forms of gardens, the number of children prevents the mother who works from approaching for help.

They can accelerate or decelerate. The key variable is the age of the children. On the whole, we are far removed from SARTRE's situation : "Huis Clos" : Hell is the others. But neighbours are the others. One can't be one's own neighbour. It is a social phenomenon, a social system which has its birth with the arrival of the first generation and its death in spite of its regeneration, in other words when new occupant arrive in the house.

With a search for identity as well, that of the mythical village which alternates between other possible identities. But at the same time, can we refer to this system without thinking of that of Meylan : local community with a territorial basis ? Has it to do with work, with the family, chums, the environments in which each couple or each individual can fit ? Every system is complicated, paradoxical, with manifold meanings.

Those neighbourhood networks—as strong and structured as they appeared don't really contradict the analysis of Louis ROUSSEL and Agnes PITROU on the permanence of family networks. Those are exchanges partly different in nature. The neighbourhood system is perhaps a partial alternative even if on a daily basis.

Perhaps we have to deal with another system, another approach. The system is being defined as an abstract intellectual construction, coherent, reasonable, with an identity of its own : the identity we chose to ascribe to it—a systematic system which does not integrate paradoxes, the total sum of the different perceptions of a family or of an individual to the other. Involvement in exchange and cooperation, in reciprocal aid......are more or less important. Interactions are organised and ruled by implicit or explicit agreements.

Implicit agreements when intimacy is impinged upon, explicit agreements for the transport of children for example. But the meanings attached to these exchanges are manifold.

But our hypothesis is that the description of this neighbourhood system will enable us to understand better the whole system of social action.

REFERENCES

Aries, P. : *L'enfant et la vie familiale sous l' ancien Regime*, Paris, coll. Point, Serie Histoire, 1973.

Barel, Y. : Le paradoxe et le systeme, essai sur le fantastique social, P.U.G., 1979.

Baudrillard, J. : Le systeme des objets, Gontheir, coll. Mediations, 1968.

Castoriadis : *Les carrefours du Labyrinthe*, Seuil, 1978.

Coing, H. : Renovation urbaine et changement social, ed. ouvrieres, 1966.

Davies, B. : Social work and social control. Discussion Paper 150, February 80. Universite du Kent.

Durkheim, E. : Les formes elementaires de la vie religieuse, P.U.F., 1979.

Ferrand, A. : Travaux pour l'A.T.P. CNRS Meylan, E.S.U., palais de I Universite, place de Verdun-38000 GRENOBLE.

Ferrand-Bechmann, D. : These : "L' anti-ville : less residences secondaires", F.L.S.H., Nanterre, 1975.

"La formation des travailleurs sociaux en Angleterre : less agents du developpement communautaire", P.U.G., 1978. Annuaire Amenagement.

Revue francaise de Sociologie, 1979 IV in Critque "L'autogestion dans 1' action sociale ? Exemple de 1' agglomeration grenobloise". Revue Rencontre, 33/80.

Gil, David G. : Ravelling social policy. Schenkman 76 Cambridge. Mass.

Godin, B. : Solutions Sociales. La Digitale, 1979.

Goffmann, E : La mise en scene de la vie quotidienne, editions de Minuit, 4, 1973, tomes.

Kerr, M. : The people of ship street, Routledge, Kegan People, 16/66.

Leat, D. : Limited Liability ? (Rapport sur les systemes ne voisinage) dans le cadre du Volunteer Centre.

Levi-Strauss, C. : Les structures elementaires de la parente, P.U.F., 1949.

Mauss, M. : Essai sur le don, Sociologie et Anothropologie, P.U.F., 1966.

Mendras, H. : Travaux de groupe de sociologie rurale F.L.S.H., Nanterre.

Meyer, P. : "Ou va le travail social", in Esprit, reed. 1978 du n° special sur le travail social de 1972.

Pitrou, A. : Revue francaise de Sociologie, XVIII, 1977.

Raymond, H. : Less Pavillonnaires, CRU, 1966, 3 volumes.

Riesman, D. : La foule solitaire, Arthaud, 1964, lere ed. en 1950.

Roussel, L. : dirigeant les enquetes de I 'I.N.E.D. : "La famille apres le mariage des enfants, etude des relatious entre generations," 1976, Travaux et Documents n° 68.

Veblen, T. : Theorie de la Classe de loisirs, Paris, Gallimard, 1970.

Verdes-Leroux, J. : "Le travail social", ed. Minuit, 1978.

Wirth, L. : "On cities and social life", Londres, 1964, edited by Albert Reiss.

Wylie, L. : Un village de Vaucluse, Paris, Gallimard, N.R.F., coll. Temoins, 1967.

Young et Wilmott : Family and kinship in East London, Routledge, Kegan Paul, 1957.

SEVENTEEN

HACHIRO NAKAMURA

THE HISTORICAL DEVELOPMENT AND FUNCTION OF CHONAIKAI
In a Comparative Perspective

INTRODUCTION

AFTER overhauling the Redfield-Wirth type of rural-urban continuum theory, the urban study turned its attention to a number of other topics and approaches, say, community power, urban social networks, quality of life, Marxian challenge to existing theories, etc. In dealing with cities in developing countries, the primate city, the culture of poverty, informal sector, core-peripheral and dependent theories and so on have been appealing to the research interest. Whichever of them may be in vogue currently, the institutionalized neighborhood organization called CHONAIKAI has constantly been the object of study for urban sociologists in Japan, though above topics and approaches have been also pursued by them on the other hand.

English translation of CHONAIKAI by Prof. R. Dore of the University of Sussex in his *City Life in Japan* (Berkeley : University of California Press, 1958) is "urban ward association". As this translation indicates, we can find one unitary CHONAIKAI in each ward of almost all urban areas of Japan. Regarding its characteristics, I have once tried a review of studies made on it and elicited the following (1) to (5) as ones that are commonly noted.

(1) The unit of membership is not the individual but the household.

Paper Presented at the "European Meeting on Applied Urban Research", Essen, Oct. 2-4, 1981.

(2) Membership is determined by residence within a defined area and is semi-compulsory. In short, it is an all-inclusive membership.

(3) There is no specialization of function (in some studies such different expressions are given to the same aspect as "multi-objective", "compound functions" and "multiple functions").

(4) They supplement the lowest-level administrative services of local government that require direct contact with people in each ward.

(5) They act as the basis for and help to preserve conservative political tradition under the leadership of the old middle class.

UNDERLYING EVALUATION OF CHONAIKAI

When one points out (1) to (3) above, it is commonly assumed that CHONAIKAI, with its all-inclusive membership allowing neither free entry into nor exit from it at the will of individuals as well as its undifferentiated function, is a social group properly belonging to the premodern age It is generally conceived that CHONAIKAI is a successor to GONIN-GUMI, or five-man team, which the Shogunate government of the feudal era compelled the townspeople to organize as a measure to supervise and control them. The absolutist government in the prewar days of Japan is said to have reinforced it or forced its establishment where it was absent, thereby mobilizing urban people for the united effort to attain the goal of the government.

Thus CHONAIKAI is a government-made organization, not in a category of the association intrinsic to the modern age, spontaneously emerging with a specialization or differentiation of function. Accordingly CHONAIKAI lacks in the autonomy submissively acting, as indicated in the characteristic (4) above, to supplement the lowest-level administrative services which the local government is supposed to perform. Little wonder that it is a stubborn stronghold of conservatism, as in (5) above, consequently working as an efficient vehicle during the last war to mobilize urban people for the home front activities,

The above are the conceptions of CHONAIKAI prevailing among many of those who study it in Japan. In the past I have conducted two field researches on CHONAIKAI, but obtained findings which disclosed evidences not wholly proving this conception, as discussed in my paper on "A Re-examination of CHONAIKAI". English translation of which is inserted in R. Pahl (ed) *Readings in Urban Sociology* (Oxford : Pergamon Press, 1968), with an introductory note by Prof. Dore. Exposition of CHONAIKAI in the way so far made, however, has to suspended here for a while to see it in another way. The aforesaid conception will be taken up again afterwards.

COMMUNITY AND CHONAIKAI IN JAPAN

In one perspective, CHONAIKAI provides a clue to examine Wirthian theory on urbanism. Although the theory assumed "the disappearance of the neighborhood", it is intact in urban Japan to such a degree as it is institutionalized into CHONAIKAI. But the examination of the theory may be out of mode today as I have referred to already.

In another perspective, CHONAIKAI may be explored in the light of the emerging international trend to seek neighborhood revitalization in the urban area. As Japan is not an exception to this trend, the quest for the neighborhood community has vehemently surged in many sectors of Japan, though it reminded me of the question posed by Norman Dennis concerning the usefulness of the idea of the neighborhood community which does not deserve the popularity given to it (Norman Dennis, "The Popularity of the Neighborhood Community Idea" in R.E. Pahl, *op.cit.*, p. 81). To comply with the quest, increasing number of local governments have been advocating the community policy, and the Ministry of Home Affairs is encouraging them to foster the community.

In this case the concept of community is understood in a normative sense, that is, comprising in its attributes solidarity of neighbors who do not lose the individuality, free will, spontaneity, the sense of responsibility and so on. With these attributes, the community is said to give a solid basis to participatory democracy. So far there has been nobody who said anything about the sort of doubt cast by J.R. Gusfield who questioned the compatibility of inner-directedness and other-directedness in his *Community : A Critical Response* (Oxford : Blackwell, 1975, pp. 101-102). As for CHONAIKAI, it is deemed not to deserve the name of community. Even so, in implementing the community policy, especially when there is a need to stir up collective activities of local people, local governments have to rely on CHONAIKAI very frequently, but with no intention of the revival of traditionalism or militarism.

In my opinion survey carried out in two suburban cities of Tokyo, overwhelming majority (89.5% and 81.1%, respectively) of respondents chose an answer "CHONAIKAI is indispensable absolutely" or "CHONAIKAI is more indispensable than not". This indicates that the popular conception of CHONAIKAI conflicts with its evaluation given by an academic circle or by a portion of people whose voices frequently appear in printed matters.

As referred to already, I have written a paper on CHONAIKAI, but, in view of such a divergence of conception still existing, another attempt to explore CHONAIKAI has been made recently. It is not a field research but a perusal of historical sources pertaining to the development of CHONAIKAI.

DEVELOPMENT OF CHONAIKAI IN PREWAR DAYS

The first inquiry in my attempt was to ask what evidences there are concerning the origin of CHONAIKAI which is alleged to date back to the feudal era of Japan. Sources disclosed that there have been such predecessors of CHONAIKAI as an organization of real property owners and their agents, parishioners' organization of a local shrine, youngsters' club, sanitary association and MUTSUMIKAI (or neighborly goodwill club), of which only parishioners' organization and youngsters' club had their origin in feudal days.

The organization of property owners and their agents emerged after the Meiji Restoration (1891). Since they had a stake in properties, mostly tenement-houses, they found it to their advantage to organize themselves as a means to preserve order among tenants in the ward. A sanitary association was established in every ward to comply with the prefectural ordinance issued in 1900 which bade ward people to establish it. In those days epidemics intermittently prevailed in a fury and the establishment of the association was regarded as an effective step to prevent epidemics. Therefore the sanitary association was government-made, but with the amelioration of sanitary conditions, it gradually disappeared in many wards soon afterwards. In some wards, it was reorganized into CHONAIKAI.

MUTSUMIKAI which accounted for the largest proportion of predecessors, seems to have sprung up now in this ward and then in another ward. Its function was to promote neighborly goodwill, thereby meeting the emotional needs of neighbors. As for the five-man team, a reliable source, i.e. Kinshiro Hiraide, *Tokyo Fuzokushi* (Records of the Folk Life in Tokyo) published in 1898, says "The system of the five-man team has entirely disappeared". The team, when it was working, was composed of agents of the property owner assigned to manage tenement-houses and tenants. The Shogunate government bade the team to take charge of lo er-level administrative work such as the registration of birth, but the new government after the Meiji Restoration abolished it. The above quotation which indicates there were no revival from then on, make it evident that the alleged origin of CHONAIKAI from the five-man team has no ground.

The above are some accounts of predecessors. Due to the lack of time I cannot afford to go further, but what must be noted are as follows.

(a) Not all unitary CHONAIKAI are successors to any one of the aforesaid predecessors, of which only parishioners' organizations and youngsters' club have a feudal origin. This means that origin of CHONAIKAI is scarcely traceable to feudal days.

(b) In the organization of property owners and their agents and the youngsters' club, it is self-evident that membership was limited to a particular group of ward people. Though not said in the above, this was the case with other types of predecessors except the sanitary association. Mostly membership was not all-inclusive but limited to the natives in a ward to the exclusion of settlers from other places.

(c) Also self-evident is the function that was specialized in the case of parishioners' organization, sanitary association and MUTSUMIKAI : the preservation of shrine and Shinto rites, the improvement of sanitary conditions and the promotion of neighborly goodwill, respectively.

(d) Except the sanitary association, no predecessors were what may be called government-made. If the persistence of CHONAIKAI could be attributed to its being government-made, the sanitary association could have also survived for a long time. As it was, however, it simply vanished or reorganized into CHONAIKAI soon afterwards.

As already suggested there are many unitary CHONAIKAI which were first established as such with no predecessors. Some historical events gave an impetus to their birth though the same events stimulated the reorganization of predecessors into CHONAIKAI, too. The first of the major events were the Sino-Japanese and Russo-Japanese Wars (1894 to 1895 and 1904 to 1905, respectively). People in a ward felt the need of their organization to give a hearty send-off to neighbors who were called up for military service and to comfort their families.

Next to be mentioned is what we call Taisho democracy in Japan, that is, the surge of public opinion to seek democracy during the latter half of the Taisho era (or from the late 1910's to the early 1920's). Since equality was stressed, those people in a ward who were excluded from the membership of the neighborhood organization came to be dissatisfied and sought open membership. Their request was accepted and many predecessors reorganized themselves into CHONAIKAI with its membership all-inclusive. In those days the complexity was increasing rapidly in urban life. To cope with such changing situation, predecessors with a specialized function found it to their advantage to add other functions to them.

By far the more intense impetus was given by the Great Earthquake of 1923 which occurred in the Kwanto district,

With the ensuing great fire, the whole area of Tokyo was reduced to ashes and social unrest spread in a fury. Ward people found it imperative to have their organization so that they could be prepared for this kind of emergency at any time.

These events thus connote that CHONAIKAI was not a product of any arbitrary policy of the central government, but that it sprouted from below among ward people stimulated be these events. In particular, the impact of Taisho democracy should not be overlooked. The all-inclusive membership and the functional undifferentiation are alleged to suggest the backwardness of CHONAIKAI, but, as we found in the above, they are attributes which CHONAIKAI came to carry to adapt itself to the progress of urban life.

As yet two more remarks remain to be said. Concerning activities during the last war, it must be pointed out that not only CHONAIKAI but also all sectors of Japan, for example, universities and religious bodies, were involved in the war-time activities. To blame CHONAIKAI in this respect is to make it a scapegoat. As for the alleged conservatism, CHONAIKAI does not always stick to a particular ideology. Evidence shows that, when the main current of public opinion leaned toward democracy and world peace in the late 1920's, there was CHONAIKAI that made democracy as its basic principle of management or one that named itself "Peace Association". Therefore it is very reasonable that CHONAIKAI comply with the community policy of the local government in these days when the quest for the neighborhood community are widely eading in Japan. As remarked by R. Dahl in his *Modern Political Analysis* (Englewood Cliffs : Prentice Hall, 1963, pp. 58-63), full attainment of participatory seems to be difficult for human beings. Those who criticize CHONAIKAI regard its activities as dull and lukewarm. Even so, optimum level, though not maximum level, of participation seems to be attained through CHONAIKAI.

What has been said so far may be summarized as follows.

1. CHONAIKAI is not a traditional type of social group. Its characteristics alleged as signs of its backwardness are the same ones that have been carried to the present to cope with the progress of urban life.

2. It is not a successor to five-man team.
3. Feudal origin of CHONAIKAI is scarcely traceable, if any.
4. It is not a government-made organization. Its persistence is not to be attributed to its being this kind of organization.
5. CHONAIKAI does not stubbornly stick to a particular ideology. It follows the change to public opinion.
6. To blame CHONAIKAI for its war-time activities is to make it a scapegoat.
7. Optimum level of participation seems to be attained by CHONAIKAI in Japan.

IMPLICATIONS FOR COMPARATIVE STUDY

To Western sociologists my hot discussion in the foregoing, I am afraid, sounds like nothing but the pros and cons debated in so narrow academic circle as that of sociologists in Japan. I may be allowed to presume that I have a privilege to have my discussion heard because participants in this meeting pursue comparative study, but little can be done if they were really disinterested. Nevertheless I would like to refer to a new area of comparative study which CHONAIKAI suggests.

In the past CHONAIKAI was assumed to be a type of social group peculiar to the urban area of Japan. Gradually it has been found, however, that there are similar organizations in the Philippines, Singapore, Hongkong and South Korea. Very possibly there may be ones in some other countries, too. A similar organization in the Philippines is the barangay and in Singapore the community center, both supported by the central government with legal provisions to reinforce them.

In Manila, a secretary of a certain barangay in a squatter area said to me to the effect that the barangay system plays an important role in the Philippines, especially in their urban area in enhancing the solidarity among people of different ethnic origins, a role which is unknown to the Japanese who are homogeneous in their ethnic composition. Other functions are also performed which include the improvement of the sanitary conditions of the environment as well as the exercise of jurisdiction over family troubles and minor disputes among neighbors, for which the barangay captain has been given a short-term training.

Because of my short stay in Singapore, I could not learn much about the community center, but the promotion of interethnic solidarity was also one of its functions. I was told there is the residents' committee besides the community center, but could not afford to obtain some knowledge about it. It might be closer to CHONAIKAI.

There is the Kaıfong system in Hongkong. A certain Hongkong student staying in Japan told me that it resembles the CHONAIKAI of Japan. I have never been to South Korea, but one of my Korean friends wrote to me that the central governments trying to foster a system of the neighborhood organization which is similar to CHONAIKAI. In Calcutta, too, there seems to be the neighborhood organization which I presume corresponds to CHONAIKAI of Japan because the description of *mohalla* by M.B. Clinard in his *Slums and Community Development* (New York : Free Press, 1966, p. 50) reminded me of CHONAIKAI. Thus, if we are careful we can find many other cases of CHONAIKAI—like organizations.

Some questions may be raised after we find them. Why, for instance, there is this type of organization in some countries and not in others ? In Bangkok there were none of this type. longkorn According to my friend, Prof. Prasart Yamklinfung of Chula University, Thailanders are poor in organizing themselves because Thailand is a loosely structured society as pointed out by J.F. Embree. Conversely speaking what my friend said seems to suggest a factor which contributes to the existence of CHONAIKAI in Japan. Probably the contributing factor is a cultural one which has made the Japanese people good at organizing themselves.

One may further ask about the merits and demerits of CHONAIKAI-like organizations. Foreign people staying in Japan often speak of the social order well preserved in the urban life of Japan. Is CHONAIKAI one of the factors contributing to such a situation ?

Yet another question may be posed regarding the bearings upon participatory democracy as I have touched on in my discussion on CHONAIKAI. In the Philippines, each unitary barangay is bestowed with the legal right to make a direct appeal to the President, though I cannot tell how this right is really exercised under Martial Law, or whether the Presidents' office has enough capacity to accept appeals when they are made by many unitary barangays at the same time.

The above are tentative questions that occur to me, but they seem to suggest a fertile maiden area open to our comparative study.

EIGHTEEN

ALBERTO TAROZZI

NEW URBAN MOVEMENTS BETWEEN ISOLATION AND INTEGRATION
Comparative Researchs in Italy and West Germany

PARTICIPATION AND SOCIAL MOUVEMENTS

FIRST OF all I would like to point out two problems of terminology which concern the word "participation" and the expression "social mouvements" and what they mean nowadays in complex societies.

What I have to say about the word "participation" is that according to me only in exceptional cases it is possible to extend the *participation* of people—with the same possibilities for everyone—to the formation of the collective political will (Habermas 1967) ; big private interests of strong corporatist groups ingrave upon public decisions in process of formation ; public institutions homologate different cultural behaviours and colonize the daily private sphere. The ground of the participation as a border field between public and private sphere is trampled by two opposed kinds of integration and intrusions (public institutions in private spheres, to reduce their complexity—private interests in public institutions, to impose orientations full of particolarism).

As far as the expression *social mouvements* is concerned, I would say that a social mouvement requires a collective identity and a wide clearness about the stake (Touraine. 1978). This clearness allows the articulation of the political will in the social action, in which it is possible to specify counterparts,

Paper Presented at the "European Meeting on Applied Urban Research" Essen, Oct. 2-4, 1981.

times, places and purposes (Offe 1980a). Nowadays we observe the identity crisis of the traditional subject of contemporary social mouvements (the working class) ; many different and distinct initiatives were born inside the working class (and inside labour relationships) and outside the working class (the purposes of the production). In the parties system, these initiatives very often find only a filtering way of communication with the administrative system ; on the other hand, it is difficult for them to express autonomous (not filtered) signals to modify the codes of the power. When this happens, we cannot foresee how many embryos will produce new mouvements and how many will produce simple phenomenes of isolation.

Are the institutional planning of the ideology and the big corporatist interests able to integrate every kind of *participation* ?

Can the legitimacy crisis be overcome by a functional differentiation of the outputs of the political-administrative system? or can it be by the isolation of each social action in the ghetto of the poverty self-management ?

Or is it possible to organize initiatives that get away from isolation and constitute a *social mouvement* ?

To give a reply to these questions it is necessary a cross-national comparative research about the rising up of phenomenes which don't express only the refusal of the political parties and of the hired labour, but also the attempt to discuss the separation between *Leisure-time and working-time*. We make the hypothesis that alternative political-cultural identities, new social relations, new forms of struggle try to determine a new *time for living* ; vindications and negotiations of next years will develop themselves between the initiatives of the social sphere and the decisions of the political system, about this problem.

THE RESULTS OF A CROSS-NATIONAL RESEARCH

Our research has been developed between 1979 and 1980 in West Germany (Ruhr-Bremen-Nieder Sachsen) and in Italy (Bologna). In Germany it has not had any purchaser, while in

Italy the purchaser was the syndicate FIM-CISL. * We want to underline the new interest of the syndicate for the analysis of the quality of life as a reason of conflict out of the factory. The object of the researches has been the *rising up* of *new* social actions ; therefore we have mainly used a qualitative approach (interview, focus interview, etc.), not to flatten the new behaviours to the low percentages of statistical results that cannot represent the trend of a rising up (Table 18.1, p. 6).

Our theoretical approach and our specific research (Bologna-Ruhr-Nuclear) suggest four comparative synthetic considerations about the examined experiences :

1. The parties system nowadays finds many difficulties in controlling the autonomies of social sphere in the legitimacy crisis of Welfare State : a) the PCI bases himself upon social situation, where to live together means also to suffer together ; new social aggregations present this contemporaneity only by chance and in little groups (precarious workers groups, alternative activities, etc.) ; b)the SPD bases its success upon inputs connected to big global issues (peace, democracy, etc.) and it leaves the load of many negotiations with the outputs of the social sphere that concerne particular quarrels (*Burgerinitiativen*, environment struggles, etc.) to the administration.
2. The initiatives of the social sphere represent a new phenomene as far as the ideology of the alternative subjects are concerned (people who have "nothing to loose"). In fact : a) they are looking for a certain level of *security* as a minimum base to succeed in their experiments ; a group or a gang identity, a professional or bodily capability, the instrumental new discovering of the couple life or of the parents, in Italy—the defense of the habitat, of an autonomous space for living, a guarantee of absence of dangers connected to the fear of the nuclear or of the war, in West Germany ; b) they are also trying to find a way thank to which they can directly act on *experimental actions* ; the syndical vindication of the amicable groups of precarious workers who live together before suffering together, the experi-

*The working group was composed by L. Altierl, P. Faccioli, and myself.

TABLE 18.1 : **Chronology of the relations between social mouvements and political system in Italy and West Germany from 1968 until today (1981)**

	ITALY	WEST GERMANY
'68	Political-social mouvement (in the University). Presence of a strong party of the working class (PCI). Rising up of new little (more or less) leninistic parties. Limited alternative experiences.	Political-social and cultural alternative mouvement with a deep ideology pro 3rd world (in the University). Limited presence of the SPD.
'69-'76	Recovery of PCI and syndicate. Failure of the new parties.	Political crisis of the mouvement, New little 'hard' leninistic parties. Limited recovery of SPD. Increase of alternative experiences.
'72-'76	New mouvements keep still sporadic explosion of vindications, out from the syndicate, in big industries and in health services.	(a) 73-74—From alternative experiences to local quarrels about urban conditions, which involve also extra '68 subjects ex : *The urban renewal in Ruhrgebiet* (*) (b) 75-76—The initiatives join themselves about issues concerning problems of urban and rural context (the nuclear).
'77-'81	(a) 77—Social revolt in urban not deeply industrialized areas (Bologna, Roma) ; refusal of political negotiation and of the parties system ; violent struggles of new social subjects for the satisfaction of their own needs.	(a) 77-81—Big quarrels about echological issues; rising up of alternative "liste" and alternative parties ; ex : *the case Gorleben* (*)

(b) 78-79—End of the revolt ; new alternative aggregation that try to overcome the traditional break *leisure-time/working-time.* Ex : *the post '77 in Bologna* (*)

(c) 80-81—Perspectives of vindications and quarrels inside and outside labour relationships, new social subjects experiment new ways of management and of negotiation (ex : the precarious workers group),

(b) 80-81—The growth of the alternative "liste" as an instrument of coordination of the initiatives. The growth of big quarrel, with partially new subjects and purposes (the immigrate people and the struggle againsts and removal of occupied houses ; the echological struggle as a struggle against nuclear rearmament and against a politics of war).

* The underlined cases have been object of my specific researche.

mental actions of alternative dcotors, musicians, booksellers, new erotic experiences, in Italy—the conversion of traditional culture into alternative culture (as an instrument of innovation), the urbanistic and architectural concrete utopias, the research of new sources of energy in West Germany.

(3) The multiplying and the autonomous joining of the initiatives goes speedlier where we register the presence of "konkurrenzpartei" (Offe 1980b) ; the process goes on slowlier where the political parties maintain their own traditional functions (communication for consent or dissent). In the first case it is easier to register the rising up of alternative "liste" as a moment of coordination among the initiatives (West Germany). In the second case the refusal of the intervention of a traditional party (also with collateral associations) coincides more frequently with the refusal of every kind of political representation (Italy).

4. When it substitutes the political parties by dealing out specific outputs, the intervention of the administrative system seems to be the reciprocal of the initiatives of the social sphere. On one hand, it deals with *specific* initiatives ; on the other hand, it is a functional *differentiation* that denies perhaps, every place of participation (Luhmann 1969). Otherwise it leaves for it only an integrated-riduced place, in the interior of a tacticistic style of planning (Lindblom 1977) ; in such a case we have an agreement with self-managed groups in fields like education (West Germany) ; rock-music, echology, theater, etc. (as the organic "piano giovani" of the "Comune di Bologna", Italy).

Is this the only kind of possible negotiation ? (a negotiation which makes possible contemporary presence of Leviathan and anarchy) ?

I think it is possible to register another kind of relationships : a relationship that includes negotiable elements (to avoid a totalitarian self-isolation of embryonic mouvements) and not negotiable elements (to evitate the integration of new social actors).

It deals with a stake which concerns several functions that can be reduced neither in the field of labour relationships, nor in the field of definition of purposes of production.

For example : a) the struggle against production of nuclear energy for peace or war in W. Germany connects economical and energetic problems, individual and "lebenswelt" problems (the fear) with echological problems (the defense of the quality of life) ; b) the struggle of the precarious young workers, in Italy, individuates a stake that does not concern only the wages or the quality of the work. In fact it concerns the overcoming of the separation between life time and labour time.

The definition of autonomous ways of daily life, which "presents itself as a material alternative of community. includes, as a subject, the articulate initiatives of the mouvements and, as a program, the built of a new system of values" (Negri 1981). Perhaps in this project it should be considered the possibility to exercise also some functions of the political party : a desultory possibility that should conjugate—situation by situation—the solidarity of new collective identity and the ability to engrave upon the decisional process. It could be a way to force the local and national political power to treat issues that, for the power, must not be an object of negotiations.

REFERENCES

Altieri, L., Caselli C., Faccioli P., Tarozzi A, (1982), *Tempo di vivere*, Edizioni Lavoro, Roma.

Habermas, J. (1967), Uber den Begriff der politischen Beteiligung. In : *Student und Politik. Eine soziologische Untersuchung zum politischen Bewusstsein Frankfurter Studenten*, Luchterland Verlag, Neuwied—Berlin.

Lindblom, C. (1977), *Politics and markets*, Basic Books, New York.

Luhmann, N. (1969), *Legitimation durch Verfahren*, Luchterland Verlag, Neuwied–Berlin.

Negri, A. (1981), Noi e l'Europa, In : *Metropoli*, Anno 3, n°6, 4-5,

Offe, C. (1980a), Nuovi movimenti, iniziative di base e identita politica collettiva nella Germania federale (intervista di A. Tarozzi). In : *La Ricerca Sociale*, Anno IX, n° 23, 37-52.

Offe, C. (1980b), Konkurrenzpartei und kollektive politische Identitat, In : *Parlamentarisches Ritual und politische Alternativen*, Campus Verlag, Frankfurt,

Touraine, A. (1978), *La voix et le regard*, Seuil, Pairs,

NINETEEN

MARGIT MAYER

THE PROFILE OF CONTEMPORARY NEIGHBORHOOD MOVEMENTS

THE NEIGHBORHOOD AND THE STATE

THE economic restructuring characterizing advanced industrial nations has far-reaching social and political consequences that are manifested at the neighborhood level. As the localized impacts of these changes in production and reproduction give rise to new sources of needs, demands, and discontent, there is a concomitant response by State authority. The hypothesis is that the state has been and is structuring this terrain in a specific way, and that this state action—the extent to which it succeeds in imposing its form over the terrain—is an important element in defining the conditions under which collective protest around urban contradictions can be transformed into an urban social movement.

A key popular response to the crisis of the 1970s and 1980s has been the neighborhood movement. The existence in the United States of thousands of community organizations does not necessarily indicate that they are a "new social movement", but it certainly represents a significant change in civil society. In West Germany, where there is a more obvious *movement* one has to ask why the housing/squatting/youth movement, crystallizes on the neighborhood level.

The United States neighborhood movement of the 1970s and 1980s as opposed to that of the 1960s—is characterized by much more diversity in terms of class and ethnic composition.

Paper presented at the "European Meeting on Applied Urban Research," Essen, Oct. 2-4, 1981,

It is constituted by a wide variety of social groups, mainly middle class, struck by the economic crisis, and receptive to environmental and consumer issues. It focusses primarily on local self-reliance and/or collective consumption issues. It is no longer so much confronted by urban renewal, rather facing more subtle forces of displacement, such as 'gentrification'. The movement can be broadly grouped into four clusters, which are not necessarily identical with real-existing groups.

The new urban neighborhood-movement

Those in which the new middle class is the social force and progressive political actor are summed up in the first cluster. The basis for this aspect of the movement is the generation of the new middle class itself. due to the expansion of the tertiary sector. They are oriented towards communal values, trying to improve the quality of their neighborhood, which means a multi-issue perspective, both urban and environmental issues are raised. Their relation to the state may range from wanting to connect with local government without changing the political institutions, but to increase their voice and power within them, to municipalization and extension of representative democracy towards grassroots democracy. Insofar as it thereby reacts to the socialization of consumption, it is in danger of becoming a corporate movement, of defending pure economic interests in the collective consumption realm, i.e. a special interest group. Quite frequently, however, it is permeated and impregnated with a cultural consciousness or goal, partially symbolized by the Back to the City Movement : the preservation or creation of new urban neighborhoods, the desire to create affordable middle class islands characterized by a conservationist use of inner city, which values urban culture and defines the city as a city to be *lived in*. The development of this specific style of life depends, in other words, upon the improvement of their urban environment.

Within this middle class cluster, there are two sub-groups, whose dynamic stems from different sources :

— in contrast to middle class strata systematically affected by the economic crisis, other "resource-rich" strata who may be confronted with a suddenly imposed major grievance or a serious infringement upon their environment (the Santa Barbara oil spill, the Three Mile Island reactor crisis, in some cases court-ordered bussing) experience a mobilization process which is much more dramatic and episodic, while the issue is perceived to be a direct and immediate one, imposed directly by the state or capital interests. Response to the issue is usually limited in scope.

— in contrast to middle class strata culturally grounded in a conservationist and preservationist ethic, are what might be understood as urban appendices to the Alternative Movement (ecology, nature, body, self-identity), whose issues may overlap with more specifically) neighborhood preservation/quality of urban life issues.

Culture and territory

A second cluster within the neighborhood movement would consist of those neighborhood groups in which local culture and territory is the driving force. This would include both groups striving to realize an autonomous ethnic norm and those striving to realize an autonomous cultural norm. Examples would be the gay community in San Francisco, and Latino communities in various large cities. That is, some "minorities", in trying to defend their cultural identity, organize on a territorial basis to achieve relative security and freedom. As their objectives are purely cultural, they face the danger of becoming cultural 'tribalists'.

The defensive neighborhood movement

The third cluster can be characterized as a defensive reaction on the part of established neighborhoods (frequently of consolidated homeowners), who are attacked either by gentrification or by deterioration, i.e. the threat of a loss of privileges constitutes the dominant force in this case.

The class composition here is mixed, predominantly ethnic white working class and WASP, as they constitute themselves as moderate-income groups to defend themselves against the urban decay of their quality of life in old industrial cities.

Such groups would also be understood as 'collective consumption' organizations, fighting around a variety of urban issues and public services, as well as organizations demanding participation in local government. Their interest base is their territory ; it is upon this basis that the need for increased control and the desire to improve the level of local and urban services is conducted.

Insofar as this is a revolt to the 'small ones against the big ones', class interest here can be directly expressed. However, and just as frequently, insofar as the stance taken is anti-taxes, anti-government (i.e. against government intrusion, state planning, redlining and disinvestment), the opposition to city plans to alter or destroy the local scene or against service cut-backs carries racist overtones and is directed against what is perceived to be a process of ethnic and racial recomposition of their territory. Their goal of local defense and control often in fact means "Keep the Blacks out", and suggests just how fluid the line between progressive and conservative attitudes here is : *any* ideology will get appropriated. The anti-bussing movement is only a particularly strong reaction of this form. Their relation to the political system is characterized by the desire to participate in the existing political institutions rather than to claim political power ; however, there is opposition to the central state, as regulator, mediator, welfare state.

Community development and service delivery organizations

The fourth cluster are those community organizations which have, to varying degrees, been administratively and technically tied into local governments and agencies, be it in the form of community development corporations or as service delivery organizations. Their class composition reflects those unorganized, "reserve" labor sectors who are systematically generated in the restructuring of labor. In the United States, it involves overwhelmingly Third World people.

Hence their interest base is both class and territory (due to the spatial segmentation process) ; i.e. they spring up in a setting which is characterized by blight devastated by arson, abandonment and disinvestment. It is not precisely a territory that is to be defended, but in order to survive, and to create a "viable community", the goals usually center around development of housing and community development programs, sometimes extending to collective consumption issues (although in a more power-oriented manner than the groups considered under "the defensive neighborhood movement". When social programs shrink, the goal becomes either to keep these going through the established linkages and pressure points on local government, or to resort to various forms of self-help and community development strategies.

These groups constitute a result of Alinsky-style organizing in the 1960s, whose success was limited to the organization's capacity to become an authoritative representative for a mobilized (usually black) community. As such, it became tied to the lower levels of the institutional system, where it was accepted and absorbed into the management of programmes they had set out to control. This, still accompanied by the claim for more political power and/or searching out interests in the private market to support their survival needs, seems the best way to get resources and to deal with the problems—thereby apparently guaranteeing social autonomy against the traditional strategy of the federal bureaucracy and also defending what was often perceived as an autonomous informal economy.

Political organizations

There is a fifth form—an attempt by political organizations (employing Alinsky ideology) to coordinate these manifestations of neighborhood discontent, in the form of the 'new citizens' movement', on local, city, and state levels. The composition of these organizations encompasses both the new urban middle classes and the defensive white working class. They are multi-ethnic, and multi-issue oriented, on the belief of the diversity of the neighborhood's interests (ranging from collective consumption issues—taxes, utilities, health care, anti-nuclear action—to environmental issues, all the way to neighborhood interaction). Territoriality is much less important than service delivery, the defense of the standard of living in the arena of public services. Their relation to the political system follows Alinsky's script : community organizations are seen as complementary to the representative institutions of liberal democracy ; so once grassroots empowerment is achieved, channels of influence and participation have been increased, the democratic institutions will work in their favor and economic interests will come under their control. So they challenge the system in order to obtain specific services, although this is secondary to their primary goal of increasing power within the institutional system.

STATE POLICY AND NEW LINKAGES

The questions addressed now are : to what extent do differing state policies impact on the structuring of the neighborhood terrain ? And how do the respective relations with the state shape the movements or condition the arena in which they operate ?

In the United States, the function of granting advocacy, interest aggregation, and articulation is to a much lesser extent performed by (weak) parties than in any of the Western European countries, so that many of these functions have been delegated to interest groups and voluntary associations, another part being taken care of by coalitional elite strategies.

This accepted tradition of extra-parliamentarian behavior of citizens groups, together with the still pervasive ideology of populism, have made for the 'institution' of voluntary organizations, understood as traditional organizations, 90% of whom are not part of a movement. However, the limits and relationship between 'the movement' and the traditional organizations are not always so clear, as traditional forms of organization impose themselves on movements, and movements often change making use of traditional organizations. Though formally outside of the state, their existence is quite complementary to the functioning of the democratic political system per se ; in addition, historically, the American state has displayed quite a capacity to expand and proliferate more and more agencies to absorb and deal with new conflicts and new interests. In turn, informal structures have evolved for interest articulation and formation to take place.

Furthermore, a large number of movement groups were spawned, fostered and shaped by the Federal programs of the 1960s (CAP, Model Cities, War on Poverty), which allowed for a common ground to emerge between blacks and citizens groups, but which—by legitimizing those interests—also channeled and limited them, specifically tying them into the institutional system.

In terms of neighborhood discontent, this process of incorporation has been reinforced during the Carter Administration by the Federal government making neighborhood organizations a central component in the "partnership to build the cities" : in the 1978 Urban Policy Statement neighborhoods were promoted as equal partners with the public and private sectors in national urban development activities ; by local governments more and more relating to these organizations as a political constituency ; by the crisis of the Democratic Party, which needed to search for a new, broader constituency, having lost its traditional labour and black base. The Democrats, moreover, had to bypass the local political machinery, which was often in the hands of the Republicans, and therefore fostered national linkages reaching down into communities.

In establishing the National Neighborhood Commission, the Carter administration attempted to initiate a movement from the federal level, to build the image of a nationwide, neighborhood movement. (It is important to note that the existence of such groups as the National People's Action, The National Association of Neighborhoods, and so on, is not evidence of the institutionalization of a *movement*, since they do not represent the community organizations to the state.)

Hence, different than in other countries which are more used to mediate political conflicts through parties, there has been a tradition and more experience in the United States, to create more and more administrative agencies, which tended to shape the movement in a corporatist form.

The question, however, is : how do different types of linkage manage or not manage to control, channel and process the conflicts and demands that are being struggled over in the neighborhood arenas.

The struggle obviously is not only over finding or developing forms which could de-thematize or successfully suppress irreducible conflicts, but also over achieving that in a form that is conducive to encouraging a 'constructive', adaptive behavior on the part of the disaffected. Therefore, in defining the respective forms and modes of state response, a criterion should be kept in mind that allows us to distinguish between :

— state policies which encourage participation, which establish new linkages to the neighborhood, do transform specific mechanisms, hence do change the urban arena, but which do so in a compatible form, that is, a form compatible with capitalist social relations ; and
— state policies, which either selectively absorb demands so as to redefine non-negotiable demands as "pathological", hence responding to those demands via repression and criminalization, or through non-decision-making. That is, state policies which divide the movement along the lines of negotiable and non-negotiable demands.

In the United States, where the terrain has been somewhat structured, a variety of responses which would fit the first category have emerged. Federal policies literally created neighborhood constituencies as spatial identities, which are, as such, presupposed to get funding. In some cases, neighborhood groups have even become legally mandated sub-units of government.

Federal policies (as with the Community Development Block Grant Program) allowed neighborhood organizations to develop 'self-sufficiency' through spawning profit-making enterprises of their own, or through small business development (funded through agencies as diverse as the Community Services Administration, the Economic Development Administration, and the Small Business Administration) as well as worker training and management training. These new organizations then combine local authority representation and community-based competitive sector interests.

Other policies encouraged neighborhood organizations to take on government functions on their own, supported by public sector employment through the Comprehensive Employment Training Act. These deliver services on their own, or engage in highly technical development projects that employ and train neighborhood residents.

"Self-sufficiency" through "self-reliance", in some cases through exploring new 'soft' technologies, is another way in which the neighborhood as a social category has entered the corporatist system of state/business/and now : neighborhoods ; frequently triggered by neighborhood self-help development programs, solar energy and energy conservation programs, former movement groups increasingly began to find themselves in such a relationship during the Ford and Carter administrations.

Collective consumption unionism, that is the extension of the wage struggle to the entire society, is a further form of change in the urban arena—specifically by finding an institutional mechanism to process neighborhood discontent through aggregating and articulating the protest against deficient public services, as with utility rates and so on.

The reprivatization and recommodification of social services (and the housing market as well in some cases) as it is supported by the current administration, is another form of response, although Reagan's strategy here is not to coopt but to diffuse social issues back to the level of local government, if not to eliminate government participation altogether.

The emergence of these forms represents a response to negotiable demands. What, however happens to demands that cannot be reduced to regulated mediation by the political system ? What happens to those forms of collective political behavior that are contrary to the functioning of the political system ? Where there is, as for example in the case of some of the German or Swiss squatters, a refusal to negotiate at all, a rejection of the "political" as such—where is the place for these needs and desires ? And what happens, then, in the case of irreducible conflicts, where the interests confronted are vital to the successful accumulation process in the respective country ?

Here I can only sum up the argument that the mode in which the state programs function has had certain effects on the ways in which citizens engage in formal collective action to solve neighborhood problems and refer the reader to S. Clark's contribution in this publication.

The existence of various programs and subsidies, which neighborhoods can qualify and compete for, such as the CDBG program, have encouraged, on the one hand, the transformation or new formation of community-based organizations as an actor in the process of urban revitalization. The CDBG program was initiated by the Federal government (as is frequently the case in the United States where social reform initiatives have emerged at the level of the central state), and was revised during the Carter administration to specify that neighbourhood organizations could be legal recipients for such funds—in contrast to the earlier Republican strategy of allocating funds only to municipal agencies. (The CDBG program can also be seen as an attempt to broaden, via locationally specific impacts, the Democratic Party's constituency). In establishing economic development a core component of public policy (in the CDBG and other block grant programs), and through the use of public funds for private profit, this urban revitalization strategy created both a new political actor and a new policy issue. With this policy response, the "ungovernable city" of incoherent and fragmented interests becomes covered with a new institutional grid of outposts of the state. Of the already existing linkages between state and neighborhood, the "corporatist', linkage seems to have become the crucial one in the area of development and production. On the other hand, bureaucratic enfranchisement (that is, the incorporation of program-specific constituencies into the bureaucratic decision making processes) will keep playing a major role in policy areas concerned with social consumption issues. Hence, while involving neighborhood-based organizations into the "urban revitalization" process, the form in which this is accomplished is essentially corporatist.

This corporatist structure is emerging at the local level, is focussed around land development and production, and does not take the form of solid, monolithic agencies, but constitutes itself through various, multiple linkages connecting the neighborhoods to a variety of bureaucracies.

The effect of these organizational responses, which provide

for designated interest representation, is that they delimit and control the participation of citizens in the policy process, and in the competition over resources. By identifying and legitimating who is such an appropriate group, the bureaucracy can at the same time establish measures to safeguard a specific policy selection process, and so define the meaning of neighborhood development itself. In the process, qualitative demands are translated into fiscal relations. Then the community-based groups have to engage in a protracted and complicated process of negotiations with the local agencies over the distribution of the federal monies (which also encourages competition between the community groups themselves). Moreover, program and policy criteria produce a selective acceptance of projects, usually in terms of self-sustenance, that is : profitability, which tends to favor groups which are not immediately accountable to their local constituency.

Even given, however, all of these elements designed to guarantee a "benign" outcome, the implementation of these policies at the local level is not without contradictions and ruptures. Funds frequently are blocked and deviated by the local agencies through which they are channeled, and can evoke unanticipated mobilizations of residents, whether around such a diversion, or over broader policy issues. Moreover, the struggles and conflicts continue within the community organizations themselves, in which the actors can attempt to define an alternative to both the direction of the community group, and of the policies to which the group is addressed (for instance, in the case of housing rehabilitation programs which had the unintended consequence of gentrification and displacement).

So, while such policies have usually succeeded in forcing local organizations to shift from organizing around 'social problems' to commercial and economic development ; while they have supported the community development corporations in "solving" the problems of decaying neighborhoods and by developing managerial control techniques over the population ; while they have given neighborhood empowerment a direction that is amenable to solving the new forms of the crisis of accumulation—at the same time, all of this does not mean anything more but that the conflicts have been displaced to a new arena that is certainly structured in a more routine and predictable manner, but one that is conflictual nonetheless.

CONSEQUENCES OF THE STATE RESPONSES ON THE STRUCTURING OF NEIGHBORHOOD ORGANIZATIONS

In the wake of the growth of funding and technical assistance programs during the Carter administration, which fostered something like a national neighborhood movement, which established agencies which related directly to neighborhood organizations and neighborhood issues, and which favored neighborhood development organizations and commercially oriented groups, a transformation of the "old line" community organizations occurred, which affected their goals and internal formal organization.

By "old line" I mean those groups which sprang up in the context of the battles around urban renewal in the 1960s, thereby confronting capital accumulation interests which were immediately clearcut. In these conflicts, the agenda was profoundly politicized, and the orientation was one of popular militancy. These groups have now differentiated into quasi-governmental bodies, new neighborhood development corporations, and into political organizations which bargain with government to influence the allocation of resources to their locality.

These groups increasingly find that their authority in the political arena is neither guaranteed, nor depends upon a direct and close relation to the grassroots. Rather, their authority emerges from their dealings with political institutions themselves. Thus, the main issue for these groups becomes gaining and maintaining " credibility" with the agencies and political officials. And for this to occur, the maintenance of the organization becomes more important than any specific issue.

The former informal leaders experience their legitimacy as informal leaders called into question, as they increasingly participate in the formal decision-making processes. They tend to get cut off from their constituency, or convert their constituency into a formal organization. This process of organizational formalization is also combined with a process of material goal displacement, as the emphasis shifts from 'social problems' to 'economic development'. Priority is increasingly placed upon the technical mastery of grant administration and management, while the problems of unemployment and blight are "solved" by eliminating—displacing—the original constituency. Especially in multi-class neighborhoods with organizations focussed on preservation, program provisions requiring that the group represent the entire locality can lead to such an outcome. In cases such as this, the bourgeois element is usually strengthened, and becomes the "representative" of the whole community. This, in turn, prepares the way for organizational involvement in gentrification.

For neighborhood groups which have become local development corporations, the goal becomes one of encouraging community reinvestment of the resources of the private sector, insofar as this could have positive spin-offs on the residential population. Hence, business retention, attraction, and expansion are seen as the best methods for local job creation. Under these circumstances of organizational self-definition, the "self-activity" of citizens is encouraged by the city, as it could have only benign effects on the social order and on investment planning. Only those issues which directly confront important accumulation interests have to be fragmented, channeled, and "processed". This occurs through the incremental incorporation of these conflicts into the policy process. In their efforts to gain access to city agencies and formal representation as political bodies, the community organizations allowed their politics to be technicized and turned into administrative problems. At the same time, competition between groups over federal and local resources is endemic to the protection of one neighborhood at the expense of another. Hence, through this double process of incorporation and competition, as well as in the transformation of organizational goals and structure, the 'state form' is superimposed on this terrain of potentially explosive conflict.

APPENDIX

This article is based on extensive research on neighborhood organizations in Chicago and the Bay Area, interviews, participatory observations and evaluations of other researchers' surveys and studies of various neighborhood organizations' developments, during a one-year research grant at Northwestern's Center for Urban Affairs and the University of California, Berkeley, Institute for Urban and Regional Development.

This is part of a larger project comparing the neighborhood movements, policy responses, and organizational effects in the United States and in West Germany—where, even without a strong tradition of neighborhood territoriality or extra-parliamentarian activity, localized troubles have also been stimulating discontent and generated demands for qualitative changes. Both, the movements, and the process of incorporation, take very different forms in West Germany than they do in the United States. The comparison, it is argued, allows a clearer understanding of the conditions, under which these new urban movements would not be turned into vehicles to increase capitalist rationality, but become fertilizers of class struggle.

TWENTY

STEPHEN HUMBLE

SOCIAL ACTION GROUPS WITH REFERENCE TO TRENDS IN THE BRITISH VOLUNTARY SECTOR

THE GROWTH OF STATUTORY SERVICE

THE period of growth in the UK since 1945 is now viewed as one of unprecedented growth in public expenditure and the statutory services. This rise of the so-called Welfare State has been much criticised. In real terms public expenditure in the UK has doubled since 1945 but expressed as a proportion of national income and private spending it has remained static. The share of expenditure on personal social services, environmental planning, education and income maintenance has also doubled, whereas housing and health's share of expenditure has not shifted. Nevertheless, greater state intervention in health, national insurance and education was supported by both Labour and Conservative parties. The long period during 1951-64 of Conservative rule has been judged not to have brought about any substantial reversal of the role of the state in social welfare, cushioned as it was by a relatively prosperous period of economic growth. The 1964-79 period witnessed the establishment of new and intricate mechanisms between the voluntary and statutory sectors, especially in the urban areas. The 1970-74 Conservative government is not considered to have reversed this statutory encroachment either. The advent of the new 1979 Conservative government does apparently herald a fresh approach, at least in the economic field with the rediscovery of so-called laissez-faire capitalism.

Paper presented at the "European Meeting on Applied Urban Research," Essen, Oct. 2-4, 1981.

What implications this approach has for social policy, only time will really tell. The government has brought overall public expenditure on social and educational items to a standstill whilst they have increased expenditure on such things as the police, prisons and defence. They have brought into sharp relief the point and purpose of state as opposed to extra-state activity.

THE GROWTH OF THE VOLUNTARY SECTOR

The tradition of voluntary action is well-established in British culture and voluntary effort has played an important role in Britain in the delivery of welfare services. The importance of its role has nonetheless varied, and it is interesting to compare the current stress being put in the UK on the voluntary provision of welfare services with the historical up's and down's of the voluntary sector as a whole. Before the 1834 Poor Law Amendment Act, poor people and working people depended in large measure upon a paternal system of welfare provision, one in which church, employer and aristocrat combined in one way or another to dispense to the needy, though a sharp distinction was drawn between the genuinely needy and the simply fickle. During the course of the nineteenth century, Britain witnessed an upsurge in the growth of voluntary organisations caring for the sick and the underprivileged, such as the foundation of the Salvation Army, settlements in the large cities, and orphanages such as Barnardo's for chilren. It was towards the end of this century that analyses were presented (e.g. by Booth, Rowntree and Marx) showing a causal relationship between industrialisation and the plight of workers, and in this period too we saw the socialist foundations of the Labour Party being laid.

The voluntary sector continued to play a major role well into the twentieth century, though marked inroads into its work were being made by the state. The state began to lay down standard provision for medical insurance, pensions, unemployment and the like. Criticism grew about the partiality of voluntary-provided services and advocates of state provision called for the establishment of comprehensive and standard service provision and recommended a supplementary role for the voluntary organisations. The real watershed was reached with the publication in 1942 of the Beveridge Report which essentially laid down the form of the welfare state in Britain as we know it today, consisting of national provision for health, education, social services, housing and employment.

The setting up of national standards and of a safety net for the under-privileged at first deprived the voluntary sector of growth-points and for a long period after the war ended in 1945, there was little apparent movement in this sector. In the 1960's and 70's, however, there were a significant number of developments which strengthened the voluntary movement :

(a) a spreading of local and national voluntary bodies ;
(b) the establishment of the Voluntary Services Unit in the Home Office as a co-ordinating arm of central government for voluntary organisations ;
(c) the specialisation of the work of voluntary organisations to carry out functions not carried out by statutory bodies, e.g. in the care of children in children's homes ;
(d) the commissioning of community development projects for inner city areas ;
(e) the growth of pressure groups, some in welfare services, such as *Shelter* in the housing field ;
(f) last, a multitude of local self-help groups, some with national headquarters, arose in an attempt to come to terms with a host of problems such as drug addiction, alcoholism and single-parent families that could not apparently be solved by the machinery of the welfare state.

THE GROWTH OF VOLUNTARY-STATUTORY RELATIONS

In the past 15 years, two sets of innovations have occurred in Britain which have considerably accelerated the pace of transactions in local voluntary-statutory relations. The first is *local government reorganisation* which took place about the middle of the fifteen-year period. The second is an *urban programme* developed by central government over the whole of the period. I start with local government reorganisation.

In the post-war period unease grew about the ability of our numerous and different local authorities to manage growth (population, planning and the like). The unease made itself felt at central government level and eventually, the length of the policy-making process being what it is, new reorganised and rationalised local authorities were instituted in 1974. I understand similar transformations occurred elsewhere in Europe. The result was a general declaration of faith in the ability of public policy decisions to be made to a degree at local level. Along with the reorganisation of the political and managerial structure within the local authorities corporate planning was introduced, which was a way of integrating the different departments within each local authority for the purpose of providing co-ordinated service delivery to local areas. Area management systems were set up, involving the decentralisation of local authority departments so as to improve their intelligence of local areas within the local authority as a whole.[1] As a consequence of local authority reorganisation, the local voluntary sector has had to adapt. Local intermediary bodies have been reorganising on geographical lines similar to the new local authorities, since they depend in large measure on local authority grants. Local voluntary organisations have been finding themselves co-opted more and more into the consultation process brought about by the strategies like area management. The second innovation which has affected local statutory-voluntary relations has come from outside, from central government and its urban programme. As a result the urban voluntary sector has experienced more change than the rural voluntary sector. The origins of the urban programme mainly aimed at ethnic groups and when Britain itself was discovering that we too had racial problems. Central government—the 1964-70 Labour government—saw itself faced with racial and educational inequalities in the urban areas. It introduced the urban programme—a poverty programme, area-based and discriminating positively in favour of the disadvantaged, not just the racially disadvantaged.[2] One of its effects was to encourage the local voluntary sector as a third force in combatting deprivation. It consisted in fact not of one programme but of several ;

- — Educational Priority Areas which included the use of volunteer activity to improve home-school relations
- — the Urban Aid Programme which involved central and local government grant-aid to voluntary and community organisations
- — Community Development Projects which were in part action-based projects to improve self-help in deprived communities
- — Central Improvement and Housing Action Areas which partly relied upon voluntary and community organisations for environmental and housing improvement
- — Inner Area Studies in three cities as part of a "total approach" to inner-city improvement and including action-based work with voluntary organisations
- — Inner City Partnerships and Programmes involving central and local authorities and the local voluntary sector in a large number of inner cities, concentrating on the regeneration of their industrial base.

The voluntary sector in inner city and other urban programme areas has received significant increases of tens of millions of pounds in recent years with a consequent growth in what I call a "local voluntary sector superstructure". This superstructure consists of paid professionals at the fringe of urban voluntary organisations and local government whose task is to support the voluntary organisations, to se k urban programme funds, to consult and make themselves available for consultation by the voluntary organisations and local authorities. This superstructure is a significant innovation in the traditional relationship between central government, local government and the voluntary sector. It exists largely on central government funds but central government appears not to have the time nor the inclination to make it accountable to it ; and it exists to serve the voluntary sector yet it is independent of it.

THE NEW PLURALISM

The growing contribution of the statutory and voluntary in urban areas has heralded a new emphasis in the UK in the overall statutory-voluntary balance. With the limits to public expenditure set by the current government has come a fresh examination of the potential of social action groups, voluntary organisations, the informal sector (neighbourhood and family care) and the self-help movement to provide welfare services. Our health minister for the first two and a half years of the new Conservative Government has written of the need to view our health and social service system as essentially a support system for the voluntary sector.[3] The voluntary sector has not been slow in taking up the challenge : Gladstone[4] for instance, writes of the necessity of "gradualist welfare pluralism", a system which voluntary organisations should play a major part in welfare service delivery. Hatch[5] advocates an "integral" model of statutory-voluntary relations, and Hadley and Hatch[6] recommend decentralised modes of service delivery and legal rights for the citizens to participate.

SOME CAUTIONARY NOTES

The political climate in Britain is therefore ripe for a re-alignment in voluntary-statutory relations. But as I come near to the end of this paper, there are some cautionary notes I would like to enter about this possible realignment.

First, the encouragement of direct action of the voluntary kind and increased public participation in the delivery of social services does not begin to tackle the problem of the distribution of income and wealth. Neither are voluntary organisations in a position to organise the equitable distribution of resources since each competes for its own area.

Second, like the urban programme before it, more emphasis on the voluntary sector means less emphasis on the statutory safety-net of support for the poor. Unless we are careful, it directs our way from the State's obligation to meet the needs of the poor and the deprived.

Third, we have had in Britain a modest programme for the voluntary sector—the urban programme—which has been found wanting in failing to increase public participation. It has had little to say about the new devices that might be open to us to allow people to feel more able to influence and organise social policy programmes,

Fourth, an accentuated voluntary sector requires more finance. The dangers of more money for voluntary organisations are obvious : it may increase their dependence on the statutory sector and the control of that sector ; it brings into question where their accountability lies ; and it helps transform them into statutory organisations in the disguise of voluntary ones.

Fifth, increased voluntary activity must rely partly upon the capacity of people in communities or neighbourhoods to care for each other. Yet this capacity may be over-emphasised. Recent work by Philip Abrams on neighbourhood care schemes in Britain has questioned the assumption on which such schemes operate.[7] His evidence is that neighbours often enter into neighbourly transactions for what they can get out of it, rather than from altruistic motives. Neighbourhood care 'networks' may thus be too fragile to cope with such schemes or to be able to deliver the right things in the right places.

Sixth, an expansion in the voluntary sector requires more volunteers. Where are they to come from ? There has been an expansion in recent times in the number of voluntary organisations and in volunteering in Britain, but there may be limits to this expansion. Commentators point as a possible scenario to the increase in time given over to leisure and recreation as a result of the introduction of micro-processors and associated technology. Another scenario might include an increasing number of unemployed whose dissatisfactions are unlikely to lead them down the path of volunteering. We are very unclear as to the motives of people in coming forward to volunteer and about the factors which influence rates of volunteering.

Seventh, the unions and unionised labour are unlikely to accept a growth in voluntary effort when it is likely to threaten jobs at the present time of increasing unemployment.

Eighth, and this is my last point, an increased emphasis on the voluntary sector will entail a growth in what I have called the voluntary sector superstructure which will cut across existing lines of accountability and responsibility between local and central government between them and the electorate. The danger is not so much that it will be more inflexible than present government but that it will provide an excuse for elected representatives to place the blame elsewhere, in a superstructure that is neither of the people nor for the people.

CONCLUSION

Social action groups, self-help groups, local protest groups and new forms of voluntary organisations have grown in part as a result of the failure in Britain for output of the welfare state to match input. The new emphasis upon the voluntary sector is partly a reaction of the state to try to harness new and inexpensive sources of welfare provision at a time of economic recession. Consequently, the voluntary sector and local action groups need to guard carefully their autonomy and right of self-determination.

FOOTNOTES

1. See Robin Hambleton, *Policy Planning and Local Government*, Hutchinson, London, 1978.
2. See John Edwards and Richard Batley, *The Politics of Positive Discrimination*, Tavistock, London, 1978.
3. Patrick Jenkin, *Economic Constraints and Social Policy* in *Social Policy and Administration*, Vol 15, No 3, Autum 1981.
4. Francis Gladstone, *Voluntary Action in a Changing World*, Bedford Square Press, London, 1979.
5. Stephen Hatch, *Outside the State : Voluntary organisations in three English towns*, Croom Helm, London, 1980.
6. Roger Hadley and Stephen Hatch, *Social Welfare and the Failure of the State*, George Allen and Unwin, London, 1981.
7. Philip Abrams, *Neighbours* papers presented to The Volunteer Centre, London, 1979.

INDEX

Administration, 277; developing bases in, 69 ; increasing computerization of, 71 ; policy analysis creeping, 63
Administrative leadership, 32, 45; recording and statistical systems, 84 ; reforms, 68
Advisory Commission Intergovernmental Relations (ACIR), 187
Adult education, 274
Agglomeration areas, 9
Aiken, M., 48
Alinstry style organisation, 315
America, 84 ; participatory thrust, 42 ; administrative system, 84 ; federal system, 84 ; local executives, 11 ; politicization of, 31 ; metropolitan area, 114
Applied urban research, 17
Australia, 94

Babchuck, N., 7
Baldersheim, Herald, 12, 45
Banerjee, Surendra Nath, 131
Baseline information, 71
Bechmann, Dan Ferrand, 23, 285
Bell, Daviel, 7
Bengal Municipal Act (1932), 122, 136 ; Improvement Act, 127
Berkeley, 324
Birmingham, 232
Bombed cities, planning expenditure, 238
Booth, A., 7
Boyd, William, 33
Bristol, 239
British India, policy of, 155; Voluntary sector, 325
Burdwan, 119, 121, 154, 165, 186 ; drainage system, 144 ; road system, 146; water supply system, 141
Business development opportunities, 219, 222

Calcutta, 119, 125 ; administration of, 124; metropolitan development authority, 120 ; urban agglomeration, 155
California, 196, 199, 324
Canada, 92, 94 ; large metropolitan areas in, 114
Catanese, Anthony J., 33
Cattle tresspass act, 126
Central-local relations implications for, 112; planning agency, 77
Chandernagar, 154, 165 ; drainage system, 145, Municipalities, 137; water supply system, 142
Chicago, 324
Chonaikai, 23, 293, 298, 299, 301; historical development, 293, 294
Christovich, Leslie J., 31
Chungi, 123
Citizen participation, 2, 6, 97, 101 ; experiments, 14 ; current tendencies in, 104 ; new approach of, 10, 276 ; socio-economic status of, 37
City, governments types of, 121 ; manager, 52 ; proposal, 55, 56 ; recommendation, 54
Civil service academy, 64
Clark, T., 7
Clinard, M.B., 1, 3, 6, 8, 301
Cloward, R.A., 195
Cohen, M.D., 48

Commerical tax, 244
Community Development, 6, 314
Community Development Block Grant (CDBG), 211, 320 Community Corporation (CDC's), 215, 222 ; programme, 315 ; projects, 215, 329
Community organizations, 315, 321 ; serivices administration, 212
Comprehensive Employment and Training Act (CETA), 211, 219
Computerized information system, 72
Conservative controlled, 243, 247
Contemporary neighbourhood movements profile of, 311
Conurbation authorities, 233, 248
Coppock, J. T., 2, 5
Council seats proportion of, 264
Criticisin, 326
Cross--national researeh, result of, 304
Crozier, M., 47

Dahl, R., 299
Darjeeling hill municipality of, 131
Data systems, 77
Davis, B., 252
Decentralization, new kind of, 16
Decision-making system, 277
Demonstration programms, 79
Derbyshire, 247
Derrick, Sewell W.R.D., 2
Dienel, Peter C., 22, 273
Discipline-oriented, 83
District Municipal Improvement Act, 126
Donnell, Patrick O., 93, 114
Dore, R., 293
Durgapur, 122, 154, 165, 168, 176; better health facility, 148 ; development Authority (DDA), 146; natural drainage system, 144 ; notified area authority, 140, 141, 144, 148, 164, 183 ; public transportation facilities and water supply system, 164

Economic development programs. 214, 225, 228; strategies, 211
Educational priority areas, 329; costs, 244 45 ; problems, 79
Elling, R.H., 200
Embree, J.F., 301
Emergency, kind of, 299
Emergency, water supply scheme, 142
Emerine, R.J., 255
Employment conditions, 253, 265; project techniques, 213 ; training programs, 212
England, 237, 252; Local Government sysetm of, 21, 232
English counties, 245
Environmental policies 67
Evaluation, 79, 83; administration contribution of, 59; program development, 74; research development of, 86; second face of, 66; strategy, 214; varies quality of, 77
Executive influence distribution of, 37
Experimental programs, 80
Explicit agreements, 290
Exploitation, 69, 277
External policy, local implementation of, 17,195

Fabricant, S., 251
Factor analysis programmes. 234
Federal, economic development projects, 65, 73, 189, 219 ; programmes, 316
Federal Republic of Germany, 78, 79, 81; citizen partcipation, problem of, 8
Financial committee, 50
Fire expenditures, 241; services, 262; estimated co-efficients, 260

Fiscal capacity (FISC), 254

Garner, Robert Ash, 195
Germany, 25; citizen participation in, 279; directions for evaluation research in, 84, 85 ; growth of evaluation in, 60, 61 ; planning call model in, 280 ; youth institute evaluation of, 80
Gladstone, Francis, 330
Goal analytical process, 76
Goal-oriented functions, 62, 63
Governmental evaluation units, 75; programs effectiveness of, 64; programmatic policy reform, 74
Greater London metropalitan authority, 93
Group Pressure Index (GPI), 34, 38
Group salience and professional tenure, 34, 38-39
Gupta, S.P., 252, 257
Gusfield, J.R., 295

Habermas, J., 303
Hage, J., 48
Halebsky, S., 200
Hampton, W., 4
Hanf, K., 66
Harder, Marvin, 214
Hellstein, Gerd-Michael, 13, 59
Hongkong, 300; kaifong system in, 301
Hooghly-Chinsura, 119, 121, 154, 165; drainage system, 145; municipalities, 137; proper road system 146,
Housing conditions, 251, 253; expenditure, 236; problems, 70
Housing and Urban Development (HUD), 211
Howrah, 121, 154, 165, 168, 176; drainage system of, 143; good street system, 146; health problem, 147; improvement trust, 139; interim water supply scheme, 141 ; municipalities, 137; water supply system, 140
Hughes, A.J., 140
Humble Stephen, 25, 325
Hutton, J.P., 252, 257

Immigrant Communities, 255
India, 120; British raj in, 123; municipal Government, principal functions of, 120
Industrial structure, 253, 255, 263
Innercity partnership and programmes, 329
Institutionalization, 1, 77; evaluation procedure, 65
Integrating manpower, 211; planning and evaluation system, 74
Inter governmental program, 213, 214
Internal formal organization, 322
Inter-organisational networks, 48
Italy, 308; political system, chronology of, 306

Japan, 294, 295, 300; Taisho democracy in, 298
Jenkins, J.C., 196
Joint federal-state educational Commission, 79
Jones, Victors, 93, 114

Kalltrop, Ove, 14
Kobrak, Peter, 19, 211
Kranse, D., 211

Labour authorities, 246
Labour 262, 264; intensive hypothesis, 190; services, 188; market policies, 86; strength, 243
Laegreid, P., 57
Lancashire, 241, 247
Landuse control, 130
Leadership as organisational control, 47
Library expenditure, 237
Liebert, Roland, 201
Lindblom, C., 308
Liverpool, 232
Local budgets, 197, 203

Local Government, 222; consolidation of, 116; re-organization, 109, 110; service provision, external mandating of, 187-192; structural reform of, 91; two-tier system of, 93
Local Labour market, 254, 256; policy environment, 213
Local-Self Government, 129, 132, 134, 137
Local urban aid programme, 225
Local voluntary sector, 328
Lord lawrences resolutions, 125
Lord Mayo's resolution, 127
Lord Ripon, resolution, 129, 130
Los Angeles country, 201
Lovell, C.H., 187
Luhmann, N., 308
Lynch, Thomas D., 4

Maars, A., 7
MacManns, Susan A., 17, 187
Management, experience of, 139; participation experiments, 101
Mandates, education, 191; package, 188; public safety, 190, pupil transportation, 190-91
Manpower, integrating, 19; programs, 212, 226
Mann, Hellmuttowell, 13
March, J.G., 48
Martial Law, 302
Mayer, Margis, 24, 311
Mazaanian, Danniel, 5
Meiji restoration, 296
Methodological developments, 82
Metropolition and regional government reform of, 91; reorganization, 92, 113
MeCarthy, James D., 195
McGivney, Joseph, 32
Minar, David W., 33
Mintuberg, H., 45
Modern democracies, 10 ; metropolis, 7 ; public administration, 31
Mogulof, M.B., 5
Motor way project, 52
Moynihan, William, 32
Municipal administration, local coordination of, 106
Municipal Govt. average annual economic base of, 176 ; income, 172 ; powers of, 135 ; sources of income, 174 ; taxatlion, 128 ; total receipt of, 169, types of, 122 ; Urban policies, 184
Mutsunikai, 296, 297
Mutual hypotheses, 287

Nakamura, Hachiro, 23, 293
National neighbourhood commission, 317
National policy environment, 213
Negri, A., 309
Neighbourhood councils, 106 ; cooperation network, 285 ; development meaning of, 321 ; organizations structure of, 322 ; system, 290
New experimental programs, 81 ; unban movements 24, 303 ; neighbourhood movements, 312
New participation technique, 284
New pluralism, 329
Newton, K., 21, 231
New York, 213
Nicnaber, Jeane, 5
Noise reduction programs, 80
Non mandated budget categories, 197 ; targeting communities, 221
Normal budgetary process, 51
Norman, Dennis, 295
North America, 21
Notified area authority, 122
Nottingham, 239, 247

Oberschall, Anthony, 195
Offe, C., 308
Olsen, J.P., 48, 57
Ontario Committee, 4
Organisational control, 12, 45, 49; increasing, 47 ; problems of, 46,

50 ; goals, transformation of, 323
Oslo, 45 ; division of authority in, 49 ; highways in, 54, 55 ; political bodies of, 50 ; problems in the transport sector, 56

Pohl, R.E., 295
Palumbo, Dennis J., 214
Parliamentary commission, 64 ; democracy, 273, 278
Participatory democracy, 273 ; experiments, 99 ; thrust, 32, 41
Perceived policy involvement distribution of, 36
Perrow, C., 196
Personal health services, 243
Philippines, 300
Planning Cell, 22, 274, 276, 278 ; technique, 279, 283
Planning evaluation cycles, 73
Planning, expenditure, 238; public service developments, 251 ; reform cycle, 73 ; Unit, 52
Police expenditure, 239, 240
Policy planning unit, 54
Political-administrative system, 304 ; factors influence of, 251 ; Influence, 204 ; organization, 199, 315 ; turmoil, 72
Population characteristics, 255 ; density, 254, 255 ; increased mobility of, 1 ; outflow of, 263
President Jimmy Carter, 20, 212, 227, 317, 319
Private, industry Council, 225 ; market sector, 183 ; sector, 218 ; initiative program, 226
Proeess oriented management tools, 67
Property tax, 187, 196
Public administrations, 218, 283 ; criticism, 24 ; demands recovery act, 133 ; expenditure, 326; opinion integration of, 7 ; participation, 4, 5, 92 ; experiments 99; objectives of, 3 ; policy determinant of, 249 ; transit systems, governmental payment for, 189

Quasi—national experiment, 195, 197

Rabinovitz, Francine F., 33
Rank Correlation Coefficient, 172, 180
Rationalization, 63
Reagan's strategy, 319
Redfield-Wirth, 293
Refuse expenditures, 336
Regional reorganization, 93, 115
Riven, F.F., 195
Rowat, Donald C., 14, 15, 91, 109
Roy, Bijoy Prasad Singh, 132
Royal army sanitary commissions, 125, 252
Rural authorities, 233 ; voluntary sector, 328

San Francisca, 313
Semi-Urban authorities, 233
Service delivery organization, 310, mandates, proponents of, 187 ; types of, 191
Sewage expenditure, 234, 235
Scharkf, F.W., 66
Scho-field, John A., 22, 251
Shorpe, L.J., 113
Sikh Dharat, 123
Singapore, 300
Singh, Arun Kumar, 16, 119,
Small business administration, 212, 318
Social services, estimated coefficients, 258 ; expenditure, 261, 279
Social work, dysfunction of, 285
Socio-economics conditions, 262 265; factors, 251
Solving emerging constitutional problems, 65
South Korea, 300

Spahn, P.B., 62
Spiegel, Hans B.C., 4
Sreerampore surface, water sources, 141
State government, 134 ; actual policy of, 183 ; indirect taxes, 179 ; major sources of income, 173 ; policy grant-in-aid, 175
Statutory service, growth of, 325
Structural reoganization, 92
Suburban environment, 40
Suburban non-metropolitian, 33
Sweden, planning and management in, 97 ; unemployment, increasing, 105

Taisho democracy, 299
Targeted Jobs Demonstration Program (TJDP), 19, 20, 21, 212, 215, 216, 224, 228 ; communities, 222 ; co-ordination among agencies, 223 ; evaluations, 216 ; implementation, 218; job opportunities under, 220
Tarozzi, Alberto, 24, 303
Theory-testing model, 83
Thompson, J.D , 45
Tobin, C.A., 187
Toronto, metropolitan government of, 114
Touraine, A., 303
Town area committees, 122 ; and country planning, 238 ; improvement act, 127
Tradition urban administration, 50 ; training system, 81
Transmitting evaluation, 70
Transport project group, 53-4
Turbulence, perception of, 39
Turk, Herman, 17, 195, 197, 203
Turke, Klaus, 8

Unemployment, 78, 331 ; problems of, 323
UNESCO conference, 76
United States, 211, 25, 76, 226, 324 ; community organizations, 31 ; social reform, 320; standard metropolitan statistical areas, 17 ; Urban institute in, 86
Unpopular problems, 283
Urban agglomerations, 232 ; aid programme, 329; amenities, 138; area, neighbourhood revitalization in the, 295 ; community development, 3
Urban Context, 39 ; crowding, 261 ; development department for, 56 ; economic development programmes, 19, 224 ; supporters of, 227 ; enterprise zone, 228 ; environment, 101, 263, 265, 312 ; local government, 121 ; municipalities population of, 111 ; policy statement neighbourhoods, 317 ; politics intersity of, 38 ; population density, 263 ; programme, 330 ; rural dictonomies, 234; services expenditures determinants of, 251; social movement, 311; network ; 293 ; voluntary sector, 328 ; Workforce, 262

Vain Horn, Carl E., 19, 211, 214
Volkswaen foundation, 278
Voluntary, associations, 105, 316, organisation, 327 ; sector, 327 ; superstructure, 331 ; statutory relations, 327

Wales, 21, 237, 252 ; local government system, 232
Weicher, J.C., 255, 257
Welfare services, voluntary provision of, 326
Welsh authorities, 245 ; counties 244, 248 ; childrens welfare of Social services, 245
Wengert, M., 3
West Bengal, 16; expenditure, major categories of, 162, 163 ; municipal governments, financial management of, 153; mun-

cipal acts features, 132, municipal legislation in, 131 ; total annual expenditure, temporal profile of, 159 ; trend of total expenditure, 156 ; types of urban government in, 121
West Europe, 21
West Germany, 13, 303, 305, 308, 309, 324 ; movement crystalizes, 311 ; political system chronology of, 306
West Yorkshire, 247
Winnipeg metropolitan area, 114
Wirt, Frederick M., 31, 32, 36, 41
Wollmann, Hellmutt, 59
Wood, Colin J.B., 7
World War II, 9, 91, 111
Wupperted research unit, 281

Yalvisaker, P.N., 2
Yamklinfung, Prasart, 301
Yates, Danglas, 42

Zald, Mayor H., 196
Zucker, Lyune G., 17, 203